WRITING IN THE DARK
THE WORKBOOK

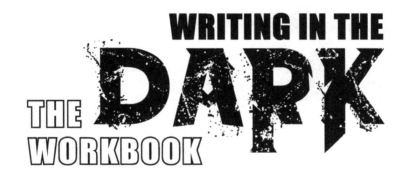

Tim Waggoner

GUIDE DOG BOOKS

Writing in the Dark: The Workbook
Copyright © 2022 by Tim Waggoner
ISBN: 978-1-947879-46-1

First GDB Paperback Edition: June 2022

rawdogscreaming.com

Cover Design © 2022 by C.V. Hunt
grindhousepress..com

Interior Layout by D. Harlan Wilson
dharlanwilson.com

Guide Dog Books
Bowie, MD

ACKNOWLEDGMENTS

Thanks to John and Jennifer at Raw Dog Screaming Press for being willing to go back to the well one more time. Thanks to author, fellow teacher, and brother in darkness Michael A. Arnzen for agreeing to write the introduction to this volume. Thanks to all the amazing writers who so graciously contributed their experience and wisdom to this book. As always, thanks to my agent and indefatigable champion Cherry Weiner. I'd especially like to acknowledge all the writers who told me how useful they found *Writing in the Dark*. I hope you find this workbook just as beneficial.

DEDICATION

This one's for my creative writing teachers—Mrs. Linnette Vagedes, Dr. William Baker, and Dr. Gary Pacernick—as well as the mentors who have helped me along the way: Laurie Eckert, Jeffrey Huberman, Donald Swanson, Dennis L. McKiernan, Thomas F. Monteleone, and Mort Castle. It's also for all the creative writing students I've worked with in classes and workshops over the last thirty years. They've not only made me a better teacher, but a better writer as well.

CONTENTS

HOW TO USE THIS BOOK

This workbook has been designed to be used either on its own or in conjunction with *Writing in the Dark,* a writing guidebook that will give you further insight into the concepts covered in these pages. While the workbook includes minimal space for composition, we strongly recommend using a writing journal or word-processing program for longer exercises. You may want to do some of the exercises multiple times, or you may be using them in a class or writing workshop, so we have provided a downloadable PDF file with extra pages that can be printed as many times as you like. Download the PDF at this address:

rawdogscreaming.com/workbook

You are welcome to use these pages and exercises however you like, but a mention of the workbook is always appreciated.

—The Editors

INTRODUCTION
TAKING STABS IN THE DARK

Michael A. Arnzen

Welcome to class. Professor Tim Waggoner is on his way to this dark room, but he's running a little late, so he asked me to say a few words to get you started before he gets here.

The lights aren't on, but you can still see, can't you? Open your books. You should have brought two with you—*Writing in the Dark*, which is Prof Waggoner's lauded instructional guide, and the accompanying sequel *Writing in the Dark: The Workbook*, a new collection of practical application and extended discussion of all the guidance given in the other.

Let's get one thing straight. There's a reason this is called a "workbook." It isn't simply meant be read, even though it is itself a very good read. No. It's called a "workbook" because you do the work. You write—directly on, inside, or alongside the book, whether on your laptop or in a college-ruled notebook or even the proverbial cocktail napkin—without worrying about who might read it. You get your hands dirty with ink and splatter the page with a mess of scrawled lines, taking a stab in the dark at things. When I think of workbooks I think of "fill in the blank" sort of study guides I had in college—the ones made of brownish coloring-book paper, with page after page of worksheets to scribble in and practice on. It was always optional homework to do, guide rails for the "train" in training—a way for the author to apply the concepts from the textbook so the learner could put them into practice.

And this is a great workbook. If you do the work that Professor W has assigned, you WILL improve as a writer and learn about what makes the horror genre tick. In fact, if you're like me, you'll have plenty of fun doing this so-called "work." Don't let your adult brain prevent you from letting your inner child go hog wild in devious delight by doing these exercises—and writing *whatever you want* in the process. Respond not just with thoughts, but with daydreams and speculations that you capture on the page. You'll be a better writer for trying, even if the results aren't immediately publishing-ready. You might even cackle maniacally as you do your homework, dying to share it with someone. In fact, you should do that, though after a little revision, of course. If you're driven to patiently submit what you write to the literary marketplace, you will no doubt produce some outstanding and publishable stories, poems, plays or whatever else it is you're doing on the dark side after walking through the many fun and fruitful exercises, the many deep and dark reflections that Tim Waggoner has in store for you.

The title is still a little misleading, however. This isn't just some humdrum classroom assignment, some "work" book, after all. Sure, you must be disciplined and put the work in to get anywhere as a writer. We all write a lot before we ever see print, let alone make money or achieve acclaim at it. Readers trust their authors to be more experienced than they are at putting ink to the page. But, no, this is *not* just a *work* book. It's much more than that. You see, this is actually … A SPELL BOOK.

Shh.

I hear footsteps. He's right down the hall. He's coming.

When he arrives, don't let Professor W know that you're on to him. He's a warlock of the written word, and he's training you in some very dark mojo here. Just do the so-called "work" that follows and secretly smile, knowing that you're being taught some amazingly powerful alchemy. Your pen might start to spark like a wand if you do it right. And after you close this amazing spell book, you will have the power to, in Waggoner's words, "spread the dark gospel of Horror" far and wide on your own, not only in print but in all forums, from convention panels to possibly even teaching a class just like him.

Never forget that this spell book is always there to assist, too, even when you think you've got it all figured out. There is power in ritual repetition and return. And of course, you can always crack the book open again any time you're stuck or just want to practice. Every spell in here could make your evil enemy—writer's block—disappear. All it takes is Tim's warm urging to think differently and wave your magic pen.

You must, however, move that pen or tickle those keys to make the magic happen. Don't fall prey to "head writing." Produce the pages. It doesn't matter if you know what you're doing before you start. Just *take a stab in the dark*. That's all it takes.

Reading this book reminded me of that core tenant of the professional writer: *Always be writing*. I got lots of ideas for stories and poems while reading *Writing in the Dark*, and it happened all over again when I first read this workbook. Reading is always a kind of icebreaker for me; it often makes me want to write—but Tim's warm, encouraging voice has a way of seducing you into wanting to put down the book, pick up a pen and start writing something amazing and deeper than you might otherwise do on your own. He's a good teacher. He motivates. And he cast his spell on me, even though I've been doing this awhile.

And one thing that makes him great at motivating us all is that he knows when to take a pregnant pause, when to back off, when to leave your brain room to breathe. He isn't overbearing, mean-spirited, holier-than-thou, or controlling. He's just wise and patient. He doesn't come at this book assuming you're only going to write novels and are woefully ignorant of the basics; he knows that horror writers are already fans who know a thing or two about horror fiction, but maybe just haven't brought the viewpoint of the writer to the page yet. But not just novels. Horror writers pen all kinds of shapes in the darkness. The genius of the approach of this book is that it allows you to apply these ideas as you will, from poetry to film scripts. This is a book for storytellers, but the scope is something you'll have to figure out on you own. It's not a book that gives you all the practical things that beginning writers think they need when it comes to outlining, word count, manuscript format or how book binding or royalty payments work … there are other books for that stuff, and it really doesn't deserve to be repeated here. No, what's great about *Writing in the Dark* and the workbook you hold in your hands is that it's mostly about horror theory and how that *supports* practice. Herman Hesse, author of *Steppenwolf*, once mused: "Theory is when one knows everything, but nothing works. Practice is when everything works, but no one knows why." This workbook brings the two into perfect harmony, with an encouraging nudge to keep going, assured that everything works *because* you know why, and you have earned that certitude, coming to know it in a very personal, informed way.

And you do write this weird shit for a reason. Never forget that. There's always a purpose lurking at the center of the chaos, like the calm eye that guides the swirling vortex. Many of the exercises in this book invite you to think about your own psyche, your own assumptions, your own experiences—not just the tropes of the genre. Horror literature is always personal, always psychological on some level, even when it's about occult spirits or some acid-tongued monster. We represent fear, and our fiction uncannily conjures the impossible to life. The genre gives the darkness *within us* shape and form. Some people don't understand how that works—but you must. Not only to defend your genre, if it ever comes to that. But because the more you know, and the more conscious you are about how your unconscious operates, the better your writing will be reviewed, received, and appreciated.

And believe me, Tim Waggoner knows what he's doing and is the perfect mentor for such a learning journey. I've seen him guide other writers for nearly three decades, while sitting beside him at book signings and convention panels. I've taught horror beside him at Seton Hill University, where we closely mentor MFA students while they work on genre novels—something most colleges don't dare allow. I've read his blog regularly, which features the instructional essays and advice that gave birth to these highly successful *Writing in the Dark* volumes. We've appeared together in several genre writing guides, among them *Writers Workshop of Horror* to *Many Genres, One Craft* (which I co-edited). I've seen him mentor new writers in the Horror Writers Association (who bestowed upon him the Mentor of the Year award—and I'm guessing it means as much to him as any of his Stoker trophies, because he truly believes in giving back and paying it forward). And of course, I've read his horror books and story collections and media tie-ins (he is so prolific!), all of which are masterful in their appeal to that creepy and surreal lizard brain that operates inside of you. I've also not only used numerous how-to guides myself across my career, but have written a books like this one and run many workshops using them (see *Instigation: Creative Prompts on the Dark Side*), so I know what works and what doesn't in a workbook. And I can report with confidence that this is one of the best writing workbooks for the horror writer ever devised, written by someone who has truly made a career of freaking people the fuck out, while also just being a nice guy who genuinely cares about the community.

You can trust him to teach you not so much how to write, *per se*, but how to *think* like a horror writer. This basically means that you'll instinctively know how to chill someone with a disturbing idea, outsmart them with an outrageous twist ending, or caution them with a clever moral lesson, and it will all come naturally to you. That's part of what makes you scary, but it isn't everything. Horror writers go places that others don't. Others fear to! We delve into the taboo and explore the backstage of reality. We are the tribesmen who venture into the dark caves that frighten the clan; we return to tell their stories. This is why Professor Waggoner emphasizes "violations" in this book. The exercise where he invites you to take virtually any topic and come at it with the mindset that "something is wrong" with it encapsulates the aim of the horror writer perfectly. It sums up what drives me to write, and many others. We dramatize "what's wrong" with a lot of things, often exploring the power of their wrongness, or the wrongness of power's abuse. Often "what's wrong" is with our minds, too, the bent ways of rationalizing evil or the corruption of thoughts by an unseen traumatizing force. Usually, wrongness is lurking in what people take for granted when they ought not to; it hides in the assumptions we pick up from hegemonic culture about the way things are or ought to be. Horror shows us the alternatives, the "Other," and encourages us to entertain, if not embrace difference, uniqueness, and alterity. This is why horror writing goes after the gross-out when it doesn't terrify or horrify (in Stephen King's infamous trinity of horror writing motives); we are ultimately seeking to disturb what people take as settled and *status quo*. But you must have a strong stomach for it. Your organs have to be lined well and resilient to always be unsettled. This book—along with simply devouring books widely and deeply in the horror genre, and at least tasting every book you can get your hands on—will strengthen your guts, but you have to practice these exercises, not just read about them. You have to swallow the theory till horror writing becomes guttural, instinctive, like muscle memory. For you see, horror is not a genre. It is a *worldview* … a dark lens through which we see, if only partially … *Hold on*. I hear the crass jiggling of a rusty knob.

Our classroom door creaks open.

Oddly, the light that pours into the room from behind him only intensifies the murky darkness we sit in.

The warlock has arrived. His features are deceptively warm beneath a straw hat. His smile is a mixture of welcoming friendship but it also contains the same dark glee that *Hellraiser*'s Pinhead expresses when he mentions having "such sights to show you."

I move to sit beside you, eager to begin. I am already under his spell and that cackling you hear in the shadows might be mine. But it also might be the darkness itself. We will remain in this chamber of darkness, but Professor Waggoner is about to show you it all, by gripping your skull, cracking it open, and holding it there for you to reach inside and turn your brain inside out.

I hear the cracking of your knuckles. I think, Good. Whatever that sound is, I love being in this black cauldron of creativity with you, and it's time to cook.

Let's get to work.

WRITING IN THE DARK
THE SEQUEL, OR, WHY ANOTHER DAMN BOOK

I finished *Writing in the Dark* in late 2019. I'd written it in something of a frenzy, rushing to get everything down on the page as fast as I could. People think I'm a fast writer, and I suppose I'm faster than some, but a big reason I seem to write drafts so fast is that I spend a lot of time thinking about what I want to write and how I want to write it before my fingers touch the keyboard. In sports, they talk about visualizing an action before you actually perform it. In your mind, you've hit the ball a hundred times before you do it in the real world. I use a similar type of visualization when I write. Since I'd been reading, watching, and studying horror all my life, I suppose it was only natural that when I sat down to compose *Writing in the Dark*, it was like I'd opened the floodgates of my mind and everything I'd ever learned about horror poured out of me.

After I sent the book to my publisher, my brain was fried, so much so that when Hunter Shea had me on his Monster Men podcast, and he asked me what two questions I'd posed to the Voices From the Shadows contributors, I honestly couldn't remember. (Not exactly the best way to impress an audience.) Eventually my memory of the book's contents came trickling back, so I didn't sound like such a dumbass during subsequent interviews—and there were a lot of them. I did more publicity for *Writing in the Dark* than any other of the fifty or so books I've written because I was determined to get this book into the hands of as many writers as possible. I'd written it to help people become better horror writers and to give something back to the genre I love so much. So not only did I do a ton of interviews, I also wrote a number of short articles about writing horror—some excerpts from the book, some new stuff—to place in various venues, such as *Writer's Digest* and *The Writer*. I talked a bunch about writing horror, and I wrote more about writing horror, and by the time all of these publicity efforts wound down, I thought I'd written and said all I had to say about horror writing. I'd accomplished what I'd wanted to with *Writing in the Dark*, and I was done. Maybe as the years passed I'd accumulate more knowledge to share and I'd contemplate writing a sequel, but for the present, my brain tank was empty and bone-dry.

As the feedback for the book began to roll in, I was gratified to see that people enjoyed it and, more important to me, found it useful. People said how much they loved reading the advice from other writers included in the book, and they also said how they got a lot out of the writing exercises included at the end of each chapter. And then my goddamned mind—which never stays quiet for long—said, *I wonder if people would like a book focused entirely on horror-writing exercises?* I was doubtful that I'd be able to come up with enough material for a follow-up, but having doubts about a project has never stopped me from plowing full-speed ahead, so I put together a short proposal, sent it to my publisher, and … well, since you're holding this book in your hands, you can guess the rest of the story.

So what can you expect from *Writing in the Dark: The Workbook*?

Since I viewed this as a companion to *Writing in the Dark*, I decided to follow the same organizational scheme of the first volume. Thus, the chapters in the workbook correspond to the chapters in the first volume, centered on the same themes. You needn't have read the previous volume to use this one. For those who haven't read *Writing in the Dark*, I start off each chapter in this book with a short recap of the corresponding chapter in the first one to get you up to speed. Of course, I think you'll get more out of this workbook by using it in tandem with *Writing in the Dark*, but since I wrote both, you'd expect me to say that, wouldn't you?

There are a lot of ways to use a workbook, and they're all good as far as I'm concerned. You can do each and every exercise in the order you encounter them. You can skip around and do whichever exercises you feel like doing whenever you feel like doing them. You can do some and not do others. You can do some now and save others for the future. You can read the exercises, contemplate them, but never actually work through them. You might not do any exercises, but they may spark ideas for your writing. You might adapt some of the exercises to your own needs, creating new exercises that might bear only a passing resemblance to the ones I created. Maybe you'll read all the way through the book now and come back to it someday to work the exercises. Like I said earlier, it's all good. *Writing in the Dark: The Workbook* isn't a school assignment. It's a tool for you to use in whatever ways you need. And as with the previous volume, I hope you find this one useful.

I wrote my own examples for many of the exercises. It's easy to write a prompt and then say, "Now you do this," but I think exercises are more effective if you can see a sample of what you're being asked to produce. I tried to do a good job creating these samples, but I wasn't attempting to write glittering prose that would last for all time. So when you read them, be kind.

One more thing. You're welcome to use any or all of these exercises in any classes or workshops you may teach, free of charge. I'd appreciate it if you give me credit, but if you want to pretend that you're the genius who came up with these amazing exercises, I won't cry about it. I wrote *Writing in the Dark*, as well as this companion volume, to help as many horror writers as possible. So if you're out there helping to spread the dark gospel, I ultimately don't give a damn whether or not you tell people where you got your exercises.

Enough of these preliminaries. Let's get to work.

VOICES FROM THE SHADOWS

One of *Writing in the Dark*'s most popular features was the mini-interviews with horror professionals that appeared at the end of each chapter. It was important to me to include these other voices because when it comes to an art form, there's no one right way to do anything. The more voices you hear from, the better, even when they contradict each other. *Especially* when they contradict each other. At the college where I teach, I sometimes have students who repeatedly take the same fiction-writing classes with me. *I really like the way you teach. You get the kind of stuff I like to write, you know?* While I'm glad these students find my classes beneficial, I always urge them to move on and study with someone else so they can get more than my perspective on their work. Creative writing education is based on an apprenticeship model, with newer writers learning from more experienced ones, but the big difference is that newer writers shouldn't apprentice with only one teacher. The more writers you learn from, the better. I asked contributors to the first volume to respond to two questions: 1) What do you think makes good horror/dark fantasy/suspense, and 2) What's the best advice you could give a beginning writer of horror/dark fantasy/suspense? I asked over two hundred horror folk, and around ninety contributed—far more than I expected to, really. Working writers are busy people, after all.

For this follow-up, I debated whether to ask for contributions from writers again. Not all writers teach and they might not be comfortable providing writing exercises. In the end, I decided to include Voices from the Shadows in this volume, and this time I asked potential contributors to provide a horror/dark fantasy/suspense craft tip they use, a writing exercise they've found useful, or a writing prompt. As with *Writing in the Dark*, I said responses only needed to be a few sentences long. As I wrote earlier, writers are busy, sometimes insanely so, and I didn't want them to have to work too hard. Plus, I figured I'd likely receive more contributions if writers could keep their responses short. I asked many of the same people who contributed to *Writing in the Dark* to contribute this time, and I also asked a number of new people in order to get some fresh voices into this volume.

As last time, more people responded than I expected. Unlike last time, many of their responses were longer than a few sentences. Sometimes a *lot* longer. These authors always told me that I was free to edit their responses to make them shorter, but why would I do that? The more you hear from other voices than mine, the better, remember? As with the first volume, there's some overlap in the responses, but I didn't edit out any repetition. If you see more than one writer offer similar advice, the more weight that advice will carry. Plus, even when discussing the same point of craft, different writers have different perspectives on it. And when you're finished reading this book, I hope you'll check out these writers' works. You'll be glad you did.

Since I'd already decided to follow the same chapter breakdown of the first volume, I decided to organize the Voices from the Shadows the same way too. The material appears at the end of each chapter, although not specifically tied to a chapter's theme. Think of these bits more as interludes, a break from listening to my voice, a chance to hear about the craft of horror writing from other professionals, some well-established and some in the early phase of their careers, some who write quiet literary horror, some who write blood-drenched extreme horror, and some who tell mind-shattering tales of cosmic terror. Horror is a big tent, after all, one filled with impenetrable shadows, and all voices are welcome there. Listen well to the arcane knowledge they whisper in your ear.

They have such wonderfully dark secrets to share.

CHAPTER ONE
WHY HORROR MATTERS

Has this happened to you? Someone asks you what you write, you tell them horror, they look at you with a blank expression, and then say, "Why would you want to write *that* stuff?" (Or some variation on this question.) Lots of people enjoy horror in its various mediums—books, movies, TV shows, comics, games—but they rarely give any thought as to why they enjoy it, and they likely don't view horror as anything more than simple entertainment. Fun, sure, but not *important*. Yet horror is as vital and meaningful as any other type of literature. Horror allows us to explore, understand, and make peace with our dark side. Through the insulating buffer of fiction, we can safely confront death, violence, cruelty, madness, distorted realities, and twisted states of mind, and ask ourselves how we would deal with these things, whether as victim or perpetrator, human or monster.

The exercises and prompts in this chapter are designed to get you to consider why horror matters to you and what you hope to achieve with your dark fiction. They'll hopefully help you determine and better articulate your own Why. That way, not only will you approach your writing with a clearer, sharper focus, you'll also have a ready answer the next time some clueless rando—or family member—asks you why you want to write *that* stuff.

BRACE FOR IMPACT

Without thinking about it too long, list five horror stories/books/films that had a significant impact on you as both a person and a writer. How you define *impact* is up to you. Maybe they were works that made you first fall in love with horror. Maybe they scared the hell out of you. Maybe they expanded your awareness of what horror could be and do. It's also okay if only part of a work impacted you. For example, when I was a kid, I saw a movie called *Earth vs. The Spider* on TV. It was an old, black-and-white flick about a giant spider terrorizing small towns. One scene (probably because the filmmakers didn't have the budget to show the spider much) depicted the aftermath of the spider's attack on a town. Cars were over-turned, buildings were smashed, and people lay dead in the street. One child survived, a blond-headed boy wearing glasses—one of the lenses was cracked—who was sobbing. The boy resembled me, which was bad enough, but this was shortly after my Uncle Red had died. Up to this point, I'd loved monster movies, and I'd never taken the deaths that occurred in these films seriously. But at that moment, seeing the boy cry, I understood that monsters killed people and made the survivors feel the same pain and sorrow I felt over losing my uncle. This one moment changed how I viewed horror forever.

1. _____
2. _____
3. _____
4. _____
5. _____

Now for each work on your list, write about what kind of impact it had on you. How did it contribute to your development as a horror fan? As a writer? As a person? Write a least a few sentences for each item on your list, but you can write as much as you wish. When you're finished, read over your responses and see what insights you can glean that might help you in your writing. For example, my experience with that one moment in *Earth vs. the Spider* taught me that horror stories aren't about monsters—they're about people. It also taught me the importance of emotional realism in horror fiction. And I began to understand the effect that dark story elements can have on an audience. I learned that the knife I wielded was sharp, and I had to be careful not to cut myself or my readers … at least, not *too* deeply. These are all important principles I follow in my writing to this day. You'll derive different insights from your list, of course, and that's exactly what you want—to become more *you*, to further hone your authorial voice.

_____
_____
_____
_____
_____
_____
_____

I THOUGHT ONLY VAMPIRES SUCKED THIS HARD

This exercise is the opposite of the last one. This time—again, without thinking about it too long—list five horror stories/books/films that disappointed you. So much that you wanted to hurl the book across the room, throw your TV out the window, or march straight to the customer service counter and demand your money back for the lousy DVD you bought, along with an extra twenty for mental and emotional damage.

1. _____
2. _____
3. _____

4. _____
5. _____

When you're finished, give yourself a few minutes for your blood pressure to return to normal, then write a few sentences (or more) about each item, this time focusing on what it was about the work that disappointed you so much. For example, I may be one of the few people who *hated* the ending of the film version of *The Mist*. I'd read the story when it first came out, and I loved the original ending in which the survivors drive through the mist into a world now filled with monstrous horrors. I had no problem with the bleakness of the film's ending, and intellectually, I can see why some view it as a bold choice. Stephen King himself said that he wished he'd had the balls to end his story that way when he first wrote it. But for me, it was a huge disappointment. The original ending opened up wonderfully dark possibilities in my imagination. What did I learn about myself from my reaction to the movie's ending? That I don't like neat, orderly endings in horror (however emotionally devastating they may be). I like endings that are more ambiguous, that make me think, that stimulate my sense of wonder. What kind of insights about yourself did you gain from your list?

_____
_____
_____
_____
_____
_____
_____

YOUR HORROR LANDSCAPE

Each of us has an internal map of the types of horror we love to read and write, but often we're not as familiar with it as we could be. Charting your individual horror landscape can not only give you a better idea of what sort of horror to write—especially if you're struggling to find a niche for yourself in the genre—it can also point out areas where your horror education may be lacking. Maybe you primarily read extreme horror, or you avoid it because it seems too icky. Maybe reading slow-burn horror seems like a dull slog to you, or maybe you love the deliberate building of dread. If you find yourself spending a majority of your time reading and writing a particular type of horror, it could be a strong indication that this a good field for you to plow. After all, don't most writers write the kind of stories they like to read? But knowing your internal horror landscape can also help you move past where you're currently at and grow as a writer. Robert Bloch, Ramsey Campbell, and Brian Lumley are just a few of the writers heavily influenced by Lovecraft when they were younger, and all of them wrote Lovecraftian fiction early on before eventually developing their own authorial voices and themes. Becoming more familiar with your horror landscape can also help you further explore why horror matters to you. Why do the types of horror you enjoy have meaning for you? Why are they important?

I first developed the concept for this exercise when I was doing publicity for *Writing in the Dark*. I was a guest on Gabriela Pereira's DIY MFA podcast, and she asked me a number of questions about the horror genre and its appeal. As I tried to explain the overall scope of the field, an image popped into my head of a map with four "directions," really basic elements of horror fiction: Real and Unreal (the vertical axis), and Quiet and Extreme (the horizontal axis). You could take any horror story, think about which directions it leaned toward, and be able to plot its position on the map. Not only does this help in discussing horror fiction by giving us more precise ways to position stories within the overall genre, if we plot the type of fiction we write on the map, it gives us a clearer way to brand our stories or even ourselves. For example, "Stefanie Queen writes realistic horror with an extreme edge."

Below are two copies of the Horror Map. One is for you to plot the type of stories you like to read. Put big X's for horror fiction you love the most, and use smaller x's for horror fiction you like okay but aren't necessarily in love with. So if you love Stefanie Queen's stories, you'd put a big X in the Real-Extreme quadrant, with the X being closer to the Real axis. If you like more than one type of horror (and most of us do), put down as many X's as you need to.

Horror Map: Reading Version
Graphic created by Christine Avery

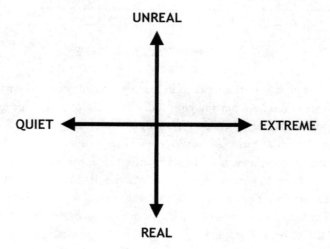

Now do the same thing with the type(s) of horror you like to write. If you really love a specific type, plot it with a big X. If you're less enamored of another type, use a small x.

Horror Map: Writing Version

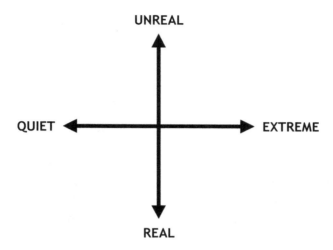

Once you're finished, look over the horror landscapes you charted and see what sort of insights you can gain from them about yourself as a horror reader and author, not only in terms of your preferences, but about why these types of horror matter to you. Spend some time freewriting about your insights.

YOUR HORROR MISSION STATEMENT

Assuming you've worked through the preceding exercises in this chapter, you're now ready to craft your Horror Mission Statement. Write a few sentences that encapsulate what horror means to you and what you want your fiction to accomplish. Here's one I've written for myself:

I want to write highly imaginative, unpredictable horror that's rich in bizarre imagery and strange incidents, while also presenting realistic characters. I want to write immersive fiction, where readers can experience what characters are thinking and feeling as events progress, and in which their fears and obsessions are manifested in the real world. I want readers to enjoy reading my horror fiction, while also having their preconceptions about what horror is challenged. I want to comment on horror tropes as I subvert them, while at the same time celebrating the genre I love so much.

A mission statement can be useful for honing in on your identity as a horror author, but it can also help with branding (which we'll discuss in a later chapter) as well as constructing an author bio (ditto).

Horror Mission Statement

_____
_____
_____
_____
_____
_____
_____

TAKE ME TO YOUR READER

Who are you writing for? And if you answer, "I write for myself," then who exactly *are* you?

Developing a profile of our ideal reader can give us even more insight into what we want to write (and how we write it), as well as helping us identify what qualities in our horror fiction we wish to emphasize and strengthen. Here's a quick sketch of who I imagine my ideal reader would be.

My ideal reader would be someone who loves horror as much as I do and is well-versed in the genre. They enjoy offbeat, sometimes experimental fiction, and they love seeing tropes reworked and twisted around. They're open to dark content—sometimes extremely dark—and they have an expansive imagination. They like meta-commentary on the genre (as long as it's not too overt), and they read for intellectual stimulation as much as to have fun.

So what does my reader profile do for me? As I said before, it can help me strengthen certain elements in my writing, but maybe just as importantly, it tells me who my ideal readers aren't. Like any other writer, I'd love it if everyone in the world bought my books, read them, and raved over them. But it's obvious from my reader profile that I'm not really interested in appealing to a large general audience. My reader profile is a very specific one, and it's no surprise that it sounds a lot like the kind of reader I am. A profile like this can help me make peace with the fact that I write for a smaller audience, which means my horror fiction will likely never see mainstream success. It can also help me identify the type of readers I want to market my fiction to. Okay, now it's your turn.

Reader Profile

_____
_____
_____
_____
_____
_____
_____

VOICES FROM THE SHADOWS

Lucy A. Snyder, Bram Stoker Award-winning author of *Halloween Season* and *Exposed Nerves*

Good descriptions are critical in creating unsettling, skin-crawling atmospheres in dark fiction. Most writers tend to focus on the sights and sounds their characters experience. But make sure to include details that relate to taste, touch, and smell. A good guideline is to make sure you're including two non-visual, non-auditory sensory details on each page.

Thinking more deeply about the world and situation of your characters is important in bringing authentic sensory details to your narratives. If you can't experience something yourself, memoirs and personal blogs can offer the specifics you're looking for. And take a page from nonfiction writers: Don't be afraid to interview people!

Alma Katsu, author of *The Hunger*, *The Deep*, and *Red Widow*

When I'm plotting and aren't sure what to do with a particular scene, I often ask "What's the worst thing that could happen?" and then write that scene. Every scene must have a purpose and that's to either advance the plot or reveal character. Also, for every scene you need to establish the POV character's goal for that scene—what is it he or she is trying to accomplish in that moment—and provide opposition. That's where "What's the worst thing that could happen?" comes in. I don't always use what I've written, but it often gets me thinking outside the box, seeing opportunities for ways to make the story trickier or richer.

Wendy N. Wagner, author of the *Locus* bestselling novel *An Oath of Dogs* and editor of *Nightmare Magazine*

Writing within a particular genre means that your reader often comes to your work with a preconception of what your story will try to do. A romance novel ought to work toward a happy ending. A sci-fi story should create an immersive world that can be explained with scientific principles. But the opening of every story makes its own unique promises that your reader will expect you to fulfill. Think about the first few scenes of the movie *The Shining*: We learn that Jack is a recovering alcoholic who hurt his son while drinking. We immediately expect alcohol to be a factor in the story, but that expectation is challenged when we learn all the alcohol has been removed from the hotel. Instead of leaving us dissatisfied, the story then introduces a phantom bartender serving phantom alcohol—which yes, causes all kinds of violence and distress. The promise at the beginning of the story was first subverted and then satisfied in an unexpected (and spooky!) way.

When it's time to edit your work, look closely at the first scene (if it's a short story) or the first fifty pages of a novel. What promises have you made? Are you meeting them? And are there any ways you can subvert the promise to help unsettle your reader even further? Revealing and resolving these promises will go a long way toward creating a satisfying reading experience.

Alan Baxter, award-winning author of *The Gulp*

For me, something I always try to remember when writing horror and suspense is to leave things unsaid. In music, it's often the gaps between the notes that have emotional weight, and it's like that with writing too. I trust in the intelligence of my readers and leave gaps for them to fill in. Then I do my best to subvert their expectations.

Matthew M. Bartlett, author of *The Stay-Awake Men and Other Unstable Entities*

Remember to craft the atmosphere of your setting so that all or most of your characters' senses are engaged. What do they see? What are the sounds? Aromas or odors? First, put yourself into the scene and gauge how you would react to all of this, and then modify them as necessary to reflect how your character reacts.

James Chambers, Bram Stoker Award-winning author of *On the Night Border*

Have confidence in your creativity. Don't self-reject story ideas because you've never seen them done before or they seem too dark, wild, or outlandish. Even ideas that don't pan out can help you find your voice.

CHAPTER TWO
THINGS UNKNOWN

At its core, horror fiction is about fear of the unknown, and the more unknown something is, the scarier it is. The more we understand about a threat, the more familiar it is, the more able we are to deal with it. I frequently use the example of the first two movies in the *Alien* franchise to illustrate this point. In *Alien*, the Xenomorph is an unknown, inhuman threat that the miners on *The Nostromo* aren't trained to deal with. Hence, *Alien* is a horror movie. But in *Aliens*, the characters—and the audience—are more familiar with Xenomorphs, and the space marines in the story are well-trained well-equipped, and well-experienced at dealing with alien creatures. Plus, there are a *lot* of Xenomorphs in that movie. The more encounters with the monsters, the less unknown they become. When all of these factors are taken into consideration, it's clear that *Aliens* is an action-adventure movie. (Side note to those of you writing a series: One of the best ways to keep a series fresh is to use different story paradigms for each installment. In my three *Nekropolis* books, I use a mystery paradigm in book one, a prison/adventure paradigm in book 2, and a war paradigm in book 3.)

Too many writers, perhaps influenced by simplistic horror films, overexplain things in their stories. What these writers don't understand is that these explanations exist to make horror stories *less* scary for the audience. Explanations provide reasons for why awful things occur in a story, reasons lead to understanding, understanding leads to a sense of control for the audience, and control equals safety. In the nineteenth century, horror stories often ended with "It was all a dream" or "The ghost was really Squire Langdon wearing a sheet." These days they might end with "Here are the rules that govern the Big Bad and which provide a way to defeat it" or "Science explains it all" or the revelation of a psycho killer's origin and motivation (in which the seed of the killer's defeat are contained). Explanations like these give the audience a feeling of control, of order being imposed upon chaos, making the Awful Thing not so awful in the end. If you don't want your audience to get *too* scared, if you want to give them some measure of relief in the end, if you want to reassure them that, despite the events depicted in your story, the world is a safe, sane, rational place after all, clear explanations—especially ones that allow your heroes to defeat the evil—work well. (All reasons why clear, comforting explanations are used in scary stories created for young children.) But horror writers pay a price for such explanations: They give up the power of the unknown—the true source of fear.

The exercises in this chapter are designed to help you harness the power of the unknown and use it in your horror fiction. How much you decide to explain in your stories is up to you, of course, but I urge you leave a little mystery and wonder in your dark tales, because that's where the magic lies.

DARKNESS STIRS

Write a scene in which some manner of dark force is present without it ever fully appearing or being named. Hints or glimpses of the dark force are okay to include, as long as it still possesses an aura of the unknown. This scene can be any type of horror you wish: Real, unreal, quiet, or extreme.

For example:

The instant Linda walked onto the Dessicks' patio she knew something wasn't right.

Jim stood at the grill, tending to some sort of sizzling meat, while Amy stood next to him, a glass of red wine in her hand. Their backs were to Linda, and neither turned as she slid the patio door shut and started walking toward them. They were two of the most outgoing and social people she knew, and usually greeted friends with loud happy voices and big hugs. Not this time. Not only didn't they acknowledge her presence, they stood so motionless they might have been mannequins. Despite the hot July day, they both wore long-sleeved shirts and jeans, the clothes looking brand-new, as if they'd just been pulled off the rack.

She couldn't see what Jim was grilling—hamburgers, or maybe chicken, she guessed—but there was something off about the smell. It was a rank odor, like leftover broccoli that had sat in the fridge too long. She heard an odd sound, soft, high-pitched, weak, and for a second she imagined that whatever was cooking on the grill wasn't quite dead yet. The contents of Amy's glass looked too dark, too thick to be wine, but what else could it be?

She felt a prickle on the back of her neck then, an atavistic warning signal urging her to leave immediately, and for an instant she stopped walking, almost turned around, rushed back into the house, dashed out the front door, jumped into her Miata, and drove the hell away as fast as she could. But she hesitated. Amy and Jim were her best friends. They'd all known each other since high school, for godsakes. She had no reason to be afraid of them.

She forced a smile and continued forward.

"Hey, you two. How's it going?"

At first, neither responded. Then they turned, moving slowly, motions deliberate, almost mechanical, and when she saw their faces—or rather the swirling mass of shadows where their faces should be—she almost screamed.

"Something wrong?" Amy asked.

She blinked and suddenly Jim and Amy's faces were restored. They were looking at her with concern.

"I … It's nothing." She smiled weakly. "Heat's getting to me, I suppose. It's been a real scorcher today."
Jim frowned. "Has it? We haven't noticed."
Amy smiled broadly displaying more teeth than should've fit into a human mouth.
"Hope you're hungry. We've cooked up something special for you."
"Very special," Jim added.

In this example, the dark force (whatever it may be) is lurking just below the surface of everyday reality, only partially visible, like the eyes and snout of a mostly submerged crocodile, watching its prey and waiting for the right moment to strike. What's really going on with Amy and Jim? Damned if I know. I just made up this example. But it's the sense of mystery, of the *unknown,* that gives this short scene its power.

Now you give it a try. When you're finished, read over what you've written, see what works and what doesn't. Were you too explicit about the nature of the dark force? Too vague? How could you change the scene to make it even more effective?

_____
_____
_____
_____
_____
_____
_____

SIRI, HOW DO YOU BANISH EVIL ENTITIES FROM DIMENSION X?

Horror stories—especially in movies and TV shows—often overexplain (or at least too easily explain) the nature of whatever threat the protagonists face. Heroes visit a professor of folklore at a nearby university, a scientist who specializes in whatever discipline is needed, a psychologist who has insight into the twisted minds of murderers to get the information required to vanquish a Big Bad … Or perhaps heroes will consult an ancient compendium of occult lore or do a quick Internet search to learn what they need to know. Whichever path they take, they end up getting something like this: *Ukor is a Baron of Hell who causes people to kill the thing they love most. According to legend, the only way to defeat Ukor and send him back to Hell is to confront him with the one thing he loves—the Archangel Seriphina. Seriphina fled Heaven after the War of the Divine, but instead of going to Hell with the other Fallen, she chose to dwell on Earth among humankind. Immortal, she's wandered the planet for untold millennia, an eternal nomad without a home. None know where Seriphina may be found or how to contact her, but it is said that if one travels to the Garden of Arcadia at Easter sunrise and says a prayer to her, she shall answer. Now to get to the Garden of Arcadia, you'll need to travel to Istanbul and hire a guide. Go to the Tavern of the Four Winds and ask for Omar the Dour—he's good and his fee is reasonable. And despite his name, he's actually a very funny guy …*

You don't have to completely avoid explanations in your horror fiction, of course, but as with everything else in fiction, less is usually more. So try the following exercise in explaining just enough. Come up with some kind of threat, whether natural or supernatural, and give it one weakness. Then write a short scene with a couple characters talking about an incident where they saw the threat demonstrate its weakness, but they don't fully understand what they saw. For example, here's a scene in which the creature's weakness is the sound of shattering glass:

"Did you see that?" Bob asked.

Kari stared at the broken window. In a small, frightened voice, she said, "Yes."

In her mind, she saw the thing—sleek like a panther but covered with sharp spines—run toward the window on all fours, leap into the air, and crash through the glass. As it went through, it let out a high-pitched shriek of agony like nothing she'd ever heard before. It sounded like a soul suffering all the torments of Hell at once.

They approached the window slowly, as if afraid the creature might leap back through and rend their flesh with its razor-sharp teeth and wickedly curved claws, but it didn't. Most of the glass had fallen outside when the creature crashed through, but a number of jagged shards still jutted from the window frame. Kari examined them, expecting to see blood on their sharp edges, but there was none. It seemed the creature hadn't been harmed when it had broken through. But then why had it cried out like that?

Why is this creature so affected by the sound of breaking glass? I don't know. I just wrote the scene for this exercise. Also, notice how I describe the monster with only a few bits of detail. Not only is this more realistic—in real life, we notice only a few details during a traumatic experience, especially when events are moving fast—it maintains a sense of the unknown about the creature.

Now you try it.

_____

_____

_____

_____

_____

_____

WHAT THE HELL WAS THAT?

In the previous exercise, I talked a bit about not depicting your story's malign presence in too much detail in order to preserve some mystery about it. In this exercise, we'll be focusing more closely on that technique. Imagine you're reading a horror story and you come across this passage:

The monster was a hairy, bipedal primate that stood eight feet, three inches tall. It was covered with thick brown fur, and its features were as much apelike as human. Its eyes were a striking amber color, and its hands and feet were huge and hairless. It weighed precisely 582 pounds, and when it opened its mouth, it displayed sharp yellowed teeth, the most prominent of which measured two and three-quarters inches. It exuded a strong odor, something like a cross between wet dog and skunk spray. The smell was so intense that any humans standing within ten feet of it would find their nasal passages burning and their eyes watering.

The above description—with the too-accurate measurements taken out—might work for a piece of adventure fiction, but it would suck the life out of a scene in a horror story. For one thing, it's presented in authorial narration as opposed to being filtered through the consciousness of a specific viewpoint character. For another, the creature is obviously a Bigfoot, and readers are well familiar with what those cryptids are supposed to look and smell like. No mystery whatsoever.

But what if I chose to write it from a character's perspective and used the technique presenting only a few striking details?

Philip noticed the smell first, a strange redolent odor that he couldn't place. There was something cloyingly floral about it, like flowers on the verge of rot, combined with a rank, earthy scent that reminded him of fresh mulch. He stopped in the middle of the trail, looked right then left, but he could see nothing through the thick forest growth. But something was out there, though. He could feel its eyes on him. Watching, measuring … trying to decide if he was a threat.

Or prey.

A sudden explosion of sound came from behind him, thrashing leaves and breaking branches. He spun around in time to see something—huge, monstrous—lumber quickly across the trail and disappear into the trees on the other side. More crashing noises as it plowed through undergrowth, but they soon stopped. It was almost as if the thing, whatever it was, could move silently through the forest when it wished, and it had purposely made sound to attract his attention. Or perhaps scare him. If that was the case, mission fucking accomplished. He was terrified.

Now that the thing was gone, he could only remember flashes of detail. Fur, teeth, and blazing amber eyes. Wait. The eyes … If he remembered seeing them, that meant the thing had turned its head to look at him as it crossed the trail. It had seen him. No, it had observed him. It had wanted a close-up look at the intruder in its realm, which was why it had made noise. So he would turn to face it. Ha-ha, made you look!

Philip felt suddenly sick, and he began trembling. He looked at the spot where the creature had vanished into the woods, breathing through his mouth so he wouldn't have to smell the awful stink of the thing.

So, still Bigfoot, right? But I avoided the usual details associated with him. No mention of big feet, and I changed the description of his body odor to make it less common. I also kept him mostly hidden in this scene, not only to preserve a sense of mystery about him, but also to make it harder to determine his motives. If you can't see him, you can't guess what he might be up to. He could be anywhere, maybe even right behind you if he can move silently when he wishes. I also let Philip guess as to the creature's motives. Maybe my Bigfoot was examining him, maybe not, but that's the impression Philip got. So even a well-used monster like Bigfoot can be made to feel unknown, depending on how you present it to readers.

Okay, pick a monster that everyone is familiar with. Vampire, werewolf, ghost, etc. Human monsters like serial killers count for this exercise too. If you have trouble coming up with a monster, pick one from a movie you love, like the shape-changing horror in *The Thing* or Michael, Jason, or Freddy. Write a short scene where a character encounters this monster, while maintaining an overall sense of the unknown about it.

_____
_____
_____
_____
_____
_____
_____

YESTERDAY UPON THE STAIR

Are you familiar with the poem "Antigonish" by William Hughes Mearns? Its first stanza is fairly famous, especially among horror folk.

> *Yesterday upon the stair,*
> *I met a man who wasn't there*
> *He wasn't there again today*
> *I wish, I wish he'd go away …*

The poem is supposedly about a ghost, but I've always interpreted it as a surreal bit of flash fiction regarding a strange presence the narrator feels but cannot detect with his or her senses. Definitely a great example of the power of the unknown at work.

For this exercise, I want you to write a short scene in which a character feels the presence of something dark and dangerous, but doesn't actually see or hear it, not completely anyway. Here's an example (and I'll use a staircase just to keep the poem's imagery going).

Evie placed her hand on the railing, but she didn't set her foot upon the first step. She stood there, frozen, unable to move forward, but also unable to remove her hand from the railing and walk away. She shouldn't be doing this. She needed to get ready for work. She'd already been late twice this week, and if it happened again, her supervisor would write her up for sure. But in the four months since she and Beth had moved into the house, she'd gone upstairs only twice, maybe three times, and only then with Beth accompanying her. She'd disliked the upstairs since the moment the real estate agent had first shown them the place. It felt colder up there than it did downstairs, and it was too quiet, skin-crawlingly so, as if the walls absorbed sound instead of bouncing it back. And then there were the dreams that had come after the showing, dreams in which the steps vanished behind her as she ascended the stairs, and when she reached the top and looked back, the entire first floor of the house was gone, nothing left but impenetrable darkness.

She'd wanted nothing to do with the damn place, would never have bought it on her own, but Beth absolutely loved *it.* It's my dream house, *she said.* I want us to grow old together there.

So Evie kept her misgivings to herself, and they moved in a short time later. Beth had wanted their bedroom to be on the ground floor, which was such a relief that Evie almost cried when Beth had told her. She tried to convince herself that she'd get used to the house, that before long it would feel like home, and the upstairs wouldn't bother her anymore. One day she'd tell Beth how she'd originally felt about the house's second floor, and they'd laugh about it. But after all this time, Evie still hadn't adjusted to the house. If anything, her feeling about the upstairs—her absolute, unreasoning dread of it—had only become stronger.

She begun trying to go upstairs by herself every morning. Beth had already begun asking her why she never went upstairs, and Evie didn't want to admit the truth to her. Beth would probably think something was wrong with her mentally, would urge her to "get help" and "see someone." Evie didn't think she could stand that. Beth left for work a half hour before she did, so once Beth was gone, Evie went to the stairs and tried to walk up them. It had taken her a week to work up the courage to touch the railing, but she hadn't managed to go any further.

Don't be such a baby, *she told herself.* You can do this. Take the step, just the first one. Do it … Do it!

She raised her right foot off the floor, only a few inches, and she kept it there for several moments. Then, with a defeated sigh, she put it down again, and she finally released her grip on the railing.

She'd try again tomorrow.

Feeling utterly defeated, she turned and headed down the hall toward the bedroom. If she hurried and got ready fast, she might make it to work on time today. That would be something, at least.

There are a couple of specific details in this example—it's colder upstairs (at least to Evie)—and sound seems deadened there. And of course, there are the dreams Evie's had. But in the scene itself, Evie experiences absolutely nothing strange about upstairs. She didn't even make it there. Yet the baleful presence of the house's second floor permeates the scene.

Your turn. Start writing.

_____

_____

_____

_____

_____

_____

VOICES FROM THE SHADOWS

V. Castro, author of *Hairspray and Switchblades* and *Goddess of Filth*.

Most of us have watched *The Shining*. Putting all the supernatural stuff aside, we see a writer who is not content with his life or himself as he recovers from alcohol addiction and a physical accident with his young son. And now finds himself doing a job he has little real interest in. He just wants to write this book. His frustration builds when it doesn't happen. I'm not a mind reader, but I can probably guess he is grumbling to himself about his misery as he stares at the blank page. Everything he is feeling and thinking churns in circles in his head instead of the free-flowing story ideas he desires. His foot is on the mental gas instead of maintaining a neutral coasting speed.

If you want to clear the mental blocks, you have to step over them for a spell OR take all those stumbling blocks in life and create a bridge. Write about it expecting nothing to come from it. Flow. Writing an essay, novella, or novel isn't just about the words. These are created by a human being. You are human. Be kind to yourself.

The biggest hinderance you can have, the greatest creativity blocks are self-limiting beliefs and internal noise. So many aspects of writing ride on validation. It is a business that thrives on validation. But if you are focusing on step ten of the journey, you will find it difficult to know where to begin step one. The longer the radio silence, the deeper the frustration and louder the noise. I know.

Here is my writing tip. Stop expecting anything from yourself or the page. Imagine step ten (opportunities, validation, reviews, feedback, etc.) doesn't even exist. Stepping away from a story or social media costs you nothing; however, consider your mental clarity and health priceless. Jack Torrance might have had the idea of his life if he stepped out of the hotel and got lost in the maze or threw himself into the snow with abandon. Just flowed with the life around him.

The greatest asset to my writing has been, hands down, a meditation practice and living life. The page is on my computer. It can't walk away. I step out of my ego and into just being a breathing human.

I hope this helps and many blessings on your writing journey.

P.D. Cacek, Bram Stoker and World Fantasy Award winner, author of *Sebastian, Second Lives* **and** *Second Chances.*

Here are three easy steps to scaring your reader:

1. Think about what makes most people uneasy. It doesn't have to be a BIG fear, sometimes the smallest things are the most frightening.
2. Let the reader do the work. Give your reader just enough information so they can fill in the details. Don't tell them they're about to be scared, let them scare themselves.
3. Write the ending first. This way you always know where the story/novel is going.

Nadia Bulkin, author of *She Said Destroy*

For me, the hardest part of writing a short horror story is sticking the landing: Creating an ending that feels satisfying and earned. I usually sketch out several options as bullet points and ask myself: Which one feels like the thematically inevitable result of the actions or priorities the main character started out with? Which one undercuts narrative convention? What mood do you want the reader to leave with—resolved (you've closed the loops) or unresolved (you've opened new loops)?

William Meikle, author of the S-Squad Series

Editing Tips …
    Cheque yure speling.
    Grammar your check.
    Remove any superfluous unnecessary adjectives.
    Remove any repeating repetitious repetition.
    Are your verbs will use the right tense?
    Never use a long word when a short individual will do.

Gaby Triana, author of *Moon Child*

Something that makes me disengage from a story is when an author reveals visual horror in favor of emotional horror. Your character isn't just a pair of eyeballs, there to describe a grisly scene to the reader. What are they thinking as they come upon the horror? What has been building in their minds up until this point? What is the emotional payoff? Even after they've given us the horrific description, don't forget to include a few lines to show what they're processing internally. I'm much more invested in a story when I connect to what characters are going through over how much blood is being spilled.

R.J. Joseph, Bram Stoker Award-nominated author

I've learned to tell the story from the point of view that best serves the story rather than forcing the POV I think should be used. The strength of a story can be determined by who's telling the story. Sometimes, that's not the character who screams the loudest inside your head. It could be the one who sits quietly, taking everything in. It could be the monster.

CHAPTER THREE
EVERYTHING YOU KNOW IS WRONG

Horror comes from a violation of what we believe to be reality. It's a distortion of society, nature, humanity, physics, space, and time that creates horror. Regardless of how realistic or unrealistic your horror is, a violation like this should lay at the heart of your story and deliver a clear message to readers: The Universe is not our friend; it's chaotic, malicious, and very, very hungry.

In the movie *The Fly*, the distortion comes from a scientist who accidentally fuses his DNA with that of the titular insect. In *Red Dragon*, the distortion comes from Francis Dolarhyde's twisted psyche. In *The Shining*, the distortion comes from Jack Torrance's susceptibility to the influence of The Overlook Hotel. Whatever type of horror story you're telling, the distortion needs to be a nightmarish one, one in which normal reality is violated. This is why a real-life horrific event—such as being taken hostage during a bank robbery—isn't by itself good fodder for horror fiction. It's an awful, traumatic experience for those involved, but it doesn't distort reality. It's a *known* event. But we don't know what a human-fly hybrid monster, a caretaker driven mad by a powerful dark force, or a psychotic, delusional serial killer will do. They're *unknown*—the stuff of nightmares.

In *Writing in the Dark*, I wrote about reading an interview Stephen King gave early in his career. He said the way he gets his ideas is by looking at something and telling himself, "There's something wrong with that." I used this as the basis for an exercise in the previous volume, and since it's a great technique for generating ideas for violations, I thought I'd at least mention it here as something you might try.

In this chapter, we're going to work through fresh exercises for creating distortions to use in your horror fiction. So get ready, get set … violate!

VIOLATION 101

We're going to start small, but many times a small violation is all you need, especially if you're writing a short story. Small violations can be useful when writing novel scenes too, as long as they're tied to the overarching threat. The moment that a violation is revealed makes a great starting point for a story or scene.

For this exercise, take an ordinary, even banal, activity, and introduce one violation to it. This violation can be real or unreal, your choice. You might consider trying a bit of each, just to see which path results in stronger ideas. I'll go first.

Ordinary Activity: Preteen child walks into the kitchen where Mom is working at the sink, presumably washing dishes.

Violation: The child walks up to the sink and sees that Mom is actually washing a severed hand.

Creepy, right? Okay, it's your turn. Go ahead, I'll wait.

Ordinary Activity: _____

Violation: _____

You back? Good. Now let's do an exercise designed to add a violation to a scene in a novel. If you're currently working on a novel, you can use that concept for this exercise. If you're not writing a novel at the moment, you can make up a concept. Either way, this concept is the seed from which the various violations spring. I'll pretend I'm writing a novel in which a recently-resurrected vampire is tormenting a family who lives in the old house that used to be his when he was alive. He plans to make them suffer for "trespassing" before he feeds on them. I'll add in the idea that in this story, vampires dement the longer they go without blood and begin acting erratically. This would explain why my vampire is so obsessed with punishing the family—and the fact that he can't think straight until he feeds makes him unpredictable and thus more dangerous, *and* it could also give the family an advantage against him. (Man, I wish these were the days when Zebra was churning out horror novels. I'd pitch this idea to them in a heartbeat!) I'll create three violations for three separate scenes.

Novel Premise: You just read it above.

Violation: This vampire is the classic kind, which can command animals to do its will. To torment the family, the vampire sends rats to scuttle around in their walls. At first, the family only hears a few noises, but they get louder and louder until the rats explode from the walls and flood the house.

Violation: Using the vampire power to psychically affect humans, the vampire enters each of the family members' dreams and puts them through different nightmarish scenarios.

Violation: Again using his psychic power, the vampire causes each of the family members to turn against each other in increasingly irrational and violent ways.

The beauty of this technique is that you can use it as a plotting/organizing tool as well. Give it a try. If you like, take it one step further and consider how you might organize your scenes into an effective sequence.

_____
_____
_____
_____
_____
_____
_____
_____

DEGREES OF VIOLATION

For this exercise, come up with a realistic scenario. It can be an everyday sort of thing, like washing dishes, or an exciting scenario filled with the potential for conflict and drama, such as the previously mentioned bank robbery. Either way, it should be a scenario that could occur in real life. You're going to take this scenario and begin introducing nightmarish elements into it, making it increasingly bizarre as you go. Allow me to demonstrate.

Starting Scenario: Taking your car to an automatic carwash.

Minor Violation: (Something out of the ordinary but still possible.) A naked man covered with tattoos from head to toe enters the carwash on foot behind you and follows you, showing no reaction as he gets blasted by soap and water.

Medium Violation: (Something weirder which might or might not be possible in real life.) The man gets into your car, sits on the passenger seat, and looks at you with a beatific smile. "Have you heard the good word about our lord and savior Purity?" You see that all of his tattoos are of various carwashes. He smells extremely clean, like a baby after a bath.

Major Violation: (Something weirder still, which more than likely couldn't happen in reality.) The man begins to half-chant, half-sing as loud as he can, and the carwash echoes the sound ten times louder, as if it's alive and answering him.

Ultra-Violation: (A violation so damn weird that it's literally like something out of a nightmare.) Before you say anything, the man's mouth opens wide, and he vomits burning-hot soapy water all over you. It hurts like hell at first, but then it begins to feel pleasant, as if all your cares are being washed away. You dissolve with a blissful sigh and the naked man slides over, takes the wheel, and—whistling—drives the car out of the carwash and down the road.

When you do this exercise, it doesn't have to be a step-by-step progression like mine so that it makes a mini-story. Mine just came out that way, probably because an automatic carwash is a beginning, middle, and end sort of scenario. Although now that I think of it, this technique could be used as a tool to help plot a short story or novel.

One of the cool things about this exercise is that you can base a story off any stage of violation—minor, medium, major, and ultra. You don't have to get any weirder than you're comfortable with. But by running a scenario through all the violation stages before you start writing, you might come up with an idea that you really like, one you wouldn't have developed without the exercise.

Bonus Exercise: Make notes for stories you'd tell based solely on each violation on your list. Which versions seem fresher and more interesting to you? Which seem like they might be more successful with editors and readers? Which ones less so?

_____
_____
_____
_____
_____
_____
_____

VIOLATION STACKING

So far, the exercises in this chapter have focused on adding one violation of reality at a time. In general, focusing on a single significant violation in a short story or novel scene works well, as the reader's suspension of disbelief isn't strained too far. If you start piling on the violations, you might well end up in Bizarro territory (which is cool if that's where you'd like to go). Not so cool, maybe, if you want your fiction to reach a broader, general audience. And too many violations at a time can make your horror fiction unintentionally humorous, so unless you're setting out to write a dark version of Looney Tunes, you might want to keep your imagination in check. But let's say you *want* to go batshit crazy with your story. This exercise will help you get there.

Violation stacking is when you start with one violation, then have something violate that, then have something violate *that*, and so on. For example …

Initial Violation: Thousands of tiny spiders come rushing out of a corpse's mouth.

Second Violation: Witnesses to this event feel an overwhelming compulsion to eat the spiders, which they begin to do, scooping up handfuls and jamming them into their mouths.

Third Violation: A human carrying an axe comes onto the scene. They scream, "No! I can't let this happen again!" and attack the affected ones.

Fourth Violation: The affected humans fight back.

Fifth Violation: One of the affected hears a chorus of tiny voices in her mind. *You must take us away from here—before he tries to reclaim us!* Her thoughts clear at the sound of the chorus, but she's too horrified by what's happening to flee right away.

Sixth Violation: The corpse sits up, sees the person with the axe, and screams, "Stay away from my children!" He then attacks and kills the axe-wielder.

Seventh Violation: The surviving affected (excluding the woman who hears the spider voices), kneel before the living corpse. "Father," they say in unison.

Eighth Violation: The Father looks at the woman standing. "Bring her to me," he says. The Children rise and start toward her. The spiders inside her scream *"Run!"* and she hauls ass out of there. The Children race after her.

As with the other samples I've created so far, I made this one up as I went. Eight isn't a magical number. Your response to the exercise can have three violations, or twenty, or however many you like. Mine just happened to reach what seemed like a good stopping point at eight. One of the ways I tried to minimize the strain on the reader's suspension of disbelief was to keep the violations related and provide a sense they're part of some larger story. It's not necessary that you do this for the exercise, but it couldn't hurt to try.

Speaking of trying, it's time you did just that. Start stacking those violations!

_____

_____

_____

_____

_____

_____

_____

VOICES FROM THE SHADOWS

Steve Rasnic Tem, award-winning author of *Figures Unseen: Selected Stories* and *Thanatrauma*

If I'm stuck for an ending for a story I go back to the beginning and ask a few questions: What is the conflict in the opening? What expectations have I set? What questions arise? What are the opening images? Have I suggested a theme or obsession? With answers in hand, I try to craft an ending which answers these questions or at least resonates in some emotionally meaningful way with what I've set up in the beginning. Finding a killer last line or paragraph is always a bonus.

Tananarive Due, executive producer of *Horror Noire: A History of Black Horror*

My advice for horror writers is the same for all writers: Compelling stories begin with deep characterization. In horror, the characters' lives, objectives and obstacles should ring as deep and true as they do in contemporary realism. One litmus test I always strive to pass: If you took away the horror element, would the readers still care about your characters? If not, go deeper. Get to know them better. Also, the reader won't be afraid if the characters are never anxious. A story is only "scary" if we feel dread for the sake of the characters.

John Shirley, award-winning author of *Stormland*

My advice to writers—turn on your flashlight. I have a flashlight. It's my attention. In a dark world, I turn my flashlight this way, that way, turn my attention here and there, and it illuminates corners of my world. My inner world, my outer world. I need more light. This flashlight only lights up small areas. I have heard there is another light, and if you can find a Certain Something to point your flashlight at, it causes another, bigger light to come on.

Janine Pipe, Splatterpunk Award-winning author of *Twisted: Tainted Tales*

Something I adhere to, especially as a woman who tends to dip her toes into the extreme, is don't be afraid to address issues such as motherhood, menstruation and menopause and then make them into something a reader might not expect. Perhaps the mother you write about eats her baby? Maybe your serial killer likes to attack during her periods and cover victims in her blood. Or you could use the metaphor of menopause and as your female creature goes through the change, she becomes human? Women can write splatterpunk and have strong women as their main characters. Make them as strong-willed and bad ass as you can. There is no rule that women have to be likeable, in horror especially. But try to ensure they're more than just a Final Girl.

Thomas Tessier, award-winning author of *World of Hurt: Selected Stories*

One tip I've found useful several times comes from Hemingway. Whether you're writing a novel or a short story, he suggested that you try to end every writing session at a point where you know exactly what the next line or lines will be. That can help you get rolling on a good start the next time you sit down to resume the work. It might seem wrong, as our instinct is usually to keep pushing on when the writing is going well, but it really can help you avoid those times when a cold start on a new paragraph or chapter just drags stubbornly.

Simon Strantzas, author of *Burnt Black Suns*

I've often found that the most ridiculous and silly ideas can become, with very little tweaking, the most bizarre and frightening parts of a story. This is likely because the root of ridiculousness and horror is the juxtaposition of the abnormal with the normal. When I find myself stuck in a story of any kind I ask myself what is the most outrageous and bonkers thing that could happen, then I take the story there to see what happens. If it doesn't work, I don't have to keep it, but even when it doesn't, I've usually learned something or unclogged something that lets me keep going. (That said, it pretty much always works.)

CHAPTER FOUR
HELLO DARKNESS, MY OLD FRIEND

Several years ago, I was on a panel at StokerCon titled "A Haunted House with Many Rooms." The topic was the richness of the horror genre, and I thought the title was an excellent way to describe how varied horror can be. In this chapter, we're going to explore some of the rooms contained within our haunted house, and see if there are some you'd prefer—or perhaps are more suited—to work in than others.

In *Writing in the Dark*, I wrote at some length about the pros and cons of consciously working in only one subgenre of horror, so I won't repeat that information here. I will say that I think it's valuable to explore different subgenres, not only because doing so can keep you from getting bored with your writing, but because you never know which subgenre might produce your best, most satisfying, and most successful fiction.

Here's a quick rundown of horror (and horror-adjacent) subgenres. Hopefully, I've covered most of them, but don't assume these are the only subgenres that exist. Who knows? You might invent your own horror subgenre someday!

Supernatural Horror: Horror caused by some kind of malign occult force.

Realistic Horror: Horror that could happen in the real world.

Psychological Horror: Realistic Horror, but with an emphasis on the characters' mental states, either protagonist, antagonist, or both.

Quiet Horror: Horror that's a slow accumulation of frightening details which build dread throughout a story.

Extreme Horror: In-your-face violent and gory horror.

Literary Horror: Horror whose aims are literary in nature—high-quality writing, character-based instead of plot-based, more subtle in terms of how the horror is presented, striving to explore deeper themes.

Cosmic Horror: Horror based on the idea that there are powers in the universe far greater than us, and who—if they notice us at all—regard us as little more than insects.

Erotic Horror: Horror with sexual elements.

Body Horror: Horror derived from alterations to one's body, whether through illness, injury, experimentation, mutilation, and some unknown force. Transformation is a major theme.

Surreal Horror: Horror that seems like a living nightmare.

Young Adult Horror: Any horror subgenre can be YA, as long as it's written for young adults.

Dark Fantasy: Horror that includes fantasy elements or fantasy that includes horror elements.

The Weird: This subgenre is a blend of horror, fantasy, and science fiction, and its goal is to create unease more than horror.

Bizarro: Dark absurdism.

Pulp Horror: A modern-day version of the entertainment-based horror that appeared in the old pulp magazines.

Creature-Feature Horror: Monsters chomping people, like in *Jaws,* or Kaiju stomping on cities.

Transgressive Horror: Horror that breaks taboos.

Gothic Horror: Horror in the tradition of stories from the nineteenth century and earlier, with a strong focus on atmosphere.

Humorous Horror: Horror mixed with humor.

Apocalyptic Horror: End-of-the-world horror.

Survival Horror: Horror in which the protagonists must battle with natural forces to survive.

Folk Horror: Horror based on rural cults and legends.

Science Fiction Horror: The horror is derived from science.

Country Horror, Small-Town Horror, Urban Horror: These are variations on a theme—the protagonist is out of his or her normal environment and is faced with unfamiliar threats.

Social Horror: Horror that comes from and comments on social issues, such as *Get Out.*

Religious/Satanic Horror: Horror derived from religious concepts, usually—but not necessarily—Christian.

Supernatural Thriller: A thriller with some supernatural elements.

Dark Crime, Dark Suspense, Dark Mystery: These subgenres are darker than usual in terms of characters, events, and themes, and because of this, they're closer to horror than regular crime, suspense, and mystery stories.

Now that we've established the subgenres, let's move on to some exercises dealing with them.

HORROR SUBGENRE SELF-ASSESSMENT

1. Which of the subgenres on the list have you read?

    _____
    _____
    _____
    _____

2. Are there any subgenres you seek out as a reader or viewer? Why? What draws you to them?

    _____
    _____
    _____

3. Are there any subgenres you actively (or perhaps subconsciously) avoid as a reader/viewer? Why? What about them repels you?

    _____
    _____
    _____

4. Which subgenres have you written in? Are there any that you tend to focus on the most? Why do they appeal to you as a writer?

    _____

    _____

    _____

    _____

5. Are there any subgenres that you've tried to write in but for whatever reason couldn't? If so, why do you think you had trouble with those subgenres?

    _____

    _____

    _____

    _____

6. Are there any subgenres you see as your "brand"? If so, why do you identify with this subgenre?

    _____

    _____

    _____

    _____

7. Are there any subgenres you'd have mixed or negative feelings about being identified with? Why?

    _____

    _____

    _____

    _____

8. Complete this sentence: _____ is the best subgenre of horror because …

    _____

    _____

    _____

    _____

9. Complete this sentence: _____ is the worst subgenre of horror because …

    _____

    _____

    _____

    _____

10. If you've received feedback on your horror fiction—whether from friends and family, beta readers, reviewers, or critics—what elements of your stories do people tend to comment on the most? What elements have they found most frightening, compelling, disturbing? Is there anything about this feedback that surprised you?

_____
_____
_____
_____

11. Is there any subgenre you've never written in but would love to try? What's kept you from exploring that subgenre?

_____
_____
_____
_____

12. After finishing items 1-11, read back over your responses. Do you see any patterns or trends? If so, did they confirm how you view yourself as a horror writer or did they give you a new perspective on yourself? Do you see any new directions you might like to explore in your work?

_____
_____
_____
_____

TIMES THREE

Take an idea from a story you've written or are currently working on. If you prefer, come up with a new idea for a story. Choose three subgenres that are different from the category your story fits into and make notes about how your core story concept would change if you wrote it in those three subgenres. Here's one of mine:

Story Concept: I'll use my short story "Mr. Punch," which appeared in the anthology *Young Blood*, published by Zebra Books in 1994. (If you're unfamiliar with Punch and Judy shows, hit Wikipedia for a quick background or go to YouTube to watch video of some performances.) "Mr. Punch" was the first story I sold for professional rates, as well as the first one where I wrote the kind of surreal dark fantasy-type horror I've become known for. In the story, a deranged serial killer who identifies with Punch from the classic puppet shows kills women who he believes are all Judys. During his latest outing, he senses that he's being stalked by the Devil, who often makes an appearance in Punch and Judy shows. At first, it appears the story is a realistic one and that Mr. Punch is delusional. By the end it's clear that the Devil—along with the combined spirit of all the "Judys" Mr. Punch has killed—has come for him. (Sorry for the spoiler, but it *is* an old story. If you'd like to the read the entire thing, you can find it in my first short story collection *All Too Surreal*.)

The story falls squarely within the Surreal Horror subgenre. Mr. Punch may be a serial killer, but there's not much overt violence in the story, so it's not also Extreme Horror. Because the events of the story might all be in Mr. Punch's mind, it has elements of Psychological Horror, and as one of my themes is women victims symbolically banding together to strike back at their male killer, it also has elements of Social Horror. I'll avoid those subgenres for this exercise and go with Science Fiction Horror, Erotic Horror, and Body Horror.

Science Fiction Horror: Across the world, a new virus causes men to start attacking and killing women. Someone in the media dubs this the "Punch Virus," and the name sticks. A new variant of the virus—the Judy Variant—makes women even more vicious so they can defend themselves.

Erotic Horror: Mr. Punch is a sex worker who specializes in S&M. He earned his nickname because of how violent he is with his clients. One day he's hired by a man calling himself the Devil and ordered to do his worst.

Body Horror: In the original story, the boy who would become Mr. Punch identified with the puppet because his features were similarly distorted. For this version, I'll have Mr. Punch look normal but seek out plastic surgery so that he'll resemble the puppet Punch. After his operation, he plans to start killing "Judys." But while he's under anesthesia, the plastic surgeon attaches parts of a woman's body to his, including the head. When he wakes, the surgeon says, "What's a Punch without a Judy?"

The Erotic Horror and Body Horror versions would work for short stories, while the Science Fiction Horror version might work for a novel. It would likely also be Extreme Horror, given the level of violence that would occur in that story. An exercise like this can be useful to play around with a concept and see if it might fit one type of horror better than another. And if you find yourself excited at the prospect of writing one version, that could indicate it's a subgenre worth exploring. Now it's your turn to try. (Bonus points if you run your core concept through all the subgenres!)

_____
_____
_____
_____
_____
_____
_____

MAKE A SCENE

Now that you have several different subgenre versions of a story idea, choose one and write a short scene from it. The scene can be the opening, something from the middle, or the end. (If you feel especially industrious, write the entire story.) Whatever you write, try to focus on the main element of that subgenre. For my Erotic Horror version of "Mr. Punch," I'd write a scene that involved sex. For the Science

Horror version, I'd focus on a woman character becoming infected by the virus and defending herself from an attack by "Punches." I might also focus on violence if I want to explore the Extreme Horror aspect of the concept. For the Body Horror version, I'd write the last scene, where Punch wakes up with a Judy attached. Once you've written your scene, ask yourself if it works better than your original idea. Also, what was your experience of writing it? Was it easier or harder than you thought? If so, why? Did you enjoy writing it more than you expected? Less? Again, why?

_____
_____
_____
_____
_____
_____
_____

HORROR FOR THE AGES

Age groups, that is.

For this exercise, take an idea for a horror story—the same one you used for the last exercise or a new one—and write several sentences about how you would adapt it for different age groups.

- Preschool Children
- Young Children
- Preteens
- Teenagers
- New Adults (18-22)
- Adults
- Middle-Age Adults
- Seniors

I'll use a new story idea for my example this time: An old tree standing next to a house is sentient and evil.

Preschool Children. This would be a picture book about a child whose bedroom is on the second floor of a house. A scary-looking tree is located outside his or her window, and the child doesn't like looking at it. One night during a thunderstorm, the child dreams about the tree—which has a (mildly) scary face on it is peering through the window. When the child wakes, they go to the window and see that the tree has no face. They also see that a family of robins—mom, dad, and babies—are sheltered from the storm by the tree's branches. The child realizes that just because something looks scary, it doesn't mean that thing is bad. The child goes back to sleep with a smile on their face. (Because this idea is geared toward preschool children, the horror element is toned way down.)

Young Children. This would be a chapter book about how the tree uproots itself and starts running through the neighborhood scaring everyone. A child who lives in the house next to where the tree once stood goes after it to try to convince it to stop misbehaving and come home. (This version would be a little scarier than the last, but still not too scary.)

Preteens. This version could be scarier, although no one would be hurt, at least not severely. The scary tree uproots itself and then starts bringing all the trees in town to life. The kid who lives in the house where the tree stood, along with a few of his or her friends, has to discover what's causing the trees to become animate and how to stop it.

Teenagers. Aside from the age of the protagonists, this version might not differ very much from one written for adults. The story could be more intense than previous versions, with a greater sense of threat toward the characters. There could be some violence and even some death, but I wouldn't depict either in graphic detail (at least, not *too* graphic). I'd add in some themes relating to teenagers—first romance, being unsure if you can handle a truly serious problem, establishing an adult identity, being part of a group or standing as an individual, etc. Maybe I'd have the tree be able to infect humans and transform them into tree people to stress the dangers of conformity.

New Adults (18-22), Adults, Middle-Age Adults, Seniors. I'd do the same basic thing for all of these groups as I did for teens. I'd have the protagonists be the same age as the readers, and I'd shape the story around ideas and themes that are important to those readers. Anyone from teens on up could read and enjoy these versions, but readers from the targeted age group would (hopefully) get the most out of them.

Now it's your turn.

Once you're finished, look over what you came up with. Do you note any major differences between the versions? Are there any you would be more interested in writing? Which do you think would be most successful for you? Least? Any other insights you can glean from this exercise?

_____

_____

_____

_____

_____

_____

VOICES FROM THE SHADOWS

Kate Jonez, author of Bram Stoker Award-nominated *Lady Bits*

Most writers are aware that a story needs big questions to answer: Who is the killer? What's the nature of the monster, etc.? If handled well, these questions add tension and suspense. Smaller questions sprinkled throughout the story can add another layer and infuse the story with a sense of unease which keeps readers on edge even if they aren't sure exactly why. Examples could be things like a package arrives and the main character doesn't open it. A phone call comes in but we don't know who's on the other end. Someone mentions an event on a future date but doesn't say what it is. Extending the time before answering questions like these infuses the story with a sense of anticipation and suspense.

Frazer Lee, Bram Stoker Award-nominated author of *Greyfriars Reformatory*

Think of what scares you most and why.
   Write it down.
   (This is where writers' neuroses can come in handy, but if you're genuinely fearless, then interview a friend.)
   Think back to when you were happiest, safest, or most contented and why.
   Write it down.
   (If you've never felt that way, my sympathies! And … interview a friend.)
   Now draw a line between the everyday memory and the frightening thing—e.g., a birthday party (fun, community) awash with maggots (fear, revulsion).
   And write a short story of 500 words or more.

Laird Barron, Shirley Jackson Award-winning author of *Swift to Chase*

Some of the best advice I've incorporated into my own process came from auditing classes by writer and teacher, John Langan. An artist's imagination is among their most powerful allies. As time passes, one's imagination, or muse, can grow stronger, more powerful. Which is to say, it can be actively developed. When we're kids, our imaginations are akin to boisterous puppies. The puppy loves to play fetch. It will bring you anything from the shoes you requested to an old bone or a chewed sock. The results can be utterly random. You train the puppy by encouraging it no matter what, and with even more praise when it brings you the right object--in this case a good idea, plot solution, etc, etc. Writers can acquire the bad habit of dismissing "absurd" or "weak" ideas. This discourages the puppy and over time might cause it to quit altogether. Don't be that writer. Pat your muse on the head and send the little sucker hunting for buried treasure. Eventually, you'll have more ideas than years to turn them into stories or novels.

Somer Canon, author of *Slaves to Gravity*

Tension is a useful tool in all genres of storytelling. It's especially important in genres that rely on making the reader uncomfortable, and horror storytelling is definitely at its best when the reader is squirming.

Tension is at its best not when it just shows up—that happens and there's nothing wrong with it—but when we're talking horror, tension is most effective when it builds. It starts at nothing and slowly, but steadily it ratchets up, like tightening a spring.

A great exercise when writing is to consider the types of tension and how they are felt and displayed. A great place to look at tension, and you might laugh, is in nature documentaries. Come on, they're plentiful and they're a great way to observe how animals react to situations that build from being normal to disastrously violent. I've found that looking at animals that, like us, are social is ideal. Prides of lions. Packs of wolves. There are social norms on full display without pretense in these groups and the great thing about tension is that it nudges and pokes at those norms and irks the group members who believe in them and thrive because of them. It's simple, yes, but it's a good starting point. I think you'd be surprised at how complex these social creatures can be … either that or we, as animals, are desperately simple. You choose your own answer on that one.

Donyae Coles, Splatterpunk Award-nominated author of "Breaking the Waters"

Don't worry about if something is "scary enough." Write it to your horrifying best. Just because you're not shaking in your boots doesn't mean it won't give the readers major heebie jeebies. So don't get hung up on it. We're all afraid of different things, just write the best dread that you can and let the readers' imaginations do the rest.

CHAPTER FIVE
STRANGE NOTIONS

So, where do *you get all your weird ideas? Your mind must be one damn crazy place, am I right?*

Non-writers always want to know where writers get their ideas, and this goes double for horror writers. In one sense, we get our ideas from the same place all artists do: Everywhere. But writers who create completely realistic fiction have it easier, I think. They can write their fiction without having the additional task of adding a violation of reality to it. But we need to inject a shot of darkness into our work, *and* we need to be mindful to avoid ideas that have been overused. (We'll discuss avoiding clichés in the next chapter.) The exercises in this chapter are designed to help you come up with those wonderfully disturbing ideas which are the lifeblood of horror fiction.

A word of caution: Some of the exercises ask you to examine your personal experiences for nightmare fuel, but this doesn't mean you have to revisit painful events from your past and retraumatize yourself. The exercises in this book are yours to do (or not do) as you wish. But if you do give the exercises in this chapter a try, remember that you never have to show the results to anyone. Hell, you don't even have to write anything down—you can just think your responses to yourself. And if you do use any painful memories in your stories, the beauty of fiction is that you can always tell people you made it up.

Jack Ketchum used to give a workshop called Writing from the Wound. (You can find a video of him reading an essay based on this workshop on YouTube. I highly recommended you check it out.) In the workshop, Ketchum discusses how some of the most powerful writing comes from the hurt and broken places inside us. But the example he uses is how he took a childhood fear of snakes and made that the basis for a story. That was a wound, yeah, but surely not among the deepest or most painful ones Ketchum had. You choose which wounds you wish to explore in your fiction and which you think are better left untouched.

One last point about using personal experience in horror: While there's undeniable catharsis in working out our pain on the page, don't treat your fiction as if it's only a therapeutic venue for purging your mind and soul. We use our experiences to help us tell the best stories we can. We're not writing autobiography. (Then again, if you're an emotionally conflicted vampire who's lived a thousand years, maybe you *are* writing autobiography. What do I know?)

A STROLL DOWN FEAR STREET

What are you afraid of? Odds are that whatever you're afraid of today is different from what you feared as a child, which in turn is different from what you'll fear in the years to come. Some fears stay with us throughout our lives, some worsen and others fade. We forget things we used to be afraid of and worry about things that may or may not happen in the future. Some fears we've faced and, one way or another, made it through the experience. However old you are at the moment you're reading these words, you have a lifetime of experience behind you, and you continue adding to it every day. It's worth putting all that experience under a microscope and seeing what you have that you can use as the basis for some great horror fiction.

As you respond to the following items, remember: This is only an exercise. You do not need to revisit traumatic memories unless you wish to.

1. What were you afraid of as a child? Do you recall any specific events in your childhood during which you were deeply afraid?

    _____
    _____
    _____
    _____

2. What were you afraid of as a preteen? Do you recall any specific events during that period in which you were deeply afraid?

    _____
    _____
    _____
    _____

3. What were you afraid of as a teen? Do you recall any specific events during that period in which you were deeply afraid?

    _____
    _____
    _____
    _____

4. What were you afraid of as a new adult? Do you recall any specific events during that period in which you were deeply afraid?

    _____
    _____
    _____
    _____

5. What are you afraid of as an adult? Do you recall any specific events during that period in which you were deeply afraid? (Depending on your age, you might wish to answer this question for your middle-age and senior years as well.)

    _____
    _____
    _____
    _____

6. What do you imagine you'll be afraid of in the next five years? Ten? Twenty? Thirty?

    _____
    _____
    _____
    _____

Once you're finished, go over your list and see if there's anything you can pull out and use as the basis for a story. Remember, you're not trying to write autobiography. Your imagination may transform a memory until it's unrecognizable to anyone but you. My mother used to tell my sister and me that when we were little, one of us was afraid of feathers, and the other was afraid of adhesive strips. (She could never remember which was afraid of which.) Over fifty years later, I wrote a story for *Weird Tales* called "Feathers." There's nothing remotely autobiographical about this surreal piece of flash fiction. I only used the concept of feathers as a frightening thing. Hopefully it won't take me another fifty years to figure out how to work fear of adhesive strips into a story!

PEERING INTO THE DARKNESS

Now it's time to get more personal.

This exercise is about delving deeper into your fears, but as I've said before, you don't have to go into any emotional territory you'd rather avoid. For this one, I want you to respond to the following items in as much detail as you wish. You can write your responses as one-word lists, short phrases, full sentences, or complete paragraphs—whichever you like.

1. Write about a time (or times) when you experienced what you consider to be true horror.

    _____
    _____
    _____
    _____

2. Write about a time (or times) when family or friends experienced what you consider to be true horror.

_____

_____

_____

_____

3. Write about a time (or times) when you felt you were in true danger.

_____

_____

_____

_____

4. Write about a time (or times) when you felt family or friends were in true danger.

_____

_____

_____

_____

5. Write about a time (or times) when you experienced something bizarre and uncanny.

_____

_____

_____

_____

6. Write about a time (or times) when family or friends experienced something bizarre and uncanny.

_____

_____

_____

_____

7. What's the worst thing that you can imagine happening to you?

_____

_____

_____

_____

8. What's the worst thing that you can imagine happening to the people you love?

_____

_____

_____

_____

9. What's the one thing that you fear becoming or doing in the future?

_____

_____

_____

_____

10. What dark part of yourself have you struggled with throughout your life?

_____

_____

_____

_____

When you're finished, take a break if you need to. (Responding to items like these can be rough!) When you're ready, come back to what you wrote and read over it. Are there any responses which spark story ideas? Do you see a pattern in the responses that suggests concepts or themes that you might use and return to in your work? (Your darkness DNA, if you will.)

TIM'S GUARANTEED NO-FAIL STORY FORMULA AND THE THREE-CUP METHOD

I have a formula I sometimes use to create horror fiction, especially short stories, and it goes like this: **Weird Observation + Seemingly Unrelated Idea + Emotional Core = Story**. For example, in my story "Forever," which appears in the anthology *Tales From the Lost 2*, my Weird Observation was the century-old gravesite of a husband and wife, enclosed by chain-link fencing, hidden within the middle of a small stretch of woods in a Virginia park. My wife grew up in the area, and during a trip there, she wanted to show me the park where she played as a child. The gravesite had a single monument erected to the couple, and there was some strange graffiti spray painted on it. My Seemingly Unrelated Idea: When my wife was young, one of her friends disappeared from the park's vicinity, and she was never found. Emotional Core: Because of both the gravesite and the story about my wife's friend, I went with homecoming, sorrow, and love as the story's key emotions. (We'll talk more about writing with an emotional core in Chapter Fifteen.) I don't consciously plot stories this way, but over the years I've come to recognize that I often employ this technique when generating ideas, and it almost always results in a good tale.

I record ideas on my phone's notes app, and I take pictures of anything interesting or strange that I see. When it's time to write a story or novel, I go over my notes and pictures and pull out three different items that at first might not seem to go together. But as I work with them, they gel into a successful story. If you don't already have a notes file to scavenge ideas from—or even if you do—consider using the Three Cup Method. You use one cup per item in the formula: Weird Observation, Seemingly Unrelated Idea, Emotional core. Then write lists for each item on paper, and when you think the lists are long enough, cut them into slips, and place them into the appropriate cup. You can continue adding items to your cups as time passes, like putting spare change into a piggy bank day after day, and when it's time for you to write a story, draw a slip from each cup and see what you can make from them. Give it a try and see if it works for you.

_____
_____
_____
_____
_____
_____
_____

IN YOUR DREAMS

Dreams can be a wonderful source of inspiration for our fiction. While we sleep, our subconscious mind comes out to play, and it can create some wildly bizarre scenarios which are perfect fodder for horror stories. Here are some techniques for capturing and using your brain's nocturnal wanderings.

Dream Journal. In college, I had a friend who kept a dream journal. Every morning when Joe woke up, he'd record as many dreams as he could remember. At first, he'd only recall one or two, but as time went by, he began to remember as many as fifteen or more. He'd been doing this since high school, and he had several notebooks filled with detailed information about his dreams. As a beginning writer, I was envious of my friend's journals. All that material he could draw from to write stories! I rarely remember my dreams, and when I do, they're usually not very interesting. And I'm usually too groggy in the morning—or maybe just too lazy—to attempt to keep my own dream journal. But I think it can be a great technique for harvesting ideas, and if you're able to function, at least somewhat, first thing after you wake, you might give it a try. My friend used a simple spiral-bound notebook which he kept by his bedside. When he woke, he'd grab the notebook and start recording his dreams before he forgot them. It might take him fifteen or twenty minutes to get them all down, so he'd set his alarm to go off a littler earlier so he'd have time to write before he'd have to start his day. Let's say that on average you recall ten dreams every morning. That's seventy dreams a week, 280 a month, and 3,560 a year. All of those dreams won't result in usable story ideas, but a lot will.

Dream Assessment. While we quickly forget most of our dreams, some of them stay with us, even if we don't record them in a journal. Following are some questions to ask yourself about those dreams that haunt you—so you can turn them into stories that will haunt us!

1. What's one of the earliest scary dreams that you can remember?

    _____
    _____
    _____
    _____

2.   What's the absolute scariest dream you've ever had?

_____

_____

_____

_____

3.   Have you had any recurring dreams? If so, were any of them scary or disturbing? Write them down.

_____

_____

_____

_____

4.   Think about the scary dreams that you've had. Are there any commonalities to them, such as settings, images, or scenarios that tend to occur? If so, list them.

_____

_____

_____

_____

5.   Think about what your scary dreams feel like to you. Describe the emotional atmosphere of these dreams. Are you isolated? Stalked by an unseen predator? Are you desperate to escape? The emotional details of your dreams can provide as many ideas for stories as the events that occur.

_____

_____

_____

_____

When you're finished, go over your responses and see what insights you can gain from them. Look for specific story ideas, of course, but be alert for any images or themes that might recur. Both can add more personalization and depth to your horror fiction.

VOICES FROM THE SHADOWS

Wesley Southard, Splatterpunk Award-winning author of *Cruel Summer*

I know that many of my peers prefer to "pants" their fiction, meaning they more or less like to wing it as they go, never really knowing where their story is going until it spills from their fingertips. That's never been my style. I tend to fully outline every piece of fiction I write—from novels all the way down to flash fiction—which gives me the opportunity to come to my laptop every day, fully prepared, and ready to focus. For me, it wipes out any second guessing with my characters and situations and allows the words to flow effortlessly. Spend some time with a pen and a notebook and get your story straightened out before you even type the first word.

Gretchen Felker-Martin, film critic and author of *Manhunt*

Think about the thing that you least want to touch. What would make you sob and scream and fall apart if you and it were shoved into the same locker?

Got it? Good. Now write about it.

Michelle Renee Lane, Bram Stoker Award-nominated author of *Invisible Chains*

Writing Prompt: A young fugitive slave lost in a blizzard in the wilds of Canada is rescued by a boy from a First Nation tribe. While returning to his settlement, they encounter a wendigo and must fight to keep each other alive.

Sidney Williams, author of *Fool's Run* and *Disciples of the Serpent*

We often laud horror mixing everyday people and events with a dash of the unreal. To find the right ingredients for an arcane brew, a "one from Column A" and "one from Column B" approach often gets the strangeness swirling.

I scan newspapers, often only headlines, so that my imagination is forced to work. When a situation nags my curiosity, I scan a list of weird images or reports of the unexplained. Then I ask: What if one of these were juxtaposed with the other?

"Murderer dies in prison, victim's family member relieved" might blend with reports of unattended gurneys in a morgue, moving mysteriously on their own. Is the killer really gone, or does a part of him live on? Did something in him feed on the victim's anguish? What happens next for the person long obsessed and suffering results of the killer's deeds?

Choose a base that piques your curiosity, add a strange modifier, stir and see what dark cocktail you create.

Simon Clark, author of *Vampyrrhic*

Invoking the sense of touch, make your writing visceral: Especially when writing horror, it is important to make the reader "feel"—that is, make the reader feel the place you are describing, or even capturing the physical sensation of the monstrous entity touching them. For example, if I'm setting a tale in an Egyptian tomb, I take a few moments to imagine what my character will feel, in a physical sense, in that subterranean vault. Will they feel cool air on their face? The unpleasant sensation of spider webs brushing against an ear as they walk along the tunnel to the mummy's sarcophagus? And surely the dust of the tomb will have been disturbed so they feel the gritty sensation of dust on their lips—and such a macabre dust. Perhaps the dust is the powdered remains of flesh and even bone floating on the air—the dust settling on their lips, on their tongue, the gritty sensation of bone dust on your character's teeth. All deeply disturbing, yes, and the feel of dust on lips is something your reader will have had experience of, even if they have never felt a powdery residue form on their lips from deep inside the mummy's tomb.

Alessandro Manzetti, two-time Bram Stoker Award-winning author

Before writing a story, I define my writing "polar stars": Location and atmosphere (to let the reader enter the story, even on a visual level); the main character of the events (strongly characterizing him, with his peculiar way of thinking, voice, ghosts of the pasts); other characters and the antagonist or villain (among which, for the supporting characters, at least one very characteristic, caricatural); the status quo of the events (the present, the stagnant pond, before rippling the waters); what happens and modifies the status quo (something that turns the table, causing reactions and actions of the protagonist, adding to that (for horror and dark fantasy tales) the element of "sense of wonder"; the intervention of the villain (human or supernatural) or of a new situation that goes beyond the human; the decisions of the protagonist (thoughts and actions that lead him to react to the received inputs, or his discoveries); the climax of the events (which must contain sequences of action scenes); the final revelation (the assumptions of which are dripped in the previous parts) that broadens the sense of wonder of the story, surprising the reader. In addition to all this, within the story I usually insert, under the surface, a current subtheme/subtopic, connected to our society, to make the reader experience not only entertainment, but also adding a metaphor of our existence. Dialogue can be added to some parts of the "polar stars," especially to rendering lifelike characters, to present the status quo, and the changes of things. Finally, I assemble the whole, taking care of the rhythm of the story, which must have changes and guide the reader's emotions, accelerating them toward the second part of the story, up to the epilogue.

CHAPTER SIX
DONE TO DEATH

One of the things that defines a genre is the use of shared tropes—ideas, images, character types, story patterns, etc.—that readers enjoy and want to experience over and over in the fiction they read. The quest to save the world in fantasy. First contact with an alien race in science fiction. The quirky genius detective in mystery. The couple who at first hate each other but eventually fall in love in romance. Tropes are familiar, and thus comforting to readers. They don't have to try to figure out what the hell they're reading, as they might with a piece of experimental literary fiction. They can just read and enjoy themselves. But remember how in an earlier chapter I said that a prime quality of horror fiction is fear of the unknown? Well, tropes aren't only known, they're *extremely* known, often to the point where they become dull, lifeless clichés. And once a trope becomes a cliché, it loses its power to affect readers, especially in horror. This doesn't mean you can't write about a haunted house or a child possessed by a demon if those are tropes you enjoy. But it does mean that you should look for fresh, new, and interesting ways to approach these tropes, and that's what this chapter is all about: giving you some tools to help you avoid clichés and write original horror.

TROPE ASSESSMENT

1. Make a list of horror tropes that you love.

_____

_____

_____

_____

2. Make a list of horror tropes that you think are overused.

_____

_____

_____

_____

3. Make a list of horror tropes that you hate.

_____
_____
_____
_____

When finished, read over your lists. It might seem counterintuitive, but the list of tropes you think are overused or which you hate will provide you the best opportunities for writing original horror. The list of tropes you love? Maybe not so much. If we love something, we tend to be less critical of it, and because of this, we gleefully use those tropes as they are with little-to-no tweaking. How many zombie apocalypse stories have you read (or maybe written) which are nothing but *Night of the Living Dead* rehashes? How many vampire, werewolf, or serial killer stories that are simplistic predator-stalks-and-kills-prey narratives? But overused tropes are ripe for reinterpretation and reinvention. Same with the tropes you hate. I've never been a fan of ghost stories. I may not hate this trope, but it tends to bore me. Ghosts are intangible spirits. What's the worst they can do? Kill someone and turn them into a ghost too? Plus, ghosts are inherently optimistic in that they provide proof of life after death. Instead of avoiding this trope, though, I've used my feelings about it to create what I hope are some original pieces of fiction.

My story "Till Voices Drown Us," which appeared in the anthology *Apprentice Fantastic*, is about a celebrity psychic who can communicate with the dead. He discovers that the dead have been keeping a secret from the living: They are all holding off a great darkness that threatens to swallow all existence. They do this to protect the living—their friends, family, and descendants—until they too die and join the eternal struggle. My novel *We Rise Again* is about a ghost apocalypse. Malevolent ghosts begin appearing across the world and wreak havoc upon the living. There's a reason behind their rising and hostile actions, but it's not what readers might expect.

Trope Revitalization. Take the horror tropes you listed and jot down ideas for putting new spins on them. Take the ones that excite you the most and use them as the basis for stories. Make plot notes or simply start writing. Don't let yourself fall back into old patterns for these tropes. Keep striving for originality.

_____
_____
_____
_____
_____
_____
_____

BREATHING NEW LIFE INTO OLD TROPES

Following are exercises that can help you revitalize worn-out tropes.

Disguise a Trope. Some of the most well-known and well-loved horror movie icons are old tropes that have been given makeovers so that they appear fresh while at the same time containing the power of their core trope. Jason Vorhees and Michael Myers are both the Grim Reaper. They each wear expressionless white masks (like skulls), wear monochromatic dark clothing (like black robes), are silent, and kill with sharp metal instruments (like scythes). Freddie Krueger is Satan. He's associated with fire, has a demonic visage, torments people with nightmarish scenarios, and wields a metal claw glove that resembles a mini pitchfork. Norman Bates from *Psycho* is a werewolf. He appears to be a mild-mannered, sweet man but he undergoes a transformation (psychologically) in which he changes his form (by donning a wig and dress), and becomes a savage killer. Hannibal Lector is Dracula. Outwardly, he appears to be a man of high intelligence, sophisticated tastes, and aristocratic bearing, but that's a disguise for a ruthless predator who feeds on humans. Pinhead is a genie. He's a magical being that can only be summoned by working a small gold metal object (like a lantern) with your hands. People summon him and his fellow Cenobites either to request a boon or by accident. But like many genies in folklore, when Pinhead grants wishes, it's never for the wisher's benefit. You can do the same thing too. Here are several common horror tropes. Try to disguise them in ways that make them seem fresh while still retaining the core power of their trope.

1. Witch

    _____

    _____

    _____

    _____

2. Monster created from parts of dead bodies.

    _____

    _____

    _____

    _____

3. Zombie

    _____

    _____

    _____

    _____

4. Evil child

    _____

    _____

    _____

    _____

5. Living murderous doll

_____
_____
_____
_____

6. Haunted House

_____
_____
_____

7. Poltergeist

_____
_____
_____
_____

8. Feel free to use the monsters I mentioned above: Grim Reaper, Satan, werewolf, Dracula, and genie.

_____
_____
_____
_____

Which of your disguised tropes do you like best? Which do you see the most story potential in?

Reverse a Trope. Another way to make a trope fresh is to reverse it. In my novel *Darkness Wakes*, a small group of people worship a creature called the Overshadow. They bring it animals—and eventually people—so it can drain their lifeforce, and in return, the Overshadow infuses its worshippers with sensations of powerful ecstasy. So intense are these sensations that the worshippers become hooked on them, and they'll do anything for the Overshadow. The Overshadow is a reverse vampire. Yes, it does feed on lifeforce like a regular vampire, but instead of taking from its worshippers, it gives them something. I don't ever use the word *vampire* in the novel, because I wanted the power of the trope—of humans in a symbiotic relationship with a supernatural being that feeds *them*—to stand on its own.

Take the tropes listed in the last exercise and reverse them. Which of the ones you came up with do you feel would make great story material?

_____
_____
_____
_____

Combine Tropes. George Romero created his famous zombies by combining several tropes: The voodoo zombie, the flesh-eating ghoul, and the disease-spreading vampire. He also gave them a vampire-like weakness, but instead of a stake through the heart, they can only be killed by a bullet through their brain. John Carpenter's the Thing is an alien, a shape-changer, and an *Invasion of the Body Snatchers*-type creator of doppelgangers. Mash-Ups like these have the potential to be strikingly original and a lot of fun, both for writers and their audience.

Take the same trope list you've been working with, only now combine two or more aspects of tropes to create a powerful hybrid concept.

_____
_____
_____
_____
_____
_____
_____

Create Your Own Tropes. Best of all is if you can create own tropes based on your experiences and imagination. You're the only you that ever was or will be (unless the Thing gets hold of you, that is), and you can create tropes that are just as individual as you are.

1. Start a list of things you encounter—whether you see them in person, on the Internet, or hear about them secondhand—that seem like they would be impactful images/tropes on their own. Keep adding to this list as time goes by and refer to it whenever you need an original trope for your fiction. For example, a while back I was driving on a street close to my house. I passed a woman mowing her front law, and out of the corner of my eye, it looked like she had a lizard head. When I looked more closely, I saw she appeared perfectly normal. I haven't used Lawn-Mowing Lizard-Head Woman in any stories yet, but I will someday.

    _____
    _____
    _____
    _____

2. Do random image searches online. For example, I just went to Google and did an image search using these words which I chose at random: *Tentacles bird fishhooks teeth.* Most of the images were general photos of birds, but there were some more interesting results: A drawing of an inside-out bird, a deep-sea squid with teeth, a fish with human teeth, a fishing tackle that looks like an eyeball with a hook emerging from the bottom, pharyngeal teeth, artwork of a toad dressed in an old-fashioned suit, a fishing tackle shaped like a small fish with hooks emerging from underneath (what if it was a real fish with hooks?), a drawing for the cover of a lit maga-

zine showing a person holding a smiling mask that they just removed, a weird (and likely Photoshopped) image of a bug that looks part ant, part spider, and part snail … I could use any of these images (with a few tweaks, perhaps) in stories, and none of them would be standard-issue horror tropes. You can do the same.

———————————————————————————
———————————————————————————
———————————————————————————
———————————————————————————

3.   Another type of Internet image search you can do is for *bizarre artwork* or *bizarre sculpture*. (You can also use *horror, dark, surreal, strange, nightmare,* and *disturbing* as search terms.) You'll encounter thousands of strange, sinister, surreal, and just plain odd images, all of which could inspire you to create original tropes for your horror fiction. They might give you ideas for entire stories as well. One year, I did an image search using the term *scary Thanksgiving* so I could find something on-brand to post on my social media feeds. I came across an old-fashioned painting of a creature created entirely from produce—pumpkin head, melon body, celery arms, ear-of-corn feet, etc. This creature struck me as a kind of pagan harvest god, and the name *Lord of the Feast* popped into my head. That name stuck with me, and it sparked an idea for a novel, which will be the next one I write for Flame Tree Press.

———————————————————————————
———————————————————————————
———————————————————————————
———————————————————————————

One warning about using images as inspiration for your writing: Don't use an artist's exact image in your story. Being inspired is one thing; exactly copying someone else's creation for your own use is another.

THIS MUST BE THE PLACE

For many writers, a strong sense of place is one of the most important elements in creating successful fiction. There are many common settings in horror, and most of them long ago became clichés: The ancient castle, the deserted graveyard, the old house with a sinister past, the mad scientist's lab, the hospital where awful things happen, the small town with dark secrets, the desanctified church, the evil forest, the fog-enshrouded street … I could list many more. But just as character tropes like vampires and werewolves need to be reworked to make them impactful for today's audience, the same goes for settings where horror stories take place.

One of the things I enjoy about writing horror fiction is that any setting can work in a story, because as soon as a violation of reality takes place there, it *becomes* a horror setting. Stephen King did this with small towns in Maine (and not the coastal ones that audiences were familiar with from movie and TV shows). Of course, after four decades of King using Maine settings, the state has become America's version of Transylvania. Same with Lovecraft's New England or Anne Rice's New Orleans. Success, unfortunately, breeds cliché. I tend to set my horror fiction in small Southwestern Ohio towns because that's the region where I've spent most of my life. But when it comes to individual scenes, I'll use an ice cream parlor or a physical therapist's office instead of a more stereotypical horror setting, such as an abandoned warehouse where something awful has taken up residence.

This exercise is about developing locations for your stories that aren't horror settings yet, but will be once you tell your deliciously creepy stories within them.

1. Make a list of places that have been important to you during the course of your life. They can be places with either positive or negative associations, or a mix of both. Or maybe they're just places that have stuck in your memory, although you don't know why. Try to think on a relatively small scale here. For example, in the town where I grew up, there was this small ramshackle grocery—an ancient little market established long before the era of convenience stores. It was one of the last places that still had glass-bottle Coke that you could buy from an old-fashioned soda vending machine. I like the way the market remained the same as the world changed around it, seeming to age much more slowly than it should. Its age gives it something in common with the old house trope, but being a small market makes it original too.

   _____

   _____

   _____

   _____

2. Make a list of the most innocuous, innocent-seeming, just plain ordinary locations you can think of, ones that are virtually anti-horror settings. Places like this can make wonderfully unexpected setting for horror stories. To get you started, I'll give you several ordinary places, and I want you to consider what sort of horror stories you might tell there. These stories can complement the setting—such as a widow trying to wash her dead husband's clothes at a laundromat to get them ready to donate to Goodwill, only the clothes have ideas of their own. Or they can contrast with the setting—such as a dentist's office where a patient keeps having visions of all the other people as shambling animated corpses.

   - A podiatrist's office
   - A dog-washing business
   - A gym
   - A streetside public mailbox
   - A DMV parking lot
   - An empty soccer field

- The hallway of an apartment building
- A petting zoo
- A planetarium
- A farmer's market
- A compost pile
- The bed of a rusted-out pickup truck
- A hardware store
- A post office
- A mini-golf course
- A dumpster filled with trash
- A backyard birdfeeder
- A kid's bedroom after he or she has moved to college
- A pizza kitchen
- A bar at closing time
- A gluten-free bakery

_____

_____

_____

_____

VOICES FROM THE SHADOWS

Graham Masterton, author of *The Children God Forgot*

My early years of training as a newspaper reporter taught me that one story can very often be illuminated and given depth and clarity by another. For instance, when a young man threw himself under a train I wrote a report not only on the scene of his suicide itself, but I went to interview his family and his friends and the colleagues with whom he worked.

From those interviews, I was able to build up a picture of why an apparently cheerful young man had decided to end his life in the most gruesome way that you can imagine. When I arrived at the station, he had been completely cut in half by the train's wheels, but was still cheerfully talking to the paramedics kneeling around him.

I have used the same technique with many if not all of my novels, even when they have been fantasies like my series *Night Warriors*, in which my protagonists fight evil forces in other people's dreams. The protagonists themselves are very ordinary people leading ordinary lives in real places.

Obviously I understand that in some fantasy novels it is both necessary and desirable to create a whole fantasy world, and that readers enjoy being taken off to Lord of the Rings land or wherever. But I believe that in horror novels it creates a greater sensation of uncertainty and downright terror if the location is real and that the characters have to deal with a problem related to their personal lives or their work that is totally realistic and believable.

I set my recent haunted house novel *The House of a Hundred Whispers* in a real house in a real village on Dartmoor, and apart from the haunting, the characters were arguing over who should inherit the house after the death of their father. My latest horror novel *The Children God Forgot* deals mainly with the vexed question of abortion, but I used the sewers under London as a setting, since there was a highly topical story in the news about fatbergs blocking the sewers—massive build-ups of solidified fat and other detritus which are incredibly difficult to remove, except with high-pressure hoses.

By telling a strong and realistic background story, I was able to give the main story a credibility which it might otherwise have lacked—especially since it was not only morally contentious but surreal in the extreme.

I am not against imaginary settings and imaginary situations. Stephen King has made a great success of Castle Rock. But personally I prefer places which my readers can actually visit for themselves after they have read the novels, like London's suburbs and Milwaukee and Baton Rouge and the wilds of Dartmoor (which Arthur Conan Doyle also used as the setting for *The Hound of the Baskervilles*.) Sometimes my characters will visit real cafés and restaurants, so readers can pick from the menus before they visit.

A woman wrote to me after she had read one of my crime novels set in Cork, and she said, "I seriously had to look out of the window to reassure myself that I wasn't in Ireland." That proved to me that real settings are incredibly effective.

So—if you're looking for a location for your next horrific adventure—simply step outside and look around you. You're there already.

Douglas Clegg, Bram Stoker Award-winning author of *Afterlife*

What makes good horror? A writer with a voice who understands imagery, story, and the effect and rhythm of language. Advice for horror writers? Write the story that is meaningful and honest to you, your understanding of human nature, and your worldview.

I suspect those can apply to any type of fiction but those are my absolute roots for writing horror fiction.

Eva Roslin, writer and librarian

Advice: One of the most helpful things that a mentor recommended to me a few years ago was to volunteer to read submissions for a magazine or press, most commonly known as a slush reader. You will learn a surprising amount about the most common mistakes to look out for in submissions, why some stories work and others don't, but most of all, you will be contributing to a community and building up relationships.

Exercise I've found useful: Some writers swear by writing sprints for productivity. One addendum I'd like to make is an accountability practice to add to this. Virtual write-ins are a great way of facilitating this because they provide a group setting in which you have the pressure of knowing that everyone else is there to write, and that you are helping keep them accountable and vice versa. If you can commit to making this a regular practice for half an hour, forty-five minutes, an hour, or even as short as fifteen minutes, it can contribute greatly to your productivity and consistency of output as a writer.

Prompt: Fear is such a subjective thing. What terrifies some will not cause another person to blink. It has been said many times, but it is crucial to make the horror you're writing about as personal to you as possible. Make no mistake, it's fraught work to do this—to try to make the fears you feel come alive for readers in a way that doesn't feel hokey or like something we've all seen dozens of times before. You may be tempted to resist going into the things that you know terrify you the most or wounds that have cut you the deepest, and it's important for you not to push yourself to a point where you're going to cause double damage to yourself, particularly if you come from a background of having suffered trauma. You will feel resistance—there's some part of you that wants to keep you safe from the pain and from re-living some of these experiences, and as I said, safety is most important. Find a way to safely push past these walls, or if you're not yet able to do that, gently take a chisel to them and chip away until the stones come down in a more gradual way.

Maurice Broaddus, author of *The Usual Suspects*

TALKING HEADS PROMPT: A married couple bumps into each other at a coffee shop when each is supposed to be at work. One has something to hide, the other something to tell. Write the conversation, but don't use dialogue tags. Each character has to be a distinct voice. Dialogue is rooted in character. You have to learn each character's voice, which is based on a variety of things (age, occupation, education, nationality, culture, etc.). Each character has an agenda, which means they may interrupt, change subject, obfuscate as a part of furthering theirs.

When you're stuck on what someone might say next, center in on what you know about the character given the context and the emotional charge of the moment. Think about what's been said and how it was said (dialogue has three dimensions: Text, subtext, and context). Also, when in doubt, think back to when you felt something similar to what your characters are feeling and write from that emotional place.

Livia Llewellyn, Shirley Jackson Award-nominated author of *Engines of Desire* and *Furnace*

Nowadays it's easy to remain fully immersed in all-things-horror: Television, movies, comics, music, and any and all visual arts. I'm guilty of this, to the point where I often feel over-saturated by what becomes repetitious themes and tropes. What helps me continue to find new ideas for stories is to take a hard break from all-things-horror on a regular basis, and seek serendipitous inspiration in unfamiliar genres, especially in books and films. Yes, favorite novels and movies can be foundational in your development as a writer, but don't forget the rest of the house you're building—you don't want all the rooms to be the same.

Matthew Holness, writer and director of *Possum*

When writing a short horror story, I sometimes plot less than usual in advance and prioritize writing "in the moment." This way I find that subconscious fears arise spontaneously and often more surprisingly. I don't think I would advocate writing a longer narrative in this way, but for the short story, a reliance on plotting can sometimes "fictionalize" the horror of the tale too much for me and dull the effect. I shape whatever I come up with in order to perfect the story's structure, but to find what really disturbs me, initially I aim to shut off the "craftsman" part of my brain and let the real monsters roam free.

CHAPTER SEVEN
WHERE NO MONSTER HAS GONE BEFORE

Monsters—whether human or inhuman—are a staple of horror fiction. But as we have discussed several times already in this book, any horror trope that is too known loses its power (and likely loses readers' interest as well). In this chapter, we're going to discuss how to build better monsters for your fiction.

First off, remember this: Horror stories aren't about monsters. They're about how characters *react* to monsters. So having a really cool monster is awesome, but it's no substitute for well-developed, interesting characters. The better your characters are, the more of a threat your monster will seem to your readers—because they care about the people it's trying to kill.

For the purposes of these exercises, a monster can be a supernatural creature (a vampire or werewolf), a creature created by science (Frankenstein's Monster, Mr. Hyde), a natural animal behaving in unnatural ways (the shark in *Jaws*, Ben the rat from *Willard*), a force of some sort (the energy of the ancient aliens in *Quatermass and the Pit*—titled *Five Million Years to Earth* in the USA), the death-force in the *Final Destination* series), or a human behaving in a monstrous way (and who likely has a monstrously distorted psyche as well). You can write about any type of monster for the exercises, but I suggest trying different ones to expand your evil monster-creating skills.

Keep in mind that a number of the exercises in the previous chapter can also be used to create more effective monsters. When I wrote *Writing in the Dark*, I debated with myself over where to put some of the information on reworking tropes. Some of it seemed to fit equally well in "Done to Death" or "Where No Monster Has Gone Before." For *Writing in the Dark*, I put most of it in the chapter on writing monsters. In this book, I put that material in the chapter on avoiding worn-out tropes. Who says you can't have your cake and eat it too when it comes to organizing material in a book?

All right—let's get monstering!

MONSTER DIAGNOSIS

Maybe you aren't that crazy about monsters, maybe you love all of them, or maybe you haven't given them much thought either way. Let's take a few minutes to find out what "monster" means to you.

Your Monster Preferences. Write your definition of a monster, then write about what you like and dislike about them. Do you think certain types of monsters are more effective than others? Do they work better or worse in different mediums, like fiction, movies, TV shows, comics, and games? Do you prefer monsters to remain offstage for the most part and used sparingly, or do you like them onstage and involved in the action throughout a story? There are no right or wrong answers here. These questions are designed to help you explore your thoughts and feelings about monsters as a trope in horror fiction.

_____
_____
_____
_____
_____
_____
_____
_____

Your Favorite Monsters. Make a list of your favorite monsters, from childhood up to now. When you're finished, look over your list to determine any similarities or themes in the kind of monsters you enjoy.

_____
_____
_____
_____
_____
_____
_____
_____

Your Least-Favorite Monsters. Make a list of your least-favorite monsters this time. Do you see any patterns in your list? What is it about these monsters that you don't enjoy?

_____
_____
_____
_____
_____
_____
_____
_____

Would You Like Fries with Your Monster? Monsters can perform different roles in different stories. Which way(s) do you enjoy your monsters?

- As Threat/Obstacle/Antagonist?
- As Metaphor/Symbol/Theme?

- As Protagobist?
- As an Object of Pity?

Write a little about why you answered as you did.

_____
_____
_____
_____
_____
_____
_____

Making the Most of the Least. Take three monsters from your list of least-favorites and jot down some notes about what sort of changes might make them interesting to you. Once you've transformed these monsters, can you see yourself writing a story about them? Why or why not?

_____
_____
_____
_____
_____
_____
_____

Now that you have a better sense of your monster preferences, it's time to …

MAKE A MONSTER

Create an original monster (or rework an existing one) for the different types:

- Supernatural
- Science-Based
- Natural Animal Acting Unnaturally
- A Force of Nature (or Unnature)
- A Human Monster

_____
_____
_____
_____
_____

And for bonus points …

- Create a monster that's a combination of two or more of the types. (Bonus-Bonus points if you can combine all the types into one monster that could actually work in a story!)

_____
_____
_____
_____
_____
_____
_____
_____

Which of the monsters that you created would you be most excited to write about? Make some notes about how you might use your monster(s) in a story.

_____
_____
_____
_____
_____
_____
_____
_____

WRITING YOUR MONSTER

You have several things to consider when it comes to using monsters in your fiction, and one of the most important is how you write scenes which are centered on your monster. Or, to put it another way, scenes in which your monster is the main character. You have a choice of three ways to write about your monster: From an objective point of view, a (slightly) closer point of view, or a close point of view.

Objective Point of View. One of the problems with writing a scene centered on a monster is that if you write from its point of view, like you would from your human characters' point of view, you risk humanizing the monster too much and damaging any sense of mystery about it. If you want to avoid that, you can use a distant point of view. You write about the monster as if you're an observer, never letting the reader see inside its head.

Here's an example from the prologue to my monster novel *Blood Island*. The Mass is an ancient lifeform that's not sentient, so I wrote about it using an objective point of view.

600 million years ago …

The sun's rays are punishingly hot, the air thick and heavy. Small fern-like plants are scattered across the inlet's rocky shore, hardy, stubborn things that have forced their way upward to claim a place in the light. The water that gently laps against the shore is stagnant soup of salt and decaying vegetable matter. Not the most hospitable of conditions, perhaps, but nevertheless, there is life here beside the little ferns. Tiny amphibious creatures that resemble what will one day be called tadpoles wriggle through the water, nibbling at bits of algae and dead fern, and if they were capable of anything approaching thought, they would consider this to be the best of all possible worlds and think themselves blessed to live in such a paradise.

These ur-tadpoles are not the only form of animal life in the water, though. Floating just below the surface is an irregularly shaped clump of cells colored a dark crimson. This small mass looks like nothing more than a bit of debris drifting in the water, perhaps a fleshy remnant of some creature that was devoured by something larger, stronger, and even hungrier than itself. But this mass is a lifeform unto itself, and despite its small size and unassuming appearance, it's the most sophisticated creature currently existing on the planet. The Mass is capable of independent movement when necessary, but for now it's content to bob in the water patiently and wait.

After a time, one of the ur-tadpoles swims toward the Mass, intending to determine if this strange object is edible. But the instant the ur-tadpole comes in contact with the Mass's substance, a thin pseudopod extrudes from the surface and whips toward the ur-tadpole lightning-fast. The barbed tip of the pseudopod stretches toward the base of the ur-tadpole's tail and pierces the animal's rubbery hide. Once inside the body of its prey, the pseudopod releases a powerful cocktail of chemicals into the ur-tadpole's bloodstream. The animal writhes in agony as those chemicals race through its body, attaching themselves to the creature's primitive nervous system and the microscopic organ that is nowhere near sophisticated enough to be called a brain. Crimson striations cover its body, as if a new network of veins has appeared beneath its skin.

The ur-tadpole grows still then, and the Mass sends a message to it through their connection. This message is a simple but powerful command, and instinctive rather than cognitive, but if it were to be translated into language, the best interpretation would be FIND FOOD.

Still connected to the Mass, the ur-tadpole wriggles off, the pseudopod thinning and lengthening as the distance between it and the Mass increases. The ur-tadpole—which is now not exactly a part of the Mass so much as a mindless slave to it—heads straight for others of its kind clustered around a glob of algae and eating, blissfully unaware that death is coming for them.

The Mass will eat well this day. It will add the ur-tadpoles' substance to its own and grow larger and stronger. It will save several of the ur-tadpoles to serve as Hunters until such time as it can find better—and bigger*—servants. Life here at the dawn of time is extremely good for the Mass.*

And it's only going to get better.

The Mass grows over the millennia, eventually becoming as large as an island (hence the book's title), and instead of using prehistoric tadpoles for hunters, it uses bull sharks. By writing about it as if I was a narrator in a nature documentary, I was still able to present a vivid scene and characterize the creature somewhat, without writing specifically from its point of view (which is good, since it doesn't have one).

Your turn. Try writing an objective point of view scene about a monster, maybe one that you created for the previous exercise.

_____

_____

_____

_____

_____

_____

_____

_____

Closer Point of View (but Not *Too* Close). If you do want to write from your monster's point of view (assuming it's at least partially sentient), but you don't want to go all the way into its head, you can keep using the nature documentary approach, only now your narration includes indications of what the monster thinks and feels (as much as it can think or feel).

Here's an example from my novel *Teeth of the Sea*. This story is about pliodons, prehistoric water creatures that are still alive today and which attack a South American island resort.

One-Eye moved down the canal as fast as he could with only three working flippers. The bullet that had hit him hadn't gone deep, but it had done enough damage to render that flipper almost useless. He had no concept of weapons, of course, but he understood pain, understood it very well, and he knew that the soft skins—which were quite tasty—could bite back when they wanted.

The injury didn't concern him overmuch. When you lived in the Great Deep, injury was an ever-present risk, even for creatures as strong and deadly as his kind were. But displaying weakness of any kind to the others in his pod ... that was dangerous. He was dominant among the nestlings. At least he had been until this injury, and all of them would view his current weakness as an opportunity to unseat him and take his place in the pod's hierarchy. Especially his brother. He knew Brokejaw was close. The two of them always hunted together, had since the day of their hatching. Several years ago, One-Eye had been attacked by an overly ambitious tiger shark. He'd bested his opponent and devoured it, but not before losing an eye—and gaining a new name. Brokejaw had challenged him then, but he'd fought off his brother's attack easily, severely wounding him in the process and giving him a new name. But losing an eye was nothing compared to losing the use of a flipper, and he needed to put distance between himself and his brother before Brokejaw—

He felt a vibration in the water off to his right, the side where his bad eye was, and he veered left just in time to evade Brokejaw's strike. Brokejaw had intended to take hold of his brother's injured flipper and tear it off, reducing his ability to maneuver enough so Brokejaw could finally kill his brother and take his place. And when the next mating season came around, he would mate with both Nub and

Whiteback, and his genes, not his brothers', would be carried into the future.

But even wounded, One-Eye was far from easy prey.

One-Eye swung back toward Brokejaw as he passed and rammed his snout into his brother's chest. Bubbles burst forth from Brokejaw's mouth as the air was forced out of his lungs, and he instinctively headed toward the surface to refill them. One-Eye didn't take advantage of the opportunity for a follow-up attack. He might still have all four of his flippers, but injured as he was, there was no way he could outmaneuver Brokejaw forever. Best to flee and regain his strength so he would be ready should Brokejaw attempt to challenge him again. One-Eye wasn't human—he had no pride and he felt no shame at fleeing. In many ways, his kind were little more than simple machines. Kill, eat, fuck, and swim so they could continue to kill, eat, fuck, and swim—this comprised the entirety of their programming. One-Eye did not view himself as running away, had not the first notion of the concept. He was surviving, and right now, that was all that mattered.

So he swam off as fast as he could, doing his best to ignore the pain of his wound as he surged through the water like a wobbly torpedo.

For *Teeth of the Sea*, I decided to make my pliodons live in small pods, and I gave them simple names based on obvious physical characteristics that animals might use to recognize each other as individuals. The times when I get a little farther into One-Eye's point of view are a bit of a cheat. I doubt a real pliodon would have even this low level of sentience, but I focused on One-Eye's basic instincts and needs as opposed to complex thought, and (hopefully) that made the point of view work for readers.

You know what's next! Write a short scene with a monster from a close (but not *too* close) point of view.

_____
_____
_____
_____
_____
_____
_____

Close Point of View. What if your monster is sentient and you want to write scenes from its point of view? You treat it like any other character and write it with a close point of view, giving readers access to its inner world—its thoughts, feelings, reactions, etc. You run the risk of humanizing your monster too much if you do this, but if you remember that you're writing from a *monster's* point of view, you should be good.

Here's an example from my novel *They Kill*, which is my love letter to the monster rally movies I loved as a kid, like *House of Frankenstein* and *House of Dracula*, so it's chock full of monsters! This excerpt is from the first scene, in which Corliss, a godlike (or if you prefer, demonlike) being sets the novel's plot in motion.

A tall, lean man known only as Corliss—to those who knew of him at all—walked down the middle of County Road 25A, roughly three miles outside the Ohio town of Bishop Hill. Dawn was only beginning to touch the eastern horizon, and the morning air was chilly, more like November than mid-September. Corliss liked the bite in the air, found it rather bracing.

An invigorating start to the morning, *he thought.*

Cornfields flanked the road on either side, the stalks swaying gently in the morning breeze, leaves rustling against each other, making it sound as if the plants were communicating in hushed whispers. Corliss scented the air. The corn was almost ready to harvest. Another few weeks. He walked up to the wood-and-wire fence on his right, reached out, and wrapped his fingers around a stalk he selected at random. He concentrated for a moment, then removed his hand, returned to the road, and continued walking. Now, whoever ate the corn from that particular plant would respond in one of two ways, depending on their temperament. They'd either fall into a deep, dark depression and kill themselves, or they would become consumed with homicidal fury and kill whoever was in their immediate vicinity at the time.

Corliss smiled. It was the little things that made his work worthwhile.

He wore a black suit and tie, which at first glance appeared perfectly normal. But the longer someone looked at his clothes, the more it seemed like the suit was an open void, a portal to some vast dark place. The observer would be tempted, almost uncontrollably so, to step forward and try to touch the suit, to prove it was nothing more than a garment made of sewn-together fabric. And if that person succumbed to this temptation, he or she would regret it, bitterly, for the few seconds of life remaining to them.

Corliss was cleanshaven, eyebrows thin, straight blond hair falling halfway down his back. His hair—almost the precise shade of corn silk, coincidentally—made a startling contrast with his dark clothing. More startling was the way his hair was always in motion, if only slightly, even when the air was still.

A third of the sun was visible by the time Corliss reached his destination. There was nothing immediately apparent about this place that marked it as special. More corn on either side of the road, uncut grass in the ditches, asphalt old, cracked, and in need of repair. Nevertheless, this was the right place. What it wasn't, however, was the right time. *But that was easily rectified.*

He made a languid gesture with his right hand, as if he were half-heartedly shoving away a bothersome insect. Daylight vanished, darkness rushed in, and with it came rain. Not a light shower, but a motherfucking deluge. *Water poured from the sky in torrents, wind blasted with gale force, thunder boomed like artillery fire, and lightning crackled as it split the dark, illuminating the area for miles in all directions with stark-white strobing flashes. It was only 6:09 p.m., but thanks to the storm, it might as well have been midnight. Corliss' head and hands became immediately drenched, but the rain that touched his suit simply kept on going, disappearing into the black expanse within. The wind grabbed hold of his wet hair, flung it this way and that, and the strands cried out in a chorus of fear and excitement. Corliss grinned, spread his arms wide, and raised his face toward the sky. This was* his *kind of weather. He stood like that for several moments, enjoying the sensation of the storm raging around him, but he soon became aware of headlights approaching from the east. He sighed. Time to go to work.*

Corliss might look human, but he doesn't *think* like a human, so when I wrote him, I did so by filtering events through his twisted mindset. This is also how I write human monsters. I also made sure not to go too far into his point of view. Corliss was human once, a very long time ago, but I don't have any memories or thoughts related to his having been human show up in this scene. This way, I can write him with a closer point of view but still keep some mystery going.

You know the drill by now. Write a scene with a monster from a closer point of view.

_____
_____
_____
_____
_____
_____
_____
_____

VOICES FROM THE SHADOWS

Stephen Volk, author of *Ghostwatch*, *The Dark Masters Trilogy*, and *Under a Raven's Wing*

A controversial one, this. Don't use CAPITALS in your screenplay outside of headings! If you use CAPITALS it soon just LOOKS like you are SHOUTING all the time. A director once told me to take out the CAPS. You lower your voice to a whisper—and the reader will lean in and listen!

Ronald Kelly, author of *Fear*, *Undertaker's Moon*, and *Hell Hollow*

Suspension of disbelief. How does a writer of horror (or science fiction or fantasy) pull off supernatural and otherworldly storylines? How do they get their readers to accept wholeheartedly or "buy into" tales of vampires, werewolves, aliens, etc.? I don't believe it has to with the monster at all, no matter how well it is described or portrayed. The burden of belief rests on the shoulders of the main characters. If they react convincingly, like real-life people would if facing some creature beyond normal comprehension, that is where the barrier of disbelief breaks down. When your most skeptical character slowly comes to the dreadful realization that the threat is real and palatable—be it a backwoods vampire, an Irish werewolf, or a snake-critter from an evil county—and faces the threat as a flesh and blood person would, that is when suspension of disbelief becomes possible. If your characters act and react implausibly or foolishly (like those teenagers in most of the slasher movies) then your creature might as well stay hidden in the shadows and remain the urban legend that the unbelieving think it is. The fear and emotion of your protagonists give the vampire its fangs and the lycanthrope its claws. Without that in its favor, the beastly antagonist—and your book or story—has no chance at all.

Christopher Golden, *New York Times* **bestselling author of** *Ararat* **and** *Red Hands*

Close your eyes. Think back to something you read or watched that genuinely made you feel dread or fear, and focus on your physical response to those feelings. How did they manifest in you? Then think about your character, who they are, what would give that specific character those feelings, and give us that. If we understand the character, their fears and dreads will carry over into the reader.

Jeffrey Thomas, author of *Punktown*

There isn't just one way for me in which a spark is struck for a story; it could be a news item or an event from my own life, some interesting place I've visited or person I've known. However, often a story has its start with an image, whether it be a painting I've seen online or a mental picture, and the story forms around that image like a pearl around a grain of sand. For instance, one of Zdzisław Beksiński's paintings directly inspired one of my short stories, whereas I am currently embarking on the inexplicable image that came to me of a titanic inverted bell, whose ring disturbs the human mind. I'm not sure yet where that's going, but it's bound to be somewhere interesting. Avoid clichés at all costs; that being said, a picture is worth a thousand words.

Mandy McHugh, author of *Chloe Cates Is Missing*

Whether it's suspense, thriller, or horror, using the senses to create strong images helps to elevate tension. Instead of using every sense to describe an item, however, choose one or two features to tighten your descriptions.

As an exercise: Choose an item near you that might not be considered dangerous (an apple, a child's toy, a picture frame, etc.). Describe the item as a weapon using every sense, then pick one or two you like best to include in your scene.

CHAPTER EIGHT
THE HORROR WRITER'S PALETTE

The name of our genre is an emotion, but horror is only one of the colors we have to work with when painting our dark works. There are five primary emotions that horror writers employ, and in descending order from highest (the most sophisticated) to lowest (the simplest and easiest), they are Dread, Terror, Horror, Shock, and Disgust. The exercises in this chapter are designed to help you gain greater facility with these "colors" so you can use any of them whenever you need to in your fiction.

First, some definitions.

- **Dread** is the mounting anticipation of a threat—nebulous and not clearly understood—drawing ever closer.
- **Terror** is a deep emotional and intellectual reaction to a threat.
- **Horror** is an immediate reaction to a threat—disbelief, denial, turning away.
- **Shock** is a surprise, an adrenaline rush.
- **Disgust** is a queasy, visceral reaction.

While they're arranged, as I said, from highest to lowest, I don't mean to imply that one is intrinsically better than another. They're arranged by the level of skill required to use them effectively. Creating Dread in a story is a lot harder than creating Disgust, but all five emotional states have their places. They're tools for us to use as we need them. Your work may tend to favor some more than others, and that's a big part of your voice as a horror author. Ramsey Campbell prefers to use Dread and Terror in his fiction, while Edward Lee uses Shock and Disgust most often. But there's nothing wrong with focusing on different emotional states in different stories, depending on the effect you wish to create. It's easier to focus on one state in a short story, while in a novel you have more room to use all five emotional states at different points in your tale.

I'LL HAVE ONE SERVING OF TERROR WITH A SIDE OF DISGUST, PLEASE

To get a sense of which emotional states you find most effective in horror, pick five horror novels/stories/films that are among the best you've ever read or seen. Then select which of the states those works tend to use the most. Try to select only one state per work, but no more than two. I want you to get a sense of the dominant emotional states the works use. (Circle your answer for each work on your list.)

The Works

1. _____ Dread, Terror, Horror, Shock, Disgust
2. _____ Dread, Terror, Horror, Shock, Disgust
3. _____ Dread, Terror, Horror, Shock, Disgust
4. _____ Dread, Terror, Horror, Shock, Disgust
5. _____ Dread, Terror, Horror, Shock, Disgust

Is there a specific emotional state that you tended to prefer in the works? If so, why do you think that is? What do you find effective about this particular emotional state?

_____
_____
_____
_____
_____
_____
_____

WAITER, I DIDN'T ORDER THIS MUCH DISGUST

Now it's time to get a sense of which emotional states you find least effective in horror. Pick five horror novels/stories/films that are among the worst you've ever read or seen. Then select which of the states those works tend to use the most. Try to select only one state per work, but no more than two. Again, I want you to get a sense of the dominant emotional states the works use. (Circle your answer for each work on your list.)

The Works

1. _____ Dread, Terror, Horror, Shock, Disgust
2. _____ Dread, Terror, Horror, Shock, Disgust
3. _____ Dread, Terror, Horror, Shock, Disgust
4. _____ Dread, Terror, Horror, Shock, Disgust
5. _____ Dread, Terror, Horror, Shock, Disgust

Is there a specific emotional state that you tended to dislike in the works overall? If so, why do you think that is? What didn't you like about this particular emotional state?

_____
_____
_____
_____
_____
_____

FUEL FOR THE FIRE

I started college as an acting major, but I quickly realized that I'd much rather write my own words than say those written by others. I still didn't know what I wanted to get my bachelor's degree in, though, so I switched my major to theater education with an English emphasis. This meant I had to take the same classes as acting majors for my freshmen and sophomore years. I don't regret those classes. I learned a lot that I've been able to apply to my writing over the years. I think an acting background can really help writers since we perform our characters' parts in our minds as we tell their stories.

One of the things I learned was that when acting in a scene, having a personal emotional touchstone to draw on can help a lot. For example, if a scene requires you to portray rage, you tap into an emotional memory of a time when you experienced rage. This way, the emotion is based on reality even if the character you're acting is imaginary. I want you to try a similar technique for this exercise. Write about times that you experienced Dread, Terror, Horror, Shock, and Disgust so that you will have emotional touchstones to use as fuel when writing scenes for your horror fiction.

A word of warning. If you're not comfortable revisiting these kind of experiences—or if you think it would be too traumatic to do so—skip this exercise. This is a workbook designed to help you write better horror fiction. It's *not* supposed to make you relive painful memories to the point of emotional injury.

If you decide to continue with this exercise, try to write more than a simple summary of your experiences. Try to capture what it felt like to live them.

Dread:

_____
_____
_____
_____
_____
_____

Terror:

_____
_____
_____
_____
_____
_____
_____

Horror:

_____
_____
_____
_____
_____
_____
_____

Shock:

_____
_____
_____
_____
_____
_____
_____

Disgust:

_____
_____
_____
_____
_____
_____
_____

You don't have to show anyone your responses, but consider keeping them handy for you to refer to when writing a scene that requires a particular emotional state.

WHAT'S YOUR DTHSD RECIPE?

Pick a short story of yours, or maybe a novel chapter—one that's representative of the kind of thing you tend to write—go through it and identify where you used the various emotional states of Dread, Terror, Horror, Shock, and Disgust. You can highlight them (use different colors if you wish), underline them, or simply make notes where they appear. When you're finished, you should be able to get a sense of your DTHSD "recipe" for this particular piece of writing.

I analyzed my story "Voices Like Barbed Wire," which originally appeared in the anthology *Tales from the Lake V* and was selected for inclusion in *Year's Best Hardcore Horror Volume 4.* I've included the story toward the end of this book in case you'd like to read it before or after I present my analysis. I am going to give spoilers from here on out, though, so be warned.

This story is a riff on the Deal-with-the-Devil trope, although my "Devil" is called Mr. Lim, and I don't use any of the usual trappings associated with the Devil. (See, I *do* practice what I preach!) My unnamed narrator is tormented by the memory of when she and her ex-husband told their young daughters they were divorcing. A friend told her about a weird restaurant called Pandora's where she went to have Mr. Lim remove a painful memory. My narrator hopes he can do the same for her. She goes to the restaurant and meets Lim, a strange man who constantly eats sandwiches made with some kind of mystery meat. My narrator must bring him something to eat as payment for his services. She buys a rabbit at a pet shop, but he refuses to eat anything alive, so my narrator has to break the animal's neck. Only then does Lim eat it and grant her wish. Her painful memory is removed. My narrator is thrilled at first, until she gets a call from one of her now-adult daughters and doesn't know who she is. She realizes this strange woman—who may well be a daughter she doesn't remember having—must be connected to the memory she had removed. She returns to Pandora's and asks Lim to restore her memory. Lim will do so—for a price. My narrator realizes what the strips of meat on his favorite sandwiches are. Others like her have regretted their deal with Mr. Lim and returned just like her. They've paid Lim's price, and so will she. Her tongue is cut off and placed on a sandwich for Lim to eat. My narrator thinks it's a small price to pay to get back what she lost.

A happy ending, right?

My analysis:

- The story starts off with Dread.
- Details of the restaurant's weirdness are presented to heighten Dread.
- Some Disgust is mixed in with these details.
- The narrator feels Terror at her memory whenever it threatens to rise to the forefront of her consciousness.
- There's more Dread and Disgust in the restaurant scene. Disgust is used sparingly, also as another way to add to Dread.

- Shock (for the reader) when she kills the bunny. Disgust when Lim eats it. A bit of Dread anticipating it.
- The narrator remembers getting barbed wire wrapped around her leg as a child. This is Disgust.
- More Dread as readers anticipate learning the effect of the narrator's removed memory.
- The narrator experiences Horror at the realization of what she's lost.
- The narrator experiences burgeoning Horror at the realization of what she has to do to get her memories back. Some Dread and Disgust mixed in.
- Terror, Horror, Shock, and Disgust are all present in the ending.

One of the things that surprised me about doing this exercise is how I weave bits of Disgust into details of mounting Dread. It's not something I've ever been consciously aware of when I write. I intentionally weave Dread, Terror, Horror, Shock, and Disgust throughout my work, but I don't follow any conscious pattern in how I do so. I suppose I'd say I use Terror and Horror the most (probably more of the former than the latter) in this story. Dread and Disgust come in a close second, with Shock being a distant third. Shock needs more of a build-up than a short story allows for. Finding out one character suddenly betrays another halfway through a novel comes as a shock if we've had time to get to know the characters. If such a betrayal happens halfway through a 5,000-word story, the impact is much less.

Now that you've read my DTHSD analysis, go perform one of your own. You can also analyze fiction from writers you find especially effective and see what proportion of these elements they use. If you feel your own use of the elements is unbalanced, play around with your "recipe" and see what it does for you. Maybe you'll find a new formula that works for you better.

_____

_____

_____

_____

_____

_____

_____

VOICES FROM THE SHADOWS

S.H. Cooper, author of *The Festering Ones*

Prompt: Look around the room you're in. Pick out an item, something totally ordinary and mundane. Ask yourself: How can I make this scary? Could it be a pen cursed to only write twisted truths? If that pillow were to grow legs, what would they look like? How would it move? Perhaps the baseball card in the nightstand starts whispering. What does it say? Take from the everyday and find a way to make it haunted.

Joe R. Lansdale, bestselling author of the *Hap and Leonard* series

One thing that I've found that helps make writing feel more exciting, helps develop more painterly scenes, or cinematic scenes, is to think of everything as alive. What I mean by this is: Consider rocks and buildings, inanimate objects, as having some sort of life. A Manitou, to use a Native American term. Think of these things as having a spirit when describing them. Don't go overboard. But if you can imagine each thing as alive and somehow aware, you can write about it, even in a realistic novel, where it pops off the pages and into the brain and leaves a mark.

Ray Bradbury had this touch, and when I read him the world inside my head explodes into colors and I feel movement and mystery. Sometimes Bradbury did this quite literally. Once you make the decision that all things are alive (rocks, tables, etc.) and that some living things, like trees and grass, have more than life, but also have awareness—in fact if all things have awareness—you're on your way to writing scenes that may well have a chance of being remembered. You need not have a rock suddenly do a dance in the desert sun, though that might be interesting, but if you think of it as alive without showing it as alive, your description of it will reveal Hemingway's iceberg theory; that if you know something, even if you leave it out, at least in a direct manner, the reader will sense it. They may not even know why "the deeps" has more impact than "water," but they will feel it. Or if we go back to Hemingway, using his story title, "Hills Like White Elephants," you've driven a glowing and welcome hot spike into the reader's brain, even if the Hills are merely symbolic of something other than hills or elephants, something else the characters are actually talking about and refuse to say literally.

These are off the top of my head, but they give some idea:

- Boulders crawled up the hill, bald and white in the sunlight.
- The frigid winds searched for us, found us huddled around a frightened fire that fluttered and lifted up on dying wings of red and gold, like doomed butterflies.
- The rain drops in the dying light looked like wet gravel.

Kenzie Jennings, author of *Reception*

One of the best exercises I've used in my teaching and in my own practice of the craft is a little pre-writing activity on abstract vs. concrete details. In the end, it opens the writer up to the old concept of showing rather than telling. You first write a statement with a dominant impression of whatever it is you want to describe. I've found it handy particularly with settings, like this:

I live next door to the creepiest house in town.

"Creepiest," or "creepy," is the abstract dominant impression, so, of course, it doesn't "show" the concrete details at all. So then you chart the house (or create a floor plan if you're that kind of writer), from the outside front walk and driveway (if there is one) to the rooms and floors inside the house, all the way to the end of the back yard. Each section of the chart, or floor plan, must use ONLY concrete details that "show" "creepy" like objective descriptors (e.g., items in the house), sensory details, and figurative bits and pieces (e.g., analogies, personification, etc.).

The end goal is to have the chart, or floor plan, filled with details that you can pull from and use in your prose somehow. If you're just writing a piece on whatever it is you're describing, it's all there for you whereas, if you're writing something longer, you have a "bank" of details you can pull from.

Kevin Lucia, author of *Through a Mirror Darkly*

My writing process is very free-flowing. As a consequence, I don't do many exercises. However, early on I discovered something which has helped me write stories from inside, not from a trope. I learned to watch the world for anything strange, and then I asked: "Why?" I started listing these things in a notebook, and I let them stew. Every few days, I'd flip open that notebook. Run my finger down the list. Feel those questions bubble. Ask myself: "Why was that decayed *Alice in Wonderland* mini-golf course so disturbing?" "Why do dark school buses parked alongside 5 a.m. countryside roads feel so … threatening?" "Those beat-up trucks that drive endlessly around town the night before garbage pick-up, looking for scrap metal … where do they go? Do they go anywhere? Or do they just keep driving forever?"

Very often, the items on this list and the questions they prompted led to very satisfying stories. Stories which arose naturally from things I saw in the world, and the weird questions I had about them.

Watch the world. Ask why. Make a list, and let it stew.

Jeff Strand, author of *Pressure*

I've written about many of the standard horror tropes (zombies, werewolves, ghosts, etc.) but I never want the reader to say, "Eh, just another werewolf novel." When I'm coming up with a concept for my next book, I often start with the trope, and then brainstorm how to give it a 90-degree twist. What about an unusual location? Can I combine it with another genre? A different type of main character? A longer/shorter timeframe? My format is usually, "It's a _____ story, but _____." "It's a creature novel, but it spans six decades." "It's a ghost novel, but also a home invasion novel." "It's a 'psychopath forces his victims to play games' novel, but half the book takes place behind the scenes."

CHAPTER NINE
THE HORROR HERO'S JOURNEY

The Hero's Journey is a common story pattern that we're all familiar with: A hero goes on an adventure, encounters a crisis point, makes a critical choice, is victorious, and then returns home a changed person. But characters in horror stories are more reactive than active. Their lives were fine until some kind of threat intruded into their reality, forcing them to react. So if the Hero's Journey pattern didn't lend itself well to horror, I wondered what sort of narrative structure did? After some thought, I came up with the *Poor Bastard's Descent into Hell* to describe a horror story's basic pattern. *The Poor Bastard* is a normal person, and *Descent into Hell* is a situation that steadily and nightmarishly worsens. After thinking about the pattern some more, I realized it had at least eight story outcomes.

Basic Pattern: The Poor Bastard's Descent into Hell. **Possible Outcomes:**

- **The Poor Bastard Escapes Hell.** The Poor Bastard gets away from the Big Bad, but the Big Bad still lives to terrorize another day.
- **The Poor Bastard Conquers Hell.** The Poor Bastard survives the Big Bad and destroys it.
- **The Poor Bastard is Eternally Damned.** The Big Bad defeats the Poor Bastard, absolutely and utterly.
- **The Poor Bastard Escapes with Severe Wounds and Scars.** The Poor Bastard escapes the Big Bad—which may or may not have been destroyed—but he or she is seriously hurt in the process, mentally, physically, spiritual, or all three.
- **The Poor Bastard is Transformed by Hell.** The Poor Bastard escapes—and perhaps defeats—the Big Bad, but he or she is irrevocably changed by the experience (and rarely for the better).
- **The Poor Bastard Carries Hell with Him.** The Poor Bastard escapes and maybe defeats the Big Bad, but he or she now carries a certain amount of Darkness within them. Darkness which may haunt them for the remainder of their lives or cause them to do bad things.
- **The Poor Bastard Drags Others to Hell or Brings Hell to Them.** The Poor Bastard escapes and perhaps defeats the Big Bad, but he or she indirectly (or even directly) causes horrible things to happen to others in the process.
- **The Poor Bastard Becomes the Devil.** The Poor Bastard escapes/defeats the Big Bad only to become just as a much a monster—or even a worse one.

You don't have to consciously follow these patterns (or any patterns, for that matter) when writing your stories. But sometimes it can be helpful to have some structure before you draft, or when you feel stuck. And having a choice of eight different outcomes can help you vary your story patterns so you don't get in a plotting rut.

WE NOW PAUSE FOR PATTERN IDENTIFICATION

PART ONE: Go through the eight horror Hero's Journey story outcomes and list all the books/stories/films you can think of that fit those patterns. For example, Stephen King's *The Dark Half* ends with the main character having defeated the Big Bad, but also having paid a heavy price = The Poor Bastard Escapes with Severe Wounds and Scars, perhaps crossed with The Poor Bastard Carries Hell with Him.

The Poor Bastard Escapes Hell:

_____
_____
_____
_____

The Poor Bastard Conquers Hell:

_____
_____
_____
_____

The Poor Bastard Is Eternally Damned:

_____
_____
_____
_____

The Poor Bastard Escapes with Severe Wounds and Scars:

_____
_____
_____
_____

The Poor Bastard Is Transformed by Hell:

_____
_____
_____
_____

The Poor Bastard Carries Hell with Him:

_____
_____
_____
_____

The Poor Bastard Drags Others to Hell or Brings Hell to Them:

_____
_____
_____
_____

The Poor Bastard Becomes the Devil:

_____
_____
_____
_____

Which of the outcomes is your favorite as a reader/viewer and which is your least favorite? Why?

_____
_____
_____
_____
_____
_____
_____

PART TWO: Pick several stories that you've written and see which of the outcome patterns they fit.

Title: _____ Pattern: _____

_____
_____
_____
_____

Title: _____ Pattern: _____

_____
_____
_____
_____

Title: _____ Pattern: _____
_____
_____
_____
_____

Title: _____ Pattern: _____
_____
_____
_____
_____

Title: _____ Pattern: _____
_____
_____
_____
_____

Did you tend to favor one story outcome more than another? Did you blend any of the outcomes? Which of the outcomes seemed to result in the most successful stories? I often use The Poor Bastard Is Eternally Damned, The Poor Bastard Is Transformed by Hell, and the Poor Bastard Becomes the Devil. Often I combine them in different proportions, especially in a novel where different characters might have different outcomes to their individual paths.

PART THREE: If there are any story outcomes you haven't used (or if you skipped Part Two), make notes on how you'd write a story ending for each of the outcomes.

The Poor Bastard Escapes Hell:
_____
_____
_____
_____

The Poor Bastard Conquers Hell:
_____
_____
_____
_____

The Poor Bastard Is Eternally Damned:

_____
_____
_____
_____

The Poor Bastard Escapes with Severe Wounds and Scars:

_____
_____
_____
_____

The Poor Bastard Is Transformed by Hell:

_____
_____
_____
_____

The Poor Bastard Carries Hell with Him:

_____
_____
_____
_____

The Poor Bastard Drags Others to Hell or Brings Hell to Them:

_____
_____
_____
_____

The Poor Bastard Becomes the Devil:

_____
_____
_____
_____

PART FOUR: Quickly create three characters that you could use in a horror novel. Don't take too much time developing them. You don't need to know much about them for this exercise. Then select one of the following basic plots (or make up a basic plot of your own):

- The characters are trapped in a house which a ghost is bound to. If one of them volunteers to switch places with the ghost, the other two can go free.

- The characters discover a dimensional rift that leads to a nightmarish alternate Earth and encounter extremely dangerous versions of themselves.
- The characters accidentally cause the death of a child on a playground and attempt to cover it up—except what they killed wasn't really a child after all. At least, not a human child.

Whichever scenario you choose, create different story outcomes for each character. If you feel ambitious, create story outcomes for the character in all three scenarios. When you're finished assess your outcomes. Do you think they'd be good endings for a novel? Do you like one story outcome for the scenario more than the others? Why?

_____

_____

_____

_____

_____

_____

_____

VOICES FROM THE SHADOWS

Craig Spector, _New York Times_ bestselling and award-winning author of _The Light at the End_ and _Underground_

My advice is, get in the skin of your characters, especially the villains. This goes against the "stay in your lane" ethos of our modern times, but it's essential: See the world through their eyes, embrace their experience, feel it the way they would. That's easier to do with a character whose worldview you agree with, much more challenging with one you find icky or even repulsive, but all the more important because of that. Research as much as you can, as much as you have to. And remember, everyone is the hero of their own drama. Very few bad guys actually think they're the bad guys; they think they're the hero. So breathe life into your characters until they come to life—a good sign of that is when they actually start arguing with you and not doing or saying what you thought they would or should, because they have their own thoughts on the matter.

Elizabeth Massie, Bram Stoker Award-winning author of _Sineater_

One thing I never do is end a day of writing by completing a chapter or a scene. I have done that before, and when I do, it can take a bit of time to rev myself up to start the new scene or chapter. However, if I stop writing in the middle of a scene or chapter, especially in the middle of a particularly exciting or terrifying scene or chapter, when I come back to it the following day, I'm immediately thrust into the excitement or terror and it's so much easier to pick up and get going again.

Daniel Kraus, *New York Times* **bestselling author**

There are so many opportunities to share your writing today and generally that's a good thing. But there's something to be said for not showing your writing and working in isolation for a time. It's human nature to try to please, so when you get feedback, you might find yourself nudging your story to generate something that will be liked by a higher percentage of readers. But that can be a dangerous thing, especially in horror. The most vital inventions won't end up in the middle of any Venn diagrams—they'll be floating off the side, their own hideous circles. My formative years were spent writing entire novels with no intent on sharing them with anyone, and I truly believe it allowed me to develop a style that indulges my own weird obsessions—and is therefore particular to only me.

Yvonne Navarro, Bram Stoker Award-winning author of *AfterAge* **and** *Highborn*

As a horror author, I bet you want to know how readers hear your work. Not read, but hear. In their heads, when the only light in the room is the one shining over their shoulder onto the page of your book. Is your writing good? Is it exciting? Captivating? To make sure, read your final draft aloud. That's right, read every word of that story, or 95,000 word novel, out loud, and do it as if you're living what you're reading. Don't drone, don't go so fast you're stumbling over words, don't mumble your phrases. Use emotion, and if the character screams, then you scream. If he moans, then you do, too. If he … you get the idea, right? Here's where you'll find your mistakes, your droning, your sentences that are so long you can't read before you get to the period. Live that writing the way you want your reader to live it.

Jennifer Loring, short fiction author and fairytale scholar

Recently I've begun to experiment with form when I'm stuck on a project. I'm especially fond of hermit-crab fiction—stories told in the format of lists, flowcharts, recipes, text messages, just about anything you can think of. So the next time you're feeling blocked, try telling the story in something other than traditional story format. The results may surprise you!

CHAPTER TEN
DOWN TO THE BONE

Horror happens inside characters, which is why the genre is most effective when written with an immersive point of view. While I think immersion is important for any type of fiction, it's absolutely vital for horror. I'd argue that immersion is what *creates* horror. If your readers can't empathize with your characters—even ones who could be considered unlikeable—the awful things that happen to these characters in your stories will have no impact on your audience. Unsure what the difference is between text that's immersive and text which isn't? Here's an explanation using a passage from my novel *The Forever House*.

Example of Distant/Non-Immersive Point of View (Not in the Novel): *A real estate agent met a family she hoped to sell a house to, but the family was weird and freaked her out.*

Example of Immersive Point of View (in the Novel): *There was something about the woman's features that disturbed Lauryn, but she couldn't say precisely what that was. On one hand, Lacresha was a plain-looking woman, so utterly forgettable that she was practically invisible. But her flesh had a mushy quality, and Lauryn felt that if she reached out and pressed a finger to the woman's cheek, there would be no resistance, and her finger would keep on going until her entire hand was lost inside the woman's head. The thought made her queasy, and she felt a bead of sweat roll down her spine.*

She told herself that there was nothing wrong with the woman, that her strange imagining was nothing more than the result of work stress combined with the emotional burden of trying to care for her mother. The rational part of her mind was eager for an explanation—any explanation—and it grabbed hold of this one and held onto it tight. The deeper part of her mind, the part that dreamed, that sometimes sensed when something bad was going to happen, the part that hadn't changed significantly since her far-distant ancestors had been small apes just starting to walk upright ... That part knew a predator when it saw one, and it screamed for Lauryn to get the fuck out of there. But her rational mind overrode her instincts, and she remained where she was, struggling to keep a pleasant, relaxed smile on her face.

An unpleasant musky odor wafted off the Eldreds. It reminded her of the stink of an animal enclosure at the zoo, rank and wild. The smell of beasts locked away in cramped quarters too long, itching to be free, to run, to bite, to kill.

She shuddered. Where on Earth had that thought come from?

You're working too hard, girl, *she thought.*

She became aware of an awkward silence then. She had no idea how long it had gone on, but now all of the Eldreds were looking at her, all of them smiling, but their gazes were empty, devoid of apparent thought or feeling. They reminded her of insect eyes—alien and unreadable. But of course, they were normal eyes. Human eyes. They just seemed *odd.*

The first example is a dry, uninteresting summary of the scene. The second example allows readers to experience the scene through Lauryn's perspective. We're *immersed* in her point of view, and it's like we live the scene alongside her. We know what her five senses tell her, as well as her thoughts, emotional and physical reactions, along with memory connections and imaginings.

This chapter presents exercises designed to help you write fiction with immersive viewpoints or, if you already do, to help you sharpen that skill further.

VIVID FICTION

The goal with immersive point of view is to simulate how humans experience the world—as an ever-changing mass of sensory data and our responses to them. We can't literally recreate the experience of consciousness on the page, but we can make readers *feel* as if they're inside a character's consciousness. To do this, provide different types of details at different points in a scene. Sometimes you'll have a lot of details, sometimes fewer, depending on which character you're writing and what he or she would be paying the most attention to at that point in the story. Here are the types of details we have to work with:

- **Sensory details.** Information gathered through sight, hearing, smell, taste, and touch. (Anything a character can experience internally, such as muscle cramps or a fever, falls under the general category of touch.)
- **Mental reactions.** Characters' thoughts.
- **Emotional reactions.** Characters' feelings.
- **Memory connections.** Something perceived in the present reminds characters of something they perceived in the past.
- **Dialogue.** Yeah, people hear dialogue, so you could make an argument that it should go under sound, but it's important enough to deserve its own category.
- **Imaginings.** Things characters think they perceive, but perhaps are mistaken about. Things characters anticipate. Imaginative comparisons such as similes and metaphors.
- **Misperceptions.** Mistaken interpretation of sensory data due to a variety of causes, including unfamiliarity, ignorance (willful or otherwise), a closed mind, a mind clouded by physical illness or injury, or mental illness.

You don't need to include all of these types of details in every scene, of course. If a character is focused on the moment, he or she will likely rely on their five senses. If a character is thinking about the past, memory connections or emotions associated with memories will be their focus.

Exercise time! Outline a short scene, then write several versions of it, focusing on only one story element at a time. These different versions may be only one page to start with. Make sure there are at least two characters in the scene. Select one to be the main character, the one whose perspective readers are supposed to experience the story through.

Write the scene as all-action, focusing on the characters' movements, on what they *do*.

_____
_____
_____
_____
_____
_____
_____

Write the scene as all-dialogue. Focus on what the characters *say* to each other and nothing else.

_____
_____
_____
_____
_____
_____

Write the scene with only the viewpoint of character's thoughts, feelings, and reactions to events.

_____
_____
_____
_____
_____
_____

Write the scene with only sensory details.

_____
_____
_____

_____

_____

_____

Write the scene with only a character's imaginings or misperceptions.

_____

_____

_____

_____

_____

_____

When you're finished, treat the individual scenes like cards in a deck and shuffle them. Combine the scenes, alternating between the different types of details to make the combined scene vivid. When you're finished, read it over. Do you usually write like this? Do you think the scene works? Is there anything you would change about it to make it even more effective?

BUT ... THAT'S IMPOSSIBLE!

In horror fiction, characters frequently encounter violations in reality. But beginning writers often forget to show their characters reacting when something awful/strange/bizarre/terrifying happens. And if their characters do react, it's after the fact. Something like this:

> *Barbara entered the bedroom. The light was off, and in the dimness a shadowy form shifted on the bed. Brian? But he should've left for work by now. Had he overslept? Was he sick?*
>
> *"Brian?" she said in a half whisper. "Are you okay?"*
>
> *No response.*
>
> *She reached for the light switch but hesitated. If he was sick, the sudden wash of light might hurt his eyes, even set off a headache. But if he'd overslept, the light might help him wake up.*
>
> *She flipped the switch.*
>
> *Crouched on the bed was a beetle the size of a large dog, so black it looked as if it had been sculpted from darkness. Its obsidian eyes fixed on her, and the creature quivered, not in fear, though. In antici-pation. It stretched out one of its front legs, placed it onto the floor. Stretched out another.*
>
> *Barbara turned and ran down the hallway. She raced out the front door, got in her Prius, turned over the engine, and began backing out of the driveway. The beetle emerged from the house, its six legs a blur as it scuttled across the yard toward her. Barbara pulled onto the street, put the car in drive, and stomped on the gas. The Prius leapt forward and she raced away from the house, gaze fixed on her*

rearview mirror so she could watch the beetle. It ran down the street after her, but large as it was, there was no way it could match the car's speed. Its form dwindled in the mirror until she could no longer see it. She didn't slow down, though, kept driving at full speed until she reached the far side of town. She pulled into the parking lot of a grocery store, slid into a space, and cut the engine.

She sat there, hands still gripping the wheel, trembling. Her pulse thrummed in her ears, and her breath came in rapid pants, like she was some small frightened animal.

What the hell was *that thing? And what had happened to Brian?*

At first, this example might seem serviceable enough. Barbara does display a physical reaction to the beetle's presence. She turns and hauls ass. She doesn't experience a mental and emotional reaction until she's parked safely on the other side of town, but that seems realistic, doesn't it? In an emergency situation, it's only natural for someone's adrenaline to kick in and for them to act instinctively. They'd only start mentally processing the event once they were out of immediate danger. But the problem with the example isn't if it's realistic or not. The problem is that it rushes past the point where Barbara is confronted with the violation of reality—the giant beetle in her bed. It doesn't fully develop the *horror* of the scene.

Here's a revised version, only this time I'm going to stay in the moment, and show Barbara reacting to the beetle more fully. I'll start from the point where she turns on the light.

She flipped the switch.

Crouched on the bed was a beetle the size of a large dog, so black it looked as if it had been sculpted from darkness. Its obsidian eyes fixed on her, and the creature quivered, not in fear, though. In anticipation. It stretched out one of its front legs, placed it onto the carpeted floor. Stretched out another.

Barbara's breath caught in her throat, and she stared as she struggled to make sense out of what she was seeing. A beetle—a giant fucking beetle—*was in her goddamned bedroom.*

The beetle's second leg touched the carpet. Then a third. The bulk of its body was at the edge of the bed now, and soon it would slide off the mattress, and all six legs would be on the floor. Would it keep coming slowly then, or would it attack in a sudden burst of speed and be upon her before she had time to react? Touching her with those hard, segmented legs, gouging her flesh with its mandibles, tearing, chewing …

Run, *she told herself. For fuck's sake, run!*

She didn't move. She couldn't tear her gaze from the thing, was mesmerized by it. She'd never been afraid of bugs, not even as a child. In fact, she'd always thought they were beautiful in their cold, inhuman way. They moved with a silent liquid grace that she found fascinating. Perhaps that was what kept her frozen to the spot, or maybe she was afraid that if she turned to flee, she'd be acknowledging the reality of the thing. Standing here, watching, she could imagine that the beetle was nothing more than a hallucination, and while that thought held its own terrors—what if she was losing her mind?—it wasn't anywhere near as frightening as the idea that this thing was real, and that it had somehow appeared in her bedroom. Real or not, there was no way she was ever sleeping on that fucking mattress again.

A short bark of hysterical laughter came out, and she pressed her lips tight to hold in the rest. If she started laughing now, she knew she wouldn't be able to stop herself, and she'd still be laughing when she felt the first feather-light touch of an insect leg against her flesh.

The beetle's last leg lifted off the bed, hovered in the air for a second, and then came down soundlessly on the carpet. The creature stood there a moment, as if regarding her, perhaps drinking in her fear and finding it sweet. And then it started forward once more.

I could go on (and I'm tempted to; writing about giant bugs is fun!), but you get the idea. Not only does staying within the character's perspective moment to moment as the scene progresses increase the tension, the slow accumulation of detail creates suspense. (We'll talk more about suspense in Chapter Eighteen).

Now it's your turn to give it a shot. Write a short scene in which a character is confronted with something awful, and make sure to remain in the character's point of view and depict their mental, emotional, and physical reactions to the awful thing. Don't worry about putting too much detail into the scene. You can always trim it down later if necessary.

_____

_____

_____

_____

_____

_____

_____

WORKING FOR A LIVING

A big part of writing from a character's perspective is understanding their worldview, the particular lens through which they view life (cultural background, religious background, family background, individual experiences, etc.) But a person's profession also affects their worldview, and this is an aspect of point of view that a lot of writers neglect. You can make an argument that some people choose a profession because of their worldview. For example, someone who believes strongly in helping others might go into healthcare. Either way, what a character does for a living can have a profound impact on how they look at people and react to different situations. When approaching a problem, a doctor might think in terms of gathering enough data to make a diagnosis and prescribe a solution. A psychologist might think in terms of working to understand the underlying reasons for a problem in order to come up with a "treatment." A police officer might approach a problem directly but cautiously, prepared for things to go bad at any moment, and ready to deal with it if they do. A bakery shop owner, who deals with customers all day, might approach a problem by speaking to others. trying to win them over with pleasant interactions.

Someone who's a manager where they work might try to take charge and boss others around, or—if they have a softer management style—might try to motivate everyone to work together. All of these characters might consciously attempt to solve problems in their various ways, but more likely they'd do it naturally, without much thought, as these behaviors have become second nature to them.

For this exercise, I'd like you to choose one of these three professions (or come up with one of your own if you prefer):

- A kindergarten teacher
- A retired boxer
- A young gung-ho soldier

Put this character into a scene where a group of people are arguing about how to solve some kind of problem. If you can't think of one right away, have them trying to deal with an infestation of giant insects (like I said earlier, writing about giant bugs is fun!). Have your character try to get the others to settle down and cooperate, using skills and behaviors suited to their particular profession.

If you'd like to take this exercise farther, after writing the first version of your scene, go back and give each of the characters a profession and have them all argue using the perspective of that profession. The simplest example of this, which we've all seen hundreds of times in movies and TV shows, is when a scientist argues with a military person over how to approach a problem, such as aliens who've landed on Earth. This technique is a great way to create conflict, even if the characters eventually end up cooperating.

_____

_____

_____

_____

_____

_____

_____

IF YOU COULD SEE WHAT I HEAR

I borrowed (okay, stole) the title of this exercise from the movie about Tom Sullivan, a blind composer. One of the things about writing with an immersive point of view is that the character you're writing about may be disabled or enhanced in some way. Their condition can be new—they've recently been injured or just developed the power to read minds—or it could be something they've lived with for a while, maybe their entire lives. The point is, these characters experience the world differently from someone who's non-disabled or non-enhanced, and you need to take that into account when writing from their viewpoints.

Disabled Characters. First off, if you're not disabled yourself—or don't have the same disability as the character you're writing about—consider whether it's a good idea for you to be writing about this character at all. I wouldn't write a story or novel seeking to portray what it's *really* like to be blind. Sure, I can do research, but I'll never come close to understanding the day-to-day reality of someone who's blind. (*If You Could See What I Hear* was based on Tom Sullivan's memoir, and he was an advisor to the production. He even had a small part in the movie playing a different character who was also blind.) But if I'm writing an ensemble novel with a cast of characters, and the story isn't about what it's like to be blind, and more importantly, what being blind *means* for an individual and for a culture, then I'm writing content based off research.

For this exercise, you can do research first if you like, or you can try it using only your imagination and empathy. You're not intending to publish the results of the exercise. You're doing it to stretch your writerly wings a bit and become more aware of the challenges writing about disabled characters.

Write a short scene about a character entering a house that's haunted. In this scene, have the character experiencing various details that indicate something supernatural exists in the house. Choose a character with a disability from the following list or select one of your own. And of course, you can write scenes for more than one character if you wish.

- Someone who's blind.
- Someone who's deaf.
- Someone who's paraplegic and uses a wheelchair.
- Someone who's partially blind or partially deaf.
- Someone who lives with chronic pain.

_____
_____
_____
_____
_____
_____
_____

How did the exercise go? Was it challenging to restrict yourself to not being able to use the full range of sensory detail or movement? Do you think that, with research, you'd be comfortable writing about a character with a disability as long as the focus of the story wasn't about living life as someone with a disability?

Enhanced Characters. These are characters with extra abilities. I don't mean superheroes—that's a different genre!—but rather people who can do certain supernatural things: Talk to dead people, predict the future, read minds, see supernatural beings others can't, sense the presence of evil, etc. Sometimes these characters are born with these abilities and sometimes they acquire them during the course of the story. What would it be like to view the world with more than five senses? What would it be like if you constantly hear the dead whispering to you, trying to catch your attention and ask a favor, 24/7? In this exercise, you'll get a chance to find out.

Write a short scene in which an enhanced character is approaching a farmhouse where, fifty years earlier, a man murdered his entire family then killed himself. Choose an enhanced character from the list or select your own.

- Someone who smells odors from the past.
- Someone who hears sounds from the future.
- Someone who can divine information by touching objects.
- Someone who can sense evil but becomes increasing ill as the presence of evil becomes stronger.

_____

_____

_____

_____

_____

_____

_____

How did this one go? I think it can be easier to write about enhanced people because since no one has special powers (that we know of) there's nobody to read our stories and say, "That is *not* what it's like to see people's auras!" But on the other hand, it can be harder to make extra abilities seem believable to readers.

Temporarily Impaired or Enhanced. Sometimes your characters may become injured during the course of a story, or they might fall under some kind of enchantment or curse. They could become temporarily impaired, even if only for the duration of a scene. They might be temporarily enhanced and have a momentary flash of the future or briefly connect telepathically to the mind of the Big Bad. These characters would have no coping skills or experience operating with an impairment or enhancement, which will definitely change how you write them.

Same drill for this exercise as for the last two. Instead of a haunted house or site of a tragic murder-suicide, this time have your character inside woods where some kind of malign entity is stalking them. Here are your character choices:

- Someone whose leg was broken not long ago.
- Someone whose mind is being probed by the malign force, which is searching for mental weaknesses.

- Although it's daytime, a sudden supernatural darkness has fallen over the woods, making a character temporarily blind.
- Someone who is suddenly able to telepathically sense what animals are thinking/feeling. (Just don't have the animals think in English. That's too Walt Disney for our purposes.)

_____

_____

_____

_____

_____

_____

How did this exercise work out? What was different writing about a character who had no experience dealing with their condition? Did it make this scene more effective than the others?

Transformed. Characters in horror (and perhaps to a greater degree in science fiction and fantasy), can find themselves changed into something other than human. With this transformation comes a change in perception, of course, but perhaps also a change in mindset. Someone turned into a vampire might suddenly find themselves looking at the world the way a predatory animal would, and depending on how the change works, they might not even be aware of their altered viewpoint. So let's work with transformation in this episode. A couple of restrictions, though. Make this transformation a profound one. Don't just give a character a random superpower, like having x-ray vision. Yeah, it's change, but not a complete *transformation*. Also, have the transformation occur before the scene starts. I want you to practice writing from the viewpoint of someone who's been transformed, not someone in the process of changing. No special scenario is needed for this exercise. You can have your character walking down a country road, walking through a city ally, walking on a beach … anything. If you want to make the exercise a bit more challenging, you can have your character trying to negotiate an object that's now difficult for him or her, such as someone who's been transformed into a snake needing to get up the side of a building and onto the roof.

Here are your choices:

- Someone who's become a basic horror trope: Vampire, werewolf, zombie, ghost, etc.
- Someone who's been rapidly aged (or youthened).
- Someone who's become symbiotically bound with a colony of insects that now live inside their body.
- Someone who's become an ambulatory plant.

_____

_____

_____

_____

_____

_____

_____

How did the writing go this time? Did you manage to really get into the viewpoint of someone who's been transformed, or did the viewpoint seem too much like that of a regular human? It can be difficult to imagine a nonhuman mindset. Try again if you like.

Altered Mental and Emotional States (Temporary and Long-Term). Maybe you're writing about a character who's temporarily hallucinating due to some occult influence. Maybe your character has contracted a virus that makes sufferers become savage killers. These examples would also count as transformations, of course, but the change has occurred to characters' mental capabilities, not their entire bodies. Readers accept these types of changes because the writer establishes their cause, and it's an unnatural one. But horror has a long tradition of portraying mental illness as monstrous. Think Poe's narrator in "The Tell-Tale Heart" or the grief-stricken, depressed man in "The Raven" (with the raven being the personification of, and maybe even a hallucination caused by, his depression). And when making a horror film it's a lot cheaper and easier to have the "monster" be a psychopathic killer than one that would require makeup or special effects to bring to life. Plus, audiences who find realistic horror more effective respond better to stories with monstrous humans as the main threat.

The problem with portraying "crazy" people as monsters in horror stories is that it continues the stigmatization of people who deal with mental illness in real life. The vast majority of people with mental illness are no threat to anyone (except themselves sometimes), and while serial killers and mass shooters exist, they are an incredibly small percentage of all the mentally ill people in the world. But if audiences see a different insane murderer on _Criminal Minds_ every week for years, they begin to believe—if only subconsciously—that all mentally ill people are potential murderers.

Yet sometimes a story calls for us to write about someone with a mental illness. I'm dysthymic, which means I experience a constant low-grade depression that, if I'm not careful, can lead to full-blown clinical depression. But with the help of meds and therapy, I do okay. I'm comfortable writing characters with depression or anxiety because I've experienced these things. Plus, those conditions don't equate with "crazy killer" in the public consciousness. If I write about characters with different mental illnesses, I do my research, and I'm careful not to create any false impressions. For example, one of my characters in _The Forever House_ was sexually abused by his father as a child, and as an adult himself, he's a pedophile. (Or at least he has pedophiliac urges; he's never actually touched a child.) Early on in the book, I made it clear that very few people who've been sexually abused ever become abusers themselves, and that my character is an exception. Pedophilia *is* monstrous, but I didn't want readers to think all sexual abuse survivors are predators in the making.

If you're going to write from the perspective of someone mentally ill, make sure you do so responsibly.

For this exercise, write about a character who's grocery shopping and thinks someone is following them. Here are your character choices:

- Someone with severe post-traumatic stress syndrome.
- Someone who has difficulty concentrating because of unwanted negative thoughts that constantly intrude on their consciousness.
- Someone who struggles with sex addiction.
- Someone with anger management issues.

_____

_____

_____

_____

_____

_____

_____

How did this exercise work for you? Any differences between writing from this viewpoint compared to the others in this chapter? Was there anything about this exercise that made you uncomfortable? Do you feel you did a good job portraying this point of view?

VOICES FROM THE SHADOWS

Gene O'Neill, twelve-time finalist, two-time winner of the Bram Stoker Award

Many writers I know go fast through first draft, getting the story down. I do it much differently. With short stories, even longer fiction, I go back each day to the beginning of the piece, editing, revising, and upgrading. I find there are at least three advantages to my method:

1. I get warmed up before attacking new material.
2. I repeatedly find grammar and spelling errors to correct each day.
3. I often change story line to fit new directions in newer writing.

This is my method and it works for me—of course I don't outline much, so this is really functional.

Ray Garton, author of *Live Girls*

When you write horror fiction—and I suppose the same is true of fantasy and, to a certain extent, some science fiction—you're writing about things that exist outside of reality, that are not a part of everyday human experience. As I see it, my first job is to make them a part of reality, of everyday human experience. Some will advise you to create the suspension of disbelief in your readers. That'll work in a pinch, but I prefer to pass suspension and go straight for outright belief, always with varying degrees of success, I suspect. I try to weave the supernatural element so tightly into everyday human experience that the two can't be separated. That usually involves building up the human part first, and once my characters are established, I insert the supernatural element, whether it's a vampire, a werewolf, a ghost—whatever it is. By that time, I hope I have engaged the readers and gained their faith, which helps a lot when I add the supernatural stuff. By now, my readers know the characters and are, if I've done my job, involved in their lives, and they care about what happens to them. Then I make those characters suffer with the supernatural.

Any story that has a supernatural element needs a set of rules for that element to follow, and those rules must be diligently observed. A supernatural story without those rules is a cheat to the reader, I think, because you're free to do whatever you want whenever you want to do it, which doesn't always make sense as a story. You have to slip the rules into the proceedings in a way that doesn't feel like a list: "You may be a werewolf IF …" followed by several signs of lycanthropy. Insert those rules in a way that the reader doesn't notice. Yeah, I know, easier said than done. Once they're in, you must follow them. Setting up rules and then violating them is just as much of a cheat to the readers as having no rules at all. But there's a narrow sweet spot between the two, and that's your goal.

Owl Goingback, Bram Stoker Award-winning author of *Crota*

How do you create a more believable monster? Give it a backstory, something to explain its existence, actions, and motivations. Tie your monster in with actual historic events, local legends, and strange sightings. Or make it seem like part of ancient folklore, like H.P. Lovecraft did with Cthulhu. You will be amazed how real your monster will feel. Just don't be surprised if readers claim to have seen your creation in the flesh; it happened to me.

Mary SanGiovanni, author of *The Hollower Trilogy* and the Kathy Ryan series

For me, writing is closely bound to artistic endeavors of all kinds—each is an act of creating something which is both a microcosm and a macrocosm of the human experience. When I get stuck, sometimes I'll seek out a piece of art online, and then imagine what is really happening in the scene, or, more darkly, beneath the scene. I'll give backstory to the figures therein, human or otherwise, and try to imagine a scenario which has led to this single, visually captured moment. You can try this with paintings, digital art, sculpture, photography—anything that inspires wonder about that one frame of time and space.

Seanan McGuire, *New York Times* bestselling author

Writing to deadline can be difficult because it feels so abstract. So I slice each deadline down to individual days, in the sense of "I can make my deadline if I do X words per day," where X is represented by some increment of 1,000. Then, each day as I sit down to work, I line up as many d10s as I need to write words that day, and turn the last one in the line down a number every time I finish 100 words. When I finish 1,000, I remove the die.

CHAPTER ELEVEN
MORE THAN MEAT

It's Creative Writing 101 to say that people like to read about characters they find sympathetic—or at least interesting—regardless of genre. But in horror, especially in stories that have a significant body count, it's too easy for writers to treat characters like collateral damage, little different than the NPC's that get mowed down in action-oriented videogames. No names, no identity, just another body that falls along the way. Sure, one way to show your Big Bad is a significant threat is to have it kill characters, and the more characters it kills—especially if it starts picking off some major ones—the higher the stakes are raised in your story. This is especially true in novels, but it can happen in short fiction as well. But deaths like these have no impact on readers if they haven't come to care about the characters, at least a little, before they go. Plus, remember what I said earlier about horror happening *inside* characters. The more developed and distinct your characters are, the more effective your horror fiction will be.

This chapter presents five exercises that address important issues regarding character that I regularly see in beginners' manuscripts, some geared specifically to horror fiction, some geared to fiction writing in general. But all of them will strengthen your ability to write characters that readers will care about and mourn when they get cut in half with a chainsaw.

So what are you waiting for? Turn the page!

REACTION VS. ACTION

As I said early in this book, horror stories tend to be reaction stories. Sure, the characters may become more active as the story continues—especially if they have no other choice—but if some dark force hadn't entered their lives, they'd have continued trucking along with no worries (at least no more worries than the average person *not* stuck in a horror story has). They react and, when finally forced to, they act. But finding the right balance of reaction and action in a horror story isn't always easy. Some beginners write stories in which their characters are active from the start, ready to battle the Big Bad and slay it. Others write stories in which their characters only react, doing nothing whatsoever to save themselves. This latter approach can work in short stories. After all, there isn't much room to show a character transitioning from reactive to active in a piece of short fiction. But even in short stories, I have my characters try to understand what's happening to them, even if they're only active mentally and emotionally.

Let's do some exercises (you knew I was going to say that, right?). We'll start with reaction.

Write a short scene depicting a character reacting—and only reacting—to a dark force of some sort. It's okay for your character to have reactions that are movements, such as closing their eyes, averting their face, running away, etc. But don't allow them to engage with whatever the dark force is. Here are some suggestions for dark forces, but as always, you're welcome to come up with your own.

- A demon that wishes to possess your character.
- Someone—or some*thing*—taunting your character from the shadows.
- Something trying to break through into our dimension.
- Something playing a horrifying game of tag with your character.

_____
_____
_____
_____
_____
_____
_____

Okay, now consider what it would take to make your character become active at this point. Is someone they care about in danger from the Dark Force? Is your character now so frightened that they become active out of desperation? Whatever motivation you give your character, write a short bit—no more than few paragraphs—showing them transition from being reactive to active.

And when you're finished with *that*, write a short scene showing your character being active. Maybe they engage the Dark Force directly, maybe they try to escape it, maybe they try to direct its attention elsewhere, etc.

_____
_____
_____
_____
_____
_____
_____

Now that you've got three parts of the same overall scene, put them together. Create any connecting material you may need so that the pieces are joined seamlessly.

_____
_____
_____
_____
_____
_____
_____

What's your reaction to this exercise? (See what I did there?) Was it more difficult for you to write one section than another? Do you think the three bits function well as one scene? Why are why not? Does one of the three sections strike you as stronger than the others? If so, why do you think it's stronger?

_____
_____
_____
_____
_____
_____
_____

DOES YOUR CHARACTER JUMP OVER HURDLES, RUN AROUND THEM, OR SAY SCREW IT AND GO HOME?

I tell students this all the time, but in the end, it doesn't matter much what your character looks like, how old they are, where they live, what their racial and cultural background are, etc. What matters—at least in terms of shaping the events of a story—is how they respond to problems, both small and large. If you know this about them, you know what they'll do (and won't do) at any point in your story. You can even use it as a plotting tool. You throw one obstacle up for your character to deal with, they deal with it, and then you throw another at them and see how they deal with that. So on and so forth. Here are some exercises designed to help you determine the ways your character will respond to the hurdles you put before them.

Problem-Solving

How does your character typically deal with problems they encounter?

1. Faces them head-on.
2. Ignores them for as long as possible and hope they'll go away.
3. Turns to their support network (friends, family, co-workers) for help dealing with the problem.
4. Goes to an authority figure (parent, boss, police officer, doctor, clergy) for help?

5. Manipulates others into dealing with the problem for them?
6. Uses verbal means?
7. Uses physical means?
8. What would it take to get your character to abandon their normal problem-solving method and select another?

Which method do you think they would try next? Why?

_____

_____

_____

_____

_____

_____

_____

Create three characters using the following questions. Make each character different from the others in the ways they deal with the issues below.

Response to Changes, Challenges, Stress

1. How does you character respond to change? Small ones? Big ones? Temporary ones? Permanent ones?
2. How does your character respond to a challenge? Do they rise to it, feel too intimidated to tackle it, don't believe they can handle it, turn away from it?

_____

_____

_____

_____

_____

_____

Breaking Point

What would it take to push your character to their breaking point and beyond? And once they reach that point, what do they do? Shut down mentally and emotionally? Completely lose their shit and go wild? Become deadly calm and start making people regret the day they were born?

Okay, once you've got three different characters designed, write a short scene in which the three of them are forced to work together to deal with the same problem. You can make up any kind problem you'd like, or you can select from the following list.

- A group of strangers are trying to break into a house where the three characters are.
- A mysterious mastermind has trapped the three characters inside a deadly maze.
- The three characters are lost in the woods and must find a way out.
- The three characters are lost at sea in a life raft, and their water and food are running out.

_____
_____
_____
_____
_____
_____
_____

How did the scene go? Did your characters find ways to cooperate? If so, how difficult was it for them? Were they in conflict and unable to work together? How serious did the conflict get? Not only is knowing how an individual character responds to problems helpful, knowing how all your characters respond to problems helps you create conflict, drama, and tension in your fiction.

_____
_____
_____
_____
_____
_____
_____

WRITING WITH AN EMOTIONAL CORE

This may be the concept I have the hardest time explaining to beginning writers, but that doesn't mean I intend to stop trying! Stories are most effective for readers when they have some kind of emotional relationship or theme underlying the events that take place. There are exceptions, of course. A short humorous story may be nothing more than an extended joke. A science fiction story may exist solely for the purpose of communicating a cool idea in fictional form. But overall, it's emotion that readers respond to most strongly. And yes, I remember telling you that horror is an emotion, and so technically I suppose you could make an argument that horror is the emotional core of dark fiction. But _horror_ by itself isn't specific enough. For a character to feel horror, they need to _feel_ it about something. And if that something is nothing more than Scary Monster is Scary, you don't have much of a story. But if the emotion lying at the core of a story is specific, such as a parent's fear of failing their children—perhaps combined with an experience when the character's own parents failed them (which explains the origin of the character's fear and intensifies it)—now you've got something to build some interesting horror from. So ...

Emotional Core: A child's parents failed them, and that experience made the child determined to never fail their own children, no matter what it takes. Now that the child is grown and a parent, their greatest fear is that no matter what they do, they will end up failing their children in the end.

Horror that Arises from the Emotional Core: Any threat that forces the parent into a situation where they may fail their kids will work. A werewolf that attacks the parents and kids during a camping trip. A zombie outbreak that occurs in the neighborhood. The Dark Old Ones return to reclaim the planet they once ruled. I prefer to connect the horror more closely to the emotional core, plus I strive for originality, and I just like weird stories—the weirder, the better. So I'd create a horror that embodies the parent's ultimate nightmare: Not only are they fated to fail their children, *all* parents are, and they have been for millions of years, all the way back to the earliest proto-humans. I'd have to figure out how I make this abstract concept more concrete for the story, but this is the kind of horror fiction I write all the time, so I'm sure I'd come up with something. The point is that no matter what the nature of the threat, the emotional core of the story remains the same. In this way, horror fiction is no different than any other kind of fiction, including mainstream and literary fiction. The emotional core is the engine of a vehicle. The specific story events are the body of the vehicle. You can make all kinds of changes to the body that you want, and outwardly the vehicle might look very different to people, but the engine inside—that thing that causes the rest of the vehicle to move—remains the same. I suppose I could strain the metaphor further and say that no matter how great the vehicle's body looks, without an engine, it's not going anywhere. So stories that are brilliantly written and constructed but have no emotional core leave most readers unaffected. (Those who read primarily to experience beautiful prose will be happy enough, though.)

I have no idea if any of that is clear or not, but we're moving on anyway.

For this exercise, I want you to follow what I did above. Come up with an emotional core—the more specific, the better. You can pick something simple, like sorrow, but if you don't specify sorrow over what, it's harder to come up with a concrete idea that will work for this exercise. Once you do that, then make some notes about three different ways you could create horror which arises from the emotional core.

Emotional Core:

_____
_____
_____
_____
_____
_____
_____

Horror Emerging from or Connected to the Emotional Core:

_____
_____
_____
_____
_____
_____
_____

If you're writing a novel, the entire story can be based on a big emotional core, and different scenes can be based on smaller emotional cores which may or may not relate to the larger one. For example, let's pretend like the parents in _Poltergeist_ were on the verge of divorce. The hurt and resentment they feel toward each other might fuel an argument that has nothing to do with the supernatural forces plaguing their house, and which eventually abduct their youngest daughter. Such a scene is still part of the overall story, and the stresses of dealing with malign spiritual entities will only exacerbate their negative emotions toward one another, but the argument is not directly caused by the ghosts.

What if you can't figure out the emotional core of your story? In that case, look to the main emotional relationship(s) in it. For example, maybe your main character has a troubled relationship with her father. It's something established about her character early on, but it doesn't really affect the rest of the story, during which she's trying to track down and kill a swamp monster. The main emotional relationship in the story isn't between the woman and the swamp monster. It's between the woman and her father. So the father needs to be a bigger part of the story. We can do this several ways. The swamp monster killed the woman's mother, and her father is going along on the hunt. The swamp monster killed her father, and despite the woman's conflicting feelings toward him, she's going to hunt the creature down and destroy it. The woman's father died long before the woman goes after the swamp monster, but symbolically—and maybe even literally toward the end—she identifies the monster with her father.

BOOM! Emotional core established. The swamp monster story has an engine now, and it's ready to hit the road.

WHAT (ELSE) IS HAPPENING?

One of the things that I see frequently in beginners' stories is the characters have no life outside whatever problem they're dealing with in the plot. No family, no friends, no pastimes, no pets, not even a job. And they don't have any problems in their lives other than the one posed by the story itself. They have a name, a gender, a general age, and that's about it. But if we want to create the illusion that our characters are real people, we need to give them more fully rounded lives. If our characters were living their lives before Something Awful came along, what exactly was happening? That's what this exercise is all about.

Is your character worried about losing their job? Are they dealing with a long-term health issue that's recently gotten worse? Is their adult child in rehab? Are they afraid they're going to have to put down a beloved pet? Do they no longer feel as close to their spouse as they once did? Are they dreading Thanksgiving dinner with relatives they don't get along with?

Think of what's going on in your life as you read these words. As I write this, it's 6:48 a.m. on a Monday. My wife's in bed with a migraine, I'm hoping I don't have a bad reaction to my second dose of the Covid vaccine, which I'm due to get at 4:00 p.m. today. I'm working on this book while periodically checking on my wife. My first class starts at 9:30 a.m., one of three I have to teach via Zoom today. I fed my two dachshunds not too long ago, and they're in the bed with my wife, snoozing while she lies awake, desperately hoping that her meds kick in. If some kind of horror-type-thing happened to me right now—say, a meteor flashes through the sky, and every animal in the vicinity starts to mutate into something nasty and dangerous—these are the conditions in which my story would take place. I'd likely hear my dachshunds make weird noises as they mutate, and my wife would surely react to their changing. I'd rush out of my writing room, run down the hall, and hurry into the bedroom to see what's happening, and the story would go on from there. Everything else would cease to matter—this book, my classes, my vaccination … My wife's migraine would still be an issue as we try to deal with our mutated dogs, get to safety, etc., (and it would be a great complicating factor in the plot), but that's it.

If my When Mutated Animals Attack scenario is a short story, I wouldn't need to add any other life details. Maybe something about my relationship to my immediate neighbors if they become involved in the story, but little more. If this story were to become a novel, though, I'd have to look at larger, more long-term factors in my life that might come into play. As soon as my wife and I were safe enough, I'd call to check on my two adult daughters (assuming I had the presence of mind to grab my phone as we were escaping my ravenous mutated dachshunds). My oldest daughter is twenty-six and lives in an apartment only a few minutes away from my house. She works at a bank, and she's probably not left yet. My youngest is twenty-one and spends half her time at my house and half the time at her mother's (my ex's) apartment. Today she's at my place (and still asleep), but to complicate my story further, I'll pretend she's at her mom's. My ex lives only a little farther away from me than my oldest daughter. My other relatives—my dad, his wife (my mom died a couple decades ago and my dad remarried), my brother, his wife, my sister, her husband, their four adult boys, and their spouses and kids all live in the same small town where I grew up, which is a forty-five-minute drive from where I'm at now. With the exception of my brother, I'm not super close to my relatives. Most of them are conservative Trumpers, and while we all love one another, we don't have a lot in common. I'd worry about whether my relatives were being attacked by mutated animals, but right now, I'd be primarily concerned about my daughters. My wife and I both take a number of medications regularly. I'm diabetic and take antidepressants, and my wife has a number of health issues. If the mutated animal attack goes on long enough and we don't have access to our meds, that will impact us eventually. Not in immediately catastrophic ways, but enough to further complicate matters.

I guess what I'm trying to show you is that the main problem in a story (in this case mutated animals attacking people) doesn't exist in a vacuum.

Enough babbling from me. It's exercise time.

Take a character from one of the stories you've already written or are currently working on. Or if you prefer, make up a new character for this exercise. Or you can do what I did in the intro to this exercise and use yourself. Provide as much information as you can about the following items.

1. What is your character concerned about/doing/dealing with at this exact moment? (In other words, before the story begins.)

   _____
   _____
   _____
   _____

2. What issues does your character have with work?

   _____
   _____
   _____
   _____

3. What issues does your character have with family and/or friends?

   _____
   _____
   _____
   _____

4. What health issues does your character or close family members have?

   _____
   _____
   _____
   _____

5. What issues does your character have with their living situation? (Late on rent, central air unit broken, basement flooded, asshole neighbors, driveway coated with ice, etc.)

    _____

    _____

    _____

    _____

6. Will any of these situations/issues get worse because they'll be interrupted/affected by the main story event? If so, how much worse? How stressed will your character become because of this?

    _____

    _____

    _____

    _____

Now that you've gotten all these details down, it's time to see how they might work in a story.

For a short story: Come up with a story idea. Use my idea of mutating animals if you like. Remember, there's not a lot of room in a short story, so choose three different life details from your list above and make notes about how they might work in a short story.

_____

_____

_____

_____

_____

_____

_____

For a novel: Come up with a novel idea (or use mutating animals again). Now you can choose as many life details to incorporate as you want. Make notes about how they might work in a novel.

_____

_____

_____

_____

_____

_____

_____

Did any of these life details help you with plotting the stories? Sometimes I think a big part of writer's block is that a writer doesn't know enough about their characters' lives to have any idea what they might do next or what might happen to them if an event interrupts their lives.

A final note: Don't feel you need to incorporate all the details you develop about your characters' lives.

In fact, I purposefully don't delve too far into the lives of characters when I write a short story so that I'm not tempted to overload the story with too much detail.

_____
_____
_____
_____
_____
_____
_____

THE WRITER GIVETH, AND THE WRITER TAKETH AWAY

One of the temptations beginning writers—especially writers of horror, fantasy, and science fiction—face is giving their characters cool stuff. Sometimes _lots_ of cool stuff. Telepathy! A magic amulet! A gun that shoots demon-killing bullets! A pet werewolf! A lover who's half fairy! A car that's alive and makes snarky comments! But one of the secrets to good storytelling is that it isn't what we give characters that make them interesting. It's what we take away from them. Superman becomes more interesting when he has someone he loves (which a villain can use against him) and kryptonite which weakens him. His complete invulnerability is taken away, or at least diminished. Batman is more interesting when he's up against a foe that has super powers (since he has none himself) or when he's severely injured but has to keep fighting anyway or when he doesn't have access to any of his tech. James Bond is more interesting when his license to kill has been revoked and he's dismissed from MI-6. Giving Superman even more powers, giving Batman even cooler, more powerful tech that can stop any criminal, and giving James Bond an entire squadron of super-spies at his command makes their jobs too easy. And in fiction, too easy is boring.

So when you create a character, or when you're putting a character through their paces in a story, consider what you can take from them that will make things even harder for them. And in the process, make your story more interesting.

1. Is there anything physical you can take away from your character? Can you give them an illness or injury? A disability? A long-term health condition, such as hypertension or stress headaches?

   _____
   _____
   _____

2. Is there anything mental or emotional you can take away from your character? Do they have any psychological issues? Any emotional ones, such as a relationship that's on the verge of

ending, or grief caused by the recent death of a family member? Trauma in their past? Have they suffered a head injury during the course of the story and now have trouble thinking clearly?

_____
_____
_____
_____

3. Is there anything you can take away from your character's support network? Are they estranged from their family? Have they recently had an argument with their lover? Does their best friend no longer trust them?

_____
_____
_____
_____

4. Is there anything you can take away from your character socially? Is their boss pissed at them? Has someone started a vicious rumor about them on social media? Are they arrested for a crime they didn't commit?

_____
_____
_____
_____

Take one item from each of the four questions above and make notes about how you might be able to use them in a single story.

Oh, and in case you're wondering, my wife's meds kicked in and she's sleeping now. And I've just about finished this chapter.

_____
_____
_____
_____
_____
_____
_____

VOICES FROM THE SHADOWS

Craig DiLouie, author of *The Children of Red Peak*

When I plan a novel, I set up goalposts for a process of discovery. These goalposts involve story architecture—plot points and character arcs—and theme. My craft tip for writers focuses on theme because it's sometimes neglected during the writing process. Often, writers will incorporate theme wittingly or unwittingly, but like anything else, if it's understood and given intent, it becomes a tool writers can use rather than a delightful accident. It answers the question "So what's your book about?" in a way that is compelling and internalized before writing begins.

Back in 2014, Gallery published my horror novel, *Suffer the Children*. I described it as a vampire novel in which the world's children die of a parasitic disease that brings them back to life needing blood to survive, and their loving parents become the story's true monsters to keep them fed. In New Orleans, I attended a Horror Writers Association conference panel in which author Leslie Klinger advised writers to find and express the nonfiction concept of the story. As a former English major who still considered theme to be homework, this was a big takeaway for me and influenced my understanding and interest in theme. As a result, I started describing the novel as being about how far parents will go for their children. I put it as a question: "How far would you go for someone you love?"

How can writers use theme? First, the don't tips that generally apply (I say "generally" because as with all writing tips, YMMV): Don't look for it or bolt it onto your work after you're done, don't overdo it, and don't be heavy-handed or turn it into an argument made by the author. Now the do's: Conceptualize it as early as possible, internalize it (try to feel it), and then let it express itself organically using the basic writing tools. Theme is usually best when it's implicit, where the author trusts the reader to grasp it and make up their own mind. (If you want to be explicit, this might be done in a debate in dialogue between characters.) While theme expresses itself organically, having been internalized to the point of being turned into a feeling, tools used to express theme include giving the protagonist a moral choice, having characters with opposing moral views, and getting creative with the story's image system—that is, its tone, symbols, motifs/leitmotifs, and figurative language.

By employing theme, writers can produce works that accomplish even more than the sum of their words, and gain another tool in their box that helps them craft compelling stories.

Scott Sigler, #1 *New York Times* bestselling author of the Infected trilogy and the Sun Symbol series

No matter what future bloggers or future Amazon reviews will say about you, remember this mantra: The author is not the character. If you're writing horror, you will inevitably be writing about awful people (or demons, ghosts, supernatch of all kinds) doing awful things. While you shouldn't be cavalier about triggers, you also need to create characters that are not you, unless you are the type that wields a straight razor in dark alleys on the regular. You can't let fear of what people might think or say about you get in the way of you uncovering those visceral scenes that will make the reader's skin crawl. If you don't disturb the reader, then what's the point?

Michelle Garza and Melissa Lason, authors of *Mayan Blue, Those Who Follow*, and *Tapetum Lucidum*

When we are having trouble writing a certain scene in our books, sometimes we just type in symbolic words of how it should feel, or settings, or trauma our characters may experience. It helps us retain the point we are trying to get across until later because sometimes we just aren't ready to write specific things how we'd like to in that moment. In our time-crunched world, sometimes we need to go back to certain scenes when we are ready to tackle them. If we sat staring at a computer, agonizing over one scene, we'd waste precious time.

Hailey Piper, author of *The Worm and His Kings*

Sometimes the secret to making a serious situation work is to give your brain permission to cut loose and think outside the box. I call it my Bigfoot Key. Why Bigfoot? Because it sounds silly in most situations, the kind of character I wouldn't want to suddenly show up in a story (that isn't already Bigfoot-related, but in those maybe swap Bigfoot for the Loch Ness Monster or something). If I'm brainstorming concepts, or scene connections, or backstory elements, writing down something like "Bigfoot uprising" or "Bigfoot killed her parents" is a way to remind my imagination that there are no bad ideas, just ideas. The Bigfoot key opens those doors, stops me from self-censoring or putting myself down before I've even put pen to paper. Obviously Bigfoot isn't a permanent solution, but it's a thought to catch my critical brain off-guard enough that I'll figure out a genuine solution to the work. Anything to lessen the stress, in my opinion. A writer already faces countless situations where we're being told, "No." We shouldn't do it to ourselves on top of all that. So I give Bigfoot a "Maybe" and that gives every other idea a "Maybe" as well, permission to come out and play and let me see what I have. I'll end up deciding what I want, or what's right, from everything that steps through the Bigfoot key's unlocked door.

Matt Cardin, author of *To Rouse Leviathan*

To empower yourself as a writer of horror or anything else, give up your power. To get ideas, stop trying to generate them and instead learn to court them. Get out of the way and get a muse or daemon. Learn to relate to your creativity as if it's an external intelligence with its own ideas. You don't have to believe this literally. Consider the muse a perfect metaphor, if you like, just a symbol of your unconscious mind. Or believe it "for real" if that feels better. The choice is yours. Either way, experiment to figure out your daemon muse's ideal work habits, productivity rate, and—above all—native subject matter. And learn to wait. Not a passive waiting, but an active waiting, an active state of listening expectantly. Meditate, or freewrite, or practice five-finger writing exercises to perfect your craft. Or do all of these. And know that through this active waiting, you invite your muse and make yourself a receptive vessel for whenever she decides to manifest and whisper into your ear. Chase her and she'll flee. Wait actively and she'll come. Wait lazily and she may leave you for somebody else. As Picasso observed, "Inspiration exists, but it has to find you working."

CHAPTER TWELVE
HURTS SO GOOD

When you get right down to it, all stories—regardless of genre—are about characters in pain. A character who experiences a deep need to make amends for a wrong they committed in the past is motivated by the pain of guilt. Peter Rabbit is hungry, so he sneaks into Mr. McGregor's garden to steal a snack. Hunger is pain, and when Mr. McGregor sees Peter and starts chasing him; Peter runs for his life. Fear is pain. Characters in a romance story meet and feel longing for each other, but they have trouble understanding and accepting their feelings. Need and confusion are pain. You get the idea. Characters don't have to engage in a fistfight to feel pain or attempt to climb down a mountain with a broken leg. Pain comes in many different forms, and all of them help make stories, well … *stories*. Otherwise, all we'd write are vignettes about characters going about their day and feeling okay about life.

But characters in horror stories encounter more pain than those in other genres. After all, horror itself is a painful emotional state. The genre is *named* for pain. And horror characters can experience a wide spectrum of pain, too, given that they often have to contend with forces that can affect their minds and spirits as well as their bodies. Most beginning horror writers understand that their characters will experience physical pain when they're being devoured by werewolves or tortured by demons. But that's often the only pain they portray in their fiction—and sometimes they do so to purposeless and self-defeating excess, but we'll talk about that more in Chapter Twenty. In this chapter, we'll go through some exercises designed to help you write effectively about all types of pain. If writers are supposed to be sadists toward their characters, we should be the best ones we can, right?

There are four types of pain characters might experience in a horror story:

- Physical
- Emotional
- Mental
- Spiritual

There's no need for me to define physical pain. Everyone knows what that is. Same with emotional pain. Mental pain can encompass psychological pain—you believe you're worthless and you hate yourself—but it can also be a realization of something awful. In Ray Bradbury's "A Sound of Thunder," when one of the time-traveling characters realizes he's made a minor mistake in the past that has altered the present in bad ways, he experiences mental pain (but not for long). Spiritual pain is when you hurt on a soul level. It doesn't matter if you believe in a literal soul or a metaphorical one—the principle is the same. In the Christian bible, Peter denies Christ three times, and when he realizes he's done exactly as Jesus foretold—a prophecy Peter assured Jesus would never come true—he feels deep spiritual pain. And various supernatural beings can attack our characters on a spiritual level, either literally wounding their souls or corrupting them like a spiritual version of cancer. To write effective horror, we need to be skilled at writing about all types of pain—and to do that, we need to explore our own pain.

I've mentioned this caveat before, but here it is again: You do not need to revisit traumatic experiences you may have lived through just to complete a writing exercise. Do as much of the following exercises as you're comfortable with or skip them altogether. Yeah, I earlier mentioned Jack Ketchum's advice to write from the wound, but he didn't say write from *every* wound or to make existing wounds worse by poking around in them so you can get material for a story. Do whatever is best for you.

PERSONAL PAIN ASSESSMENT

I'm not a big proponent of the advice that writers should write what we know. If we did that, we'd write only autobiography. But being able to draw on our personal experiences allows us to make our work feel more real, more *honest*, to readers. So if you want to write honestly about pain, it helps to review your history with it, and that's what this exercise is all about.

Below are the four pain categories. Think back over your life and write down some information on your most memorable experiences with pain. I want you to write about your own direct experience, but if an experience in which you witnessed another's pain or supported them while they went through pops into your head, it's okay to jot that down, too.

Physical Pain:

_____

_____

_____

_____

_____

Emotional Pain:

_____

_____

_____

_____

_____

Mental Pain:

_____
_____
_____
_____
_____

Spiritual Pain:

_____
_____
_____
_____
_____

Which pain experience stood out most in your memory? Which type was it? Were you more likely to remember pain that lasted a short time or did a long-term experience (such as years of dealing with back pain) stand out more? How did you do coping with pain in the various experiences you wrote about? How—or even if—characters can function while coping with pain is important to know in a horror story, since our protagonists (and antagonists) can get hurt in all kinds of ways in our fiction.

_____
_____
_____
_____
_____
_____

Now that you've taken a look at the role of pain in your life, it's time to do the same for your characters. Or at least one of them. Pick a character from a story you've already written or make up a new one for this exercise. Do the same as you did last time, only now for this imaginary person.

CHARACTER PAIN ASSESSMENT

Physical Pain:

_____
_____
_____
_____

Emotional Pain:

_____
_____
_____
_____
_____

Mental Pain:

_____
_____
_____
_____
_____

Spiritual Pain:

_____
_____
_____
_____
_____

How did this exercise turn out? Was inventing pain experiences more difficult than you thought it would be or was it easier than relating your own? Let's take this exercise a step further.

_____
_____
_____
_____
_____
_____

HOW DOES THIS CHARACTER COPE WITH PAIN?

1.   How does this character deal with immediate/short-term pain? (Like a shallow cut or twisted ankle?)

_____
_____
_____
_____
_____
_____
_____

2. How does this character deal with longer-term pain? (Such as an injury that will take hours, weeks, or even months to recover from.)

_____

_____

_____

_____

_____

_____

_____

3. How does this character deal with long-term pain? (Such as a chronic medical condition that could last years or even a lifetime.)

_____

_____

_____

_____

_____

_____

_____

PAIN AS STORY FODDER

Look over your character's pain assessment. Are there experiences that could form the basis for a story? For example, my mother suffered from anxiety and depression, and as a result, she became agoraphobic. I've used this experience—being the child of a mentally-ill parent—several times in my fiction. Another example: I almost drowned when I was nine, and that experience, or at least the idea of water as a threat, has appeared often in my stories, so much so that I had enough for a collection—*A Little Aqua Book of Marine Stories* from Borderlands Press.

Story Ideas Based on Character's Pain:

_____

_____

_____

_____

_____

_____

_____

_____

_____

_____

THE WORST OF THE WORST

I've already said that the characters in horror stories usually experience more pain than characters in other types of stories, and that pain can get *bad*. But our characters don't just have a difficult time in our fiction. They experience nightmares, sometimes literally. (I'm looking at you, Krueger!) Whatever type of pain (or combination of types) a horror character experiences is often the worst they've ever encountered, and maybe beyond anything they've ever imagined.

Your Personal Worst. For this exercise, I want you to contemplate the worst pain you can imagine that you've never experienced. Write responses for all four categories of pain.

Physical Pain:

_____
_____
_____
_____
_____

Emotional Pain:

_____
_____
_____
_____
_____

Mental Pain:

_____
_____
_____
_____
_____

Spiritual Pain:

_____
_____
_____
_____
_____

Their Personal Worst. For this next part, you need to use a character that's already developed. Pick one from a story you've written or one you're familiar with from other stories—a book, a film, a TV show. Once you've selected a character, do the same thing you did for yourself in the last part. Write about the worst pain they can imagine but have never experienced.

Physical Pain:

_____
_____
_____
_____
_____

Emotional Pain:

_____
_____
_____
_____
_____

Mental Pain:

_____
_____
_____
_____
_____

Spiritual Pain:

_____
_____
_____
_____
_____

The point of this exercise is that the worst pain we can imagine is exactly the kind of pain a character in a horror story should be put through. Several years ago, I was watching a true-crime show on TV which was about people who went missing and were never found. As a father, my first reaction was, *What if one of my daughters went missing? God, I don't know how I could handle that.* That worst pain of mine became the basic scenario for my novel *The Mouth of the Dark.* A father is searching for his missing adult daughter and discovers that she's involved in an aspect of our world called Shadow, and she isn't who he thought she was. For that matter, he discovers *he* isn't who he thought he was either. So whether you use one of your worst pains or make up one for a character, worst pains can make strong foundations for horror stories. Now that I've said that …

Do Your Worst. Choose one of the worst pains on your list or the character's. Make notes about how you could use that pain as the basis for a piece of fiction. If you'd like to take this exercise further, come up with story ideas for each pain category: Physical, emotional, mental, and spiritual.

_____

_____

_____

_____

_____

_____

_____

How did it go? Come up with any ideas that you think would make for a great story? Why not take a break from this book to go write it? (I'll still be here when you get back, promise!)

VOICES FROM THE SHADOWS

S.P. Miskowski, author of *I Wish I Was Like You*

Be your own wiki. Never throw anything away. Keep your notes. Jot down every premise, every character history, every idea for style, POV or action. Keep your notes in any form and any condition that will suit you and serve your needs. Scribble in notebooks or on index cards, in a Word document or Dropbox files. Organize your notes within an inch of their lives or keep them randomly or use a system only you understand. Flip through them whenever you get stuck and need ideas or a change of direction.

Eric LaRocca, author of *Things Have Gotten Worse Since We Last Spoke*

One of the most arduous aspects of the writing process can be generating a concept—the initial spark of a compelling and dynamic idea. Though my own process varies depending on a myriad of circumstances, I'm usually most inspired by a compelling title. In fact, I typically keep a list of potential titles in my notes section on my phone. I think the most compelling, unique titles for works of horror are poetic, beautiful, grotesque, etc. My challenge to you would be to start writing a poem—a stream of consciousness—comprised of the most beautiful, obscene, provocative language you can conjure. Then, when you're finished with your poem—pull a sentence from your piece and consider what kind of story might accompany this if it were a title. This, of course, may take a few tries. Also, if the language you've conjured doesn't inspire a story, at least you have a completed a poem to submit to a journal or online zine! This process was how I came up with the titles for *Things Have Gotten Worse Since We Last Spoke*, as well as my unpublished piece "I Look for You Until My Lungs Sprout Metal." Although I primarily write dark fiction, I've had the privilege of seeing some of my works for theater performed on the stage. At a recent playwriting workshop

I attended, one of the more difficult (yet inspiring) writing challenges was to remove a crucial symbol, plot point, character, etc. from your piece (mine, for instance, was a small pine box that housed my play's dark secret/grand reveal) and see how the removal of this item informs your revision process. This challenge was difficult to say the least; however, it made me realize certain aspects of my play I hadn't considered before. Reflect upon the heart of your project's narrative—it could be a character, a theme, an object—and then remove it. You'll be surprised how your narrative changes in new, exciting ways.

Paul Kane, author of *Darkness and Shadows*

One exercise I've found works really well for people, and can be quite fun, is to pick a favorite scene from a TV show or movie. Then you write that scene as prose, from one character's point of view; maybe even one that you wouldn't expect. Obviously you wouldn't be able to use it for anything, but it really helps with description, characterization, and POV, especially if you try it from several different ones.

Similarly, you could take a favorite scene from a book or story and rework that from a different character's POV. Or maybe even first person, if it isn't already. Try to make the scene your own and write it in a different way than the original author.

Regina Garza Mitchell, author of *Shadow of the Vulture*

Write down a phrase from a song or poem that speaks to you in some way. It might be two words, or it could be an entire line. Think about the phrase itself, the images and feelings it evokes, rather than how it is used within the context of the song or poem. Now use that phrase as the starting point for a story.

Briana Morgan, author of *The Tricker-Treater and Other Stories* and *Unboxed*

The Four A's of Characterization:

1. Actions. What risks has the character taken in the past? How has he or she treated family and friends? What about enemies? What hobbies does he or she enjoy? What has your character done? What is he or she doing in the story?
2. Attitudes. How does the character feel about gay marriage, abortion, religion, and other hot-button issues? What are your characters' views on the world?
3. Artifacts. What are your characters' prized possessions? What shelter do they have? What cars do they drive? What's the first thing they'd save in the event of a fire?
4. Accounts. What are some noteworthy anecdotes about these characters? What do other people have to say about them? What rumors have been circulated?

CHAPTER THIRTEEN
THE PHYSIOLOGY OF FEAR

Fear has more than a psychological effect on us. We physically react, too, and as horror writers, we need to be able to depict both types of fear realistically. In order to do that, though, we need to understand the physiology of fear. I covered this topic in detail in *Writing in the Dark*, and I'm not going to repeat all of that information here. But if

I had to summarize my advice for writing about the physical effects of fear, I'd say it's important to depict the effects in specific detail rather than write something general like *Marty was gripped by terror and froze in place.* Exactly what does *gripped by terror* feel like? There's no way for readers to know unless they're shown. The exercises in this chapter will hopefully help you do that.

WANNA FEEL SOMETHING *REALLY* SCARY?

Think back to different times in your life when you experienced fear. What did you physically feel during those events? Write down as many specific details as you can remember for times when you experienced mild fear, medium-level fear, and intense fear. (I'll offer the same caveat here as I have for other exercises. If revisiting times you experienced fear is too emotionally difficult for you, feel free to pass on this exercise.)

Mild Fear:

_____

_____

_____

_____

Medium-Level Fear:

_____

_____

_____

_____

Intense Fear:

_____
_____
_____
_____

How many specific details could you recall? Sometimes during a fear experience we can remember the smallest details, but other times our memories are hazy, and while we may remember an event happened, details elude us. Don't get frustrated if you can't recall many specifics. Maybe try choosing other fear events in your life to write about, or perhaps try substituting research for personal experience. Reading or watching accounts of people who've been in life-threatening situations might provide the details you need to write convincingly about physical reactions to fear. However you do it, once you have a list of physical fear responses, you can use it to provide the details you need whenever your characters are scared.

DEGREES OF FEAR

Our characters aren't always in extreme "Confronting the Unspeakable Horror" situations, but even ordinary events can spark a fear reaction in us, with the accompanying physical sensations. Following is a list of situations, some life-threatening, some less so. Using a combination of experience and imagination, describe the physical sensations someone in each situation might experience.

1. Meeting a blind date.

    _____
    _____
    _____
    _____

2. Hearing an unexpected sound in your home in the middle of the night.

    _____
    _____
    _____
    _____

3. Receiving a diagnosis of a terminal illness.

    _____
    _____
    _____
    _____

4.   Lover/partner/spouse saying they want to break up.

_____

_____

_____

_____

5.   Learning you're being fired from your job.

_____

_____

_____

6.   Your car starting to slide as you're rounding a curve on a rain-slick road.

_____

_____

_____

_____

What was similar about your descriptions of physical fear reactions for each situation? What was different? Did you write long descriptions or short ones? In my experience, the more normal a fear situation is, the fewer physical details I'll provide for it. But for major events—such as a diagnosis of a terminal illness or losing control of your car in the rain—I'll provide more details. The car scenario would receive the most details from me because it's a life-threatening moment-by-moment experience, and I would want to make it exciting and suspenseful for readers.

_____

_____

_____

_____

_____

_____

_____

FIGHT OR FLIGHT

It doesn't get more basic than this, does it? The animal in us—the part of our brains that has remained the same for millions of years—has an instant binary response to fear: Run like hell or beat the shit out of whatever is threatening us. This response is so strong and so immediate that—unless we have very specific training—we can't control it. And in general, that's a good thing, because if we had the capability of contemplating our choice, we'd hesitate, and maybe end up dead. And until we're in a specific situation, we have no idea which way we'd react, and in horror, our characters are usually everyday people who've never been in a deadly situation necessitating a flight or fight response. They have no clue how they—or any companions of theirs that are sharing the situation—will react. As writers, even we might not know until we start to draft a scene, and we may have to try a scene both ways—fight or flight—to see which version will serve the story better. That's what this exercise is about.

I'm going to give you a choice of scenarios. I want you to choose one and then, using the same character, write two short scenes based on the scenario, one in which the character experiences a flight reaction, one in which the character experiences a fight reaction. You can use a character you developed in a previous exercise, use one from a story you've already written, or base the character on someone you know or even yourself. As usual, bonus points if you choose to write a scene based on all three scenarios.

Scenario One: Your character is walking down a city sidewalk when a masked maniac wielding a very large and very sharp knife emerges from an alley to block their way.

\
\
\
\
\
\
\
\

Scenario Two: Your character is walking through the woods during the night of a full moon, hunting a werewolf. They're carrying a pistol loaded with silver bullets, but they're unfamiliar with firing guns. They hear a twig snap behind them followed by a soft growl.

\
\
\
\
\
\
\
\

Scenario Three: Your character is one of the few survivors of a zombie apocalypse. They're a normal person, not some bad-ass survivalist who's long been preparing for the end of the world. They have no clue how to survive long-term in this situation. They're just doing their best to get from one moment to the next without becoming zombie chow. Zombie vision is terrible, especially at night, so your character waits for dark to sneak into a convenience store in hope of finding some food and water. Once they're inside, they hear the sound of shuffling footsteps and know that a zombie is in there with them.

\
\
\

_____

_____

_____

_____

How did your character do in the scenario you chose? Which version—flight or fight—seemed truer to the character? Which version (if either) was easier to write? Which version do you think was more effective? Which do you think readers would enjoy reading more?

YOU TAKE THE LOW ROAD AND I'LL TAKE THE HIGH ROAD

High road and low road are ways to describe the two levels of fear response. The low road is an immediate, physical reaction. The high road is slower, more rational. Both occur at the same time. Your body reacts first, but your mind quickly follows. The high road can modify or even counteract the low road. For example, a solider will experience an instantaneous low road reaction when a battle begins, but their training will kick in, allowing them to deal with the fear and do what they have to do. Knowing your characters' low road and high road reactions allows you to write about them facing dangerous situations more effectively.

So let's explore roads both high and low.

High and Low Road Exercise

Take what you wrote for the fight or flight exercise, and revise it to take the high and low road reactions to fear into account. You likely already have low road reactions in the scene you wrote, so all you'll need to do is add in high road reactions, depicting your character's rational side kicking in. Here's an example (using one of the scenarios I gave you for the previous exercise):

Olivia heard a twig snap, the sound loud as a shotgun blast in the night's silence. Cold fire surged in her chest, and her fingers tightened painfully around the Glock's hard surface. Run! *her mind screamed at her.* Run, you stupid bitch! *And she almost did, went so far as to take a single step forward, but she stopped herself. If she ran, she'd let the wolf know she was aware of it. More, her sudden burst of speed might trigger it to attack. She needed to keep walking slowly, draw the wolf in close enough so she could get a good shot at it, without causing it to run at her full speed. She drew in a shuddering breath, held it for a ten count, and then slowly released it. Her panic didn't subside—her nerves still felt raw and inflamed—but she thought she'd be able to control herself now. She lifted a foot, put it down, lifted another, did the same. Her legs were shaky, but they held her up, and that was all that mattered right now.*

She continued walking, listening intently for the next sound that would indicate the wolf was closing in.

One of the great things about high and low road responses to fear is that they add a different level of conflict to a scene. Not only is there the conflict of Olivia hunting—and being hunted—by a werewolf, but she's also conflicted about her reaction to hearing that it's approaching. This conflict adds more tension and suspense to the scene. A word of warning: When writing a scene like this, don't have your character think too much. If I'd had Olivia go into a five-page reverie about the time she saw a wolf at the zoo when she was a child, and how she can't believe the beautiful, peaceful animal she saw then could be a cousin to the thing that's stalking her now, not only would it bore readers, it would seem grotesquely unrealistic. Sure, people can have odd thoughts when they're afraid, but in general they stay focused on the present danger.

All right, it's your turn. Write your own high road and low road scene.

_____

_____

_____

_____

_____

_____

_____

LONG-TERM PHYSICAL EFFECTS OF FEAR

If you're writing a story or novel where a character has been in a fear situation for a long time—say, a story about a haunting that's been going on for days, weeks, or months—that stress will eventually start to take a physical toll on them. Here's a list of reactions they might experience:

- More colds and infections
- Sexual disorders
- Aches and pains
- Fatigue
- Loss of appetite

And if your character has been severely traumatized, they'll likely experience PTSD (post-traumatic stress disorder), which can have the following physical effects:

- They might have elevated stress hormones in their body on a longer-term basis, resulting in faster and more dramatic fight or flight responses.
- They may experience fear reactions when situations don't warrant them.
- They might have a fear response when reminded of the traumatic event.
- Their bodies have trouble turning off the fight or flight response.

- Depression.
- Substance abuse as they attempt to self-medicate.
- Problems thinking and remembering.

For this exercise, write two short scenes: One in which a character is experiencing a long-term effect of fear (perhaps more than a single effect, too), and one in which a character is showing signs of PTSD. Do your best to stick with physical reactions more than psychological ones for this exercise.

On your mark … get set … go!

1. SCENE ONE: Longer-Term Effects of Fear.

_____
_____
_____
_____
_____
_____

2. SCENE TWO: PTSD Effects.

_____
_____
_____
_____
_____
_____

How did these exercises turn out for you? Was it easier writing about longer-term effects of fear or PTSD? Which do you think would lead to more possibilities in a story? Could you see yourself maybe basing an entire story, chapter, or scene on one of these effects?

VOICES FROM THE SHADOWS

Lee Murray, five-time Bram Stoker Award nominee and author of *Grotesque: Monster Stories*

At school visits, when students ask me how to overcome writer's block, I tell them there's no such thing and that all they need to do is write a placeholder word, something dry and boring, and keep writing it until a more interesting idea jumps into their head. I usually suggest they write Weet-a-bix. Occasionally, they'll leave those placeholders in their story, and I'll get instances of Weet-a-bix, Weet-a-bix, Weet-a-bix scattered throughout their prose—a delightful insight into a child's writing process. Of course, as horror writers, we'll need something more sophisticated than Weet-a-bix. Perhaps a cliché? Yes, a cliché might work. Hence, my tip: In case of writer's block, write "double, double, toil and trouble," until otherwise inspired.

John Palisano, Bram Stoker Award-winning author of *Ghost Heart*

One of the methods I use to combat writer's block is to really get to know the characters. We create descriptions based upon looks, but often don't explore their emotional journeys. Knowing how a character would act when facing extraordinary situations can really pull the plug and let the story flow.

Hunter Shea, author of *Faithless*

One of the fun things about writing horror is tearing away at people's vulnerabilities and seeing if they're fighters or victims in the face of evil. Now, don't get me wrong, it's a blast to knock some perfect all-American man or woman down a few pegs (especially if they like to party, have premarital sex, indulge in drugs or underage drinking or say inane stuff while in the car driving to that cabin their uncle lent them for the weekend). I call them the low-hanging fruit. The truth is, the vast majority of us are not the all-American man or woman. We have weaknesses, issues, shortcomings and regrets. One of the things I like to do is take a "normal" character who I know is going to face some seriously nasty doo-doo around page 146 and make things even more difficult for them. How? I give them what others might consider a fatal flaw. It could be a disease that's cutting their time short even before the killer/monster/alien shows up. Or maybe they have a disability that will make it difficult for them to flee from their tormentor. Perhaps they're hard of hearing and won't know when the beast is creeping up on them. Whatever you do, please don't give them diabetes with no access to insulin. That's been done to death. By all means, be creative with giving your characters physical flaws. Your readers might identify with them just a little bit more, and will either cheer louder when they elude certain death, or wail at the moon when they succumb to a bloody axe. Because aren't we all flawed?

J.A.W. McCarthy, author of *Sometimes We're Cruel and Other Stories*

For me, horror is most effective when it's rooted in the truth. My best stories are the ones where I took a personal experience and embellished it, blowing up the horror I experienced and pushing it into something that is fictional, but is true to what I was feeling at the time. If you can recall not only the sights and sounds of that personal experience but also how you felt, you've got the seeds of a successful story.

J.H. Moncrieff, author of the bestselling *Ghost Writers* series and *Return to Dyatlov Pass*

Tip: Don't begin at the beginning, and don't feel you need to tell us everything a character does. Anything irrelevant to the plot slows down the pace and kills suspense. We don't need to see them waking up in the morning, brushing their teeth, or going to bed at night. All the mundane stuff is implied. Focus on the interesting, the relevant, the unusual.

Prompt: You've booked an isolated cabin for a writing retreat, but soon realize it isn't empty.

CHAPTER FOURTEEN
TELL ME A SCARY STORY

The corresponding chapter in *Writing in the Dark* discussed a number of different techniques for plotting horror fiction, and it was one of the longest in the book. But rather than creating exercises for each bit of advice in that chapter, I've chosen to highlight certain areas that I feel most writers likely aren't familiar with—*and* I've added an entirely new technique as well! (What can I say? I'm a generous guy.)

Much of the plotting advice in *Writing in the Dark* can be applied to any type of fiction, and the same goes for the exercises in this chapter. Different genres—literary fiction included—might have different basic plot designs that they tend to follow, but overall, fiction is fiction. However, there also are several exercises here designed specifically for writers of the dark stuff.

Whenever writers start talking about plotting, a debate—sometimes congenial, sometimes less so—usually breaks out. It goes something like this:

"Plotting is essential to creating well-constructed fiction."

"I never plot! It's too artificial and panders to an audience reared on simplistic entertainment designed for the masses. *I* let my characters shape my stories!"

"What the hell is wrong with you? Are you some kind of lunatic?"

"Eat shit and die, plot-head!"

I use a combination of plot-based and character-based story-shaping when I write, so I stay out of the plot vs. character arguments. No technique is better or worse than another. Techniques are tools, and tools are good for some tasks and not others. And some craftspeople happen to work better with some tools and not others. As long as the job is done well, who cares exactly how it was done?

Well … *we* do. Fellow craftspeople. We love to know how others of our tribe do their work and hope we can gain insights (otherwise known as stealing) from their techniques. So if you have an innate dislike—even full-blown revulsion—at the very notion of plotting, you can of course skip this chapter. But I urge you to at least read through it. The following exercises don't offer step-by-step formulae for how to plot a horror story. They present several tools that you might find useful in your work, no matter how you prefer to approach it.

THE END IS ONLY THE BEGINNING

One of the things I noticed early on in my career as a creative writing teacher was that student stories were often preludes designed to set up the Cool Thing at the End. The Cool Thing would be an image or concept—such as a plot twist (that usually wasn't very surprising) or the reveal of a supposedly terrifying monster. These stories always fell flat, of course. Who wants to read ten pages of throat-clearing just to get to a couple paragraphs of interesting material at the end? Why not begin with the Cool Thing and have your story become even cooler as it goes along? So I invented The End Is Only the Beginning exercise. After students finished a draft of a story, I asked them to take the ending image/situation and imagine it as the beginning of a new story. I had them make notes about how this story would go, and then we'd discuss the results in class. One of the biggest surprises students discovered was how little of their original story they needed in the first place. All the information that they thought was vital to set up the ending was either completely unnecessary or could be related in far fewer words, sometimes as little as a paragraph or even a single line of prose. The other surprise was how original the new stories were. They took off in interesting, sometimes wild, directions that the authors had never anticipated. And the stories were full of life and energy, where before they'd been dull and listless. Since then, I always make sure to pass along The End Is Only the Beginning technique whenever I teach a class or conduct a workshop.

And now I'm passing it along to you.

Classic Movies Reimagined

For this exercise, you're going to take a classic movie, use its ending as the beginning for a new story, and make notes about what that story would be like. I'm not talking about coming up with sequel ideas, but rather a brand-new story. For example, let's take the first *Star Wars* movie (*A New Hope*). It ends with Leia giving Luke, Han, and Chewie medals for destroying the Death Star. The Empire has a spy within the rebel alliance, though, and as payback for destroying their new weapon, the Empire orders the spy to detonate a bomb during the medal ceremony. The spy does, killing most of those present (including himself). Luke survives—perhaps because his Force powers instinctively shielded him—but he's terribly wounded. He needs some prosthetic parts and his face was badly mangled. Doctors fix him, more or less, but he no longer resembles the young man he was. Luke decides to avenge his friends by waging a one-man war on the Empire. He becomes a ruthless, barely-trained cyborg-Jedi who mercilessly destroys anyone and anything related to the Empire, risking losing himself the Dark Side along the way.

Get the idea?

Here's a list of movies to choose from, but you can pick your own movie if you'd like. And if you don't think the movies I chose qualify as "classics," that's fine. This isn't a film criticism class. It's just a writing exercise. Ignore any sequels that were made to the movies on my list and come up with your own

CHAPTER 14 / Tell Me a Scary Story   **147**

original story ideas. Write notes on how you'd tell this new story, and you're welcome to do more than one movie if you want.

- *Back to the Future*
- *Jaws*
- *Psycho*
- *The Texas Chainsaw Massacre*
- *The Wizard of Oz*
- *Get Out*
- *The Silence of the Lambs*
- *Titanic*
- *Alien*

_____
_____
_____
_____
_____
_____
_____
_____

How did your new story go? Did it take off in any surprising directions? If you did more than one, which do you think would make the most successful story if you decided to write it?

Try One of Yours

Do the same thing as in the last exercise, only this time use one of your stories or novels. Take the ending and imagine it as the beginning of a brand-new story. Write notes about how you'd tell that story. If you'd like to do this exercise for several of your stories, that's fine. When you're finished, ask yourself what you learned from this exercise in terms of how you've plotted stories before and how you might plot them in the future. Will you change anything because of this exercise? Why or why not?

_____
_____
_____
_____
_____
_____

SCENE AND SEQUEL

At the beginning of this chapter, I told you I wasn't going to give you any specific formulae for plotting stories, but I lied. (Hey, I'm a fiction writer—it's what we do.) Actually, this technique is more about constructing scenes than writing entire stories, but you can use it to plot a story from start to finish if you like. You can also use it to just start writing and see where the story takes you. Whether you're a plotter, pantser, or somewhere in between (a plottsner?), Scene and Sequel can get you where you want to go, and it will help you keep your scenes tight and focused along the way.

I learned of this technique when I went to one of my first science fiction conventions in my twenties. I attended every panel on writing that I could and soaked up every bit of knowledge the speakers had to share. One of the things they kept mentioning was a technique called Scene and Sequel, which they'd learned about from a book called *Techniques of the Selling Writer* by Dwight V. Swain. After the convention, I hauled ass to a nearby bookstore, found a copy, bought it, went home, and read it cover to cover. You can still find Swain's book today, but there's plenty of information on the Internet about Scene and Sequel as well.

To understand the technique, you need to forget the common definitions of *scene* and *sequel*. Scene is a unit of a story where a character takes action to obtain a subgoal that furthers their overall story goal. Sequel is a unit of a story where a character processes the outcome of a Scene and decides on their next move, which leads into a new Scene, and so on. It goes something like this:

Character: Jim.

Character's Overall Story Goal: Jim believes he's possessed by a demon that wants him to become a serial killer, and he wants to get rid of the demon before it makes him actually hurt someone.

Subgoal: Jim decides to visit a psychic in town who has a reputation for being the real deal. He hopes she can exorcise the demon and free him, or—failing that—give him an idea of who or what can help him do the job.

Scene: Jim visits the psychic. He doesn't tell her his problem at first. He wants to see if she can sense what's wrong with him. She does, and although she's shaken by being in the presence of such a powerful demon, she invites Jim to sit down. He does and they talk about what might be done to rid Jim of the demon. As they talk, the demon takes control of Jim's right arm, snatches the psychic's crystal ball off the table, and beats her with it. Jim desperately tries to assert control over his body and stop the demon, but he can't, and the psychic dies. Once she's dead, the demon relinquishes control of Jim's body. (The Scene ends here, but the action continues from this point as it transitions into a Sequel.)

Sequel: Horrified, Jim stares at the psychic's dead body. He feels overwhelming guilt too. If he hadn't come here to consult her, she would still be alive. He's so disturbed by what's happened that he can't think straight. All he knows is he needs to get out of here before anyone sees him and realizes he killed the psychic. He knows he technically didn't—unless the demon isn't real and he's crazy—but no one will believe his story. He decides to flee and does so. (End Sequel.)

Subgoal: Jim wants to get the hell out of there as fast as he can.

Scene: Jim is in his car, driving down the road, constantly checking in his rearview for signs of pursuit by a police vehicle. When he becomes convinced no one is following him, he relaxes a little. (End Scene.)

Sequel: As he drives, Jim thinks about what his next move should be. If he seeks out anyone else's help, the demon might just kill them too. But Jim doesn't think there's any way he can get rid of the demon on his own. Jim's not religious, but he figures if demons exist, maybe God—or at least some version of the power of Light and Good—exists too. He decides he'll go to the nearest church and see if a pastor or priest can help him.

I could keep on going, but you get the point. Scenes end in **Disasters** of some sort (whether major or minor) which set the character back and make them work harder. Sometimes, such as in a fight sequence, characters have no chance to process what's happening until later, after the fight is over and there's time to think. Then you have **Deferred Sequels**. The rule is that for every Scene you have a Sequel, but they don't always have to be back-to-back (although usually they are).

As I said earlier, this technique helps keep your story tight and focused, and it can be used for plotting as well. I can make an entire short story, novella, or novella out of Jim and his problem simply by planning out Scenes and Sequels, one after the other, until his story is finished. I've been writing fiction for so long that I don't think consciously about Scene and Sequel when I write, but I use this technique naturally, the same way a veteran baseball player doesn't consciously think about hitting a ball when it's pitched to them.

Now it's your turn to give this technique a try. I'll give you several characters with overall goals, you pick one, and then start writing a chain of Scenes and Sequels for it. Try to develop at least five sets of Scenes and Sequels, but if you want to plot out an entire story, go ahead. If you don't like any of the situations I've given you, come up with one of your own.

- Holly's grandmother recently died, and her sister took the necklace Grandma promised to Holly. Holly wants to get it back.
- Ethan's boyfriend has just broken up with him, but Ethan wants to repair their relationship—no matter what it takes.

- Salvador owns a deli that's on the verge of going out of business. He took out a loan from a loan shark, and now the money is due to be repaid—with significant interest. Salvador decides the only way out of his situation is to kill the loan shark.
- Kira was turned into a vampire fifteen years ago. Ever since then, her twin sister has been hunting her. The sister wishes to kill Kira and free her soul from the curse of vampirism. Kira likes her "curse" just fine, though. Kira wants to find a way to stop her sister without killing her or turning her into a vampire.

_____

_____

_____

_____

_____

_____

_____

What was it like for you to structure a story using Scene and Sequel? Did it make plotting easier and more natural for you? Or did you find it awkward and artificial? If you did find it awkward, can you think of any way that you might be able to adapt the technique so it would work better for you?

Now take one of your finished stories. Read over it and see if you could strengthen it by applying the Scene and Sequel technique. Make notes about how you might do that, and if you're feeling industrious, rewrite the story. When you're finished compare the two versions. Which one is more effective?

_____

_____

_____

_____

_____

_____

ACTION-IDEA

For years, I noticed a problem in the novel manuscripts of students I taught or advised. I understood what was wrong: There was little-to-no sense of main conflict, story focus, or forward story movement. Whenever I would say this to students, they would nod as if they understood, but I could tell by the look in their eyes (not to mention their revisions) that they didn't. I kept thinking there had to be a simpler, clearer way to express the concept, but I couldn't come up with one.

Until I read Michael Tierno's *Aristotle's Poetics for Screenwriters*. In it, he discusses a concept he calls the Action-Idea. An Action-Idea is the foundation upon which a story rests, and it provides focus and direction. It's one sentence long, describes the main action of the story, and whoever takes the lead in the action is the protagonist. Everything in the story relates to the Action-Idea in one way or another, and the Action-Idea should contain the potential for catharsis as well. One of the examples he used was *Jaws*:

> **Jaws is about a man trying to stop a killer shark.**
> **Sheriff Brody is the hero.**

The potential for catharsis is embedded in the Action-Idea. If Brody stops the shark, he will save lives, and the audience will find that outcome cathartic. (The great big KA-BOOM! At the end of the movie doesn't hurt either.) Tierno says that we can think of the Action-Idea as the story's mission statement, and I think that's a great way to describe it.

I started teaching students about the Action-Idea, and their novels immediately improved. (And of course an Action-Idea can work for short stories, novellas, scripts, etc.) And now it's your turn to give it a try. We'll start off by writing Action-Ideas for five well-known popular horror movies:

The Thing:

_____

_____

_____

Halloween:

_____

_____

_____

The Exorcist:

_____

_____

_____

The Shining:

_____

_____

_____

The Birds:

_____

_____

_____

How did your Action-Ideas turn out? Did you manage to keep them limited to one sentence? If so, was it difficult to summarize the movies to that degree? Were clear actions embedded in your Action-Ideas? What about the potential for catharsis?

Next, use a novel you've already written, have partially written, or have contemplated writing. Write an Action-Idea statement for it. Here's an example for one of my novels:

Your Turn to Suffer is about a woman trying to discover what wrong a mysterious cult believes she committed so she can make amends for it and end the cult's harassment.

Now you try.

Novel Title:

_____

Action-Idea:

_____

_____

_____

How did it go this time? Since this was your story, was it easier to write an Action-Idea for or harder? If you had difficulty writing an Action-Idea for your book, it may be a sign that you aren't really sure what your story's about or you have too much going on for one story. If that's the case, consider revising your novel concept until you can write an Action-Idea for it.

ANTICIPATION, CONFRONTATION POINT, AFTERMATH

This is a new concept that doesn't appear in *Writing in the Dark*. Because of that, I'm going to go into more detail about it than I have for other exercises in this volume.

Like the Horror Landscape Map I discussed in Chapter One, I came up with this concept while speaking with Gabriela Pereira on the DIY MFA podcast. I can't recall the specific question she asked me—something about how horror stories are structured, most likely—and (as often happens to me in the process of struggling to articulate something about writing) the concept just popped into my head.

Horror stories are built from three important elements:

1.   ANTICIPATION: The fear that something awful is approaching.

   • A threat of some sort exists.
   • It may or may not be clearly defined.
   • It's drawing nearer.
   • It's inescapable.

- The character's mental, emotional, and/or physical state worsens as the threat draws ever closer.
- A sense of Impending Doom.

2. CONFRONTATION POINT: The moment that something awful arrives and must be dealt with—if it can be dealt with at all.

- This is the point where a character, despite their best efforts, has no choice but to face the threat.
- They can choose to confront the threat or the threat may catch up to them at last.
- The Confrontation Point—especially in short fiction—may be the culmination of the story, and it may be implied.
- The story may end at a point of Suspension, with the character on the verge of the Confrontation Point, suspended in a state of absolute terror.
- Shirley Jackson's "The Summer People" is an excellent example of ending in a state of suspended terror. So are Edgar Allen Poe's "A Cask of Amontillado" and "The Tell-Tale Heart."

3. AFTERMATH: What occurs after the Confrontation Point.

- The effects on the character, friends, family, community, world, etc. that occur after the Confrontation Point.
- In general fiction-writing terminology, this could be lumped in with Denouement: Falling Action.
- The most common—and clichéd—Aftermath in horror fiction is the main character's death.
- The character losing their sanity is probably second-most common.
- Not very long, if it's shown at all.
- The character can defeat the threat, escape the threat, survive the threat, be destroyed by the threat (spiritually, mentally, emotionally, physically), be transformed by the threat, join with the threat, take the threat's place, become a worse threat, be devastated by a choice they made or price they paid to defeat, escape, or survive the threat, etc.

Horror stories can focus primarily on any one of these elements:

- A focus on Anticipation.
- A focus on the Confrontation Point.
- A focus of the Aftermath.

Novels and novellas have a *lot* more room, and so they can contain an overarching structure of Anticipation, Confrontation Point, and Aftermath, and while also having numerous individual scenes which focus on Anticipation, Confrontation Point, and Aftermath throughout.

Horror stories can begin with any of these elements:

- ANTICIPATION: The character can become aware of the threat or they can already be aware of threat and dreading it.
- CONFRONTATION POINT: A story like this might focus entirely on the Confrontation Point, perhaps with a small hint or even a flashback of the approach to the Confrontation Point.
- AFTERMATH: A story like this would grow out of how a character is affected by the Confrontation Point. How have they been changed? What do they do next? How do they go on? How do they live with what actions they may have taken during the Confrontation Point?
- Short stories tend to start as close to the climax as possible.

You can write individual scenes in a longer work using this pattern:

- A novel can have an overarching structure of Anticipation, Confrontation Point, and Aftermath.
- But scenes within the novel can use this structure as well.
- Think of Stephen King's *It*. Each of the children have a separate encounter with Pennywise which consists of its own Anticipation, Confrontation Point, and Aftermath, while the larger story uses the same structure.
- In fact, since *It* takes place in the past and the present, it has two large Anticipation, Confrontation Point, and Aftermath structures that are intertwined, with numerous individual scenes that follow the pattern as well.

Exercise time! Here are three prompts:

1. Write a short scene—just a few paragraphs—in which a character is anticipating an unknown threat. Make the scene vivid and impactful, even though "nothing happens."

   _____
   _____
   _____
   _____
   _____
   _____
   _____

2. Write a short scene in which a character comes up to the edge of a confrontation point and which ends in a frozen moment of suspended terror.

_____

_____

_____

_____

_____

_____

_____

3. Write a short scene in which a character is processing/experiencing/dealing with some effect of surviving a Confrontation Point with a threat.

_____

_____

_____

_____

_____

_____

_____

What was your experience with this pattern like? Did it help you focus more clearly on different aspects of horror storytelling? Can you see yourself using this technique the next time you write a piece of fiction? Why or why not?

MONSTROUS ARCS

In Chapter Seven, I presented several exercises for writing from a monster's point of view, whether that monster was human or inhuman. Now I'd like you to consider the role of monsters in your stories. Specifically, I want you to consider giving them their own character arcs. If you're unfamiliar with the term *character arc*, it refers to a specific character's inner journey during the course of a story. Every character within a story can have their own arc, from your main protagonist down to the most minor supporting character. Now just because all characters *can* have their own arcs doesn't mean they *should*. Your book could be thousands of pages long if you did that. (Although this can work well for epic fantasy series, where the arcs have much more room to play out than in a single novel.)

Giving your story's antagonist their own character arc can keep them from being flat and uninteresting. Even simple arcs can work. In *Lord of the Rings*, Sauron wants to conquer Middle Earth, he starts a great war while he seeks the One Ring, he fails to get the ring before it's destroyed, and instead *he's* destroyed. Sauron is never portrayed as a character in the books, more like a foul force of unnature, but his arc is what gives shape to the overarching narrative. Some horror movies recycle common antagonist character arcs. The momma monster that wants to get her egg/baby back from the humans who took it. The long-lived ancient being who desires to be reunited with the reincarnation of their lost love. The crazed revenge-seeker looking to extract justice by killing those they believe wronged them. The demonic being seeking to obtain a mystical object that will break down the dimensional barriers and which will allow its kin to flood into our reality and claim it for their own.

I'm not saying your monsters always need arcs. For the most part, both Michael Myers and Jason Vorhees have no character arcs in their respective movie series. They function as mindless avatars of Death. And creatures/people that are evil might be solely motivated to serve evil by committing evil acts and corrupting others so they become evil. (What can I say? It's always evil, evil, evil with these guys.) But giving your monsters character arcs can make your stories something more than another tale in which a person hires a prostitute only to discover that they're a vampire, werewolf, succubus, or serial killer—a predictable cliché.

Simple character arcs for monsters (again, human or otherwise) are primal things like:

- Survival
- Food
- Reproduction
- Defending territory
- Fighting off a threat or rival
- Finding a home
- Protecting their offspring

More sophisticated arcs for monsters would be similar to arcs for humans. They're just, well … more *monstrous*.

- Love/companionship
- Justice/revenge
- Satisfying a desire
- Making one's self known
- Communicating with others
- Gaining fame (such as serial killers wanting their crimes covered by the media)

And I'm sure you can think of many, many more. Your monster's arc can take place mostly behind the scenes if you like, or it can show up periodically during the course of the story. The most important thing is that *you* know their arc, and you can use it to shape your overall story. Here are a couple examples from my own work.

In *Teeth of the Sea*, the pliodon Brokejaw and his pod—mother, father, brother, and two females—have returned to their ancestral breeding grounds on the island of *Las Dagas* to mate. (The two young female pliodons are from a different pod. The pliodon population mixes like this to avoid inbreeding.) They discover that since the last time they visited, humans have created a resort on the island. The pliodons want to make the humans leave, and Brokejaw wants to assert his dominance over the other three young pliodons because he believes he's the smartest and strongest.

In my novel *They Kill* (huge spoiler alert!), the powerful being Corliss belongs to a group called the Multitude, mystic beings whose only purpose is to make the complete entropic collapse of the universe occur as soon as possible. Corliss is on the verge of retiring, and he's come to a small Southwestern Ohio town seeking a young woman he thinks might be a good replacement for him. He creates nightmarish scenarios to test her to see if she's got what it takes to become one of the Multitude.

Try it. Create a monster—or choose one from a story you've already written, or maybe one you wrote about for the exercises in Chapter Seven. Make some notes on how you would give that monster its own character arc without making it *too* human or sympathetic. When finished, read over what you wrote. Could you see yourself using this arc in a short story or a novel? If not, why? If you did write a story or novel using this character arc, how often would you show your monster on stage? Would your story be more effective with more monster action or less?

_____

_____

_____

_____

_____

_____

_____

VOICES FROM THE SHADOWS

Christine Morgan, Splatterpunk Award-winning author of *Lakehouse Infernal*

Writing tip: Utilize ALL the senses to evoke emotional response or set mood ... don't just go with what can be seen and heard like when watching a movie ... give us smell, taste, touch, temperature, texture. In horror, for instance, there's a big difference between sticking your hand in a puddle of warm, fresh blood vs. cooled, congealed blood. Scent can be a shortcut link to a host of memories and experiences pre-laden with atmosphere and baggage: Attic smells, classroom smells, outdoor smells, fairground smells, etc. Get right in there, immerse the reader, make 'em FEEL it.

Paolo Di Orazio, author of "Hell" in Ellen Datlow's *The Best Horror of the Year: Volume Seven*

Once I've found out my very basic idea, I start writing down the complete biography of the main characters. The more I write about them, the more they will act by their consistency. And more: This method is strongly helpful to accelerate the plot's development. Then, I try to think just like all of my characters, as if I were inside my story, too, throughout them. It's a real transfer. Because for me, every hero and every villain (or monster) is human and every one of them is me. When I enter the villain's mind, I think about everything that's impossible to do in real life, the baddest, the bloodiest thing, even if the villain's a freaky almost-human-reptile or an evil slasher. The same, when I enter the main character's mind, the good one, I think how I could win over the problem, and fight all for all (making him do everything I can't in life: Shooting, knife or fire or poison handling, and so on). In a few words, I play all the roles in my story, and that's easier only when I create a large biography of every character. Heroes, monsters, killers, madmen, whoever they are, male or female. We must be all of them. Not only their writers.

Meghan Arcuri, Bram Stoker Award-nominated author and Vice President of the Horror Writers Association

General writing exercise: Often when I begin a story, I'll write lines and lines of dialogue—no attributions, no setting, nothing. Just the chatter. This helps me figure out who my characters are (or who I want them to be). It also helps me develop voice, which leads me to characterization. Then I have someone I begin to understand, and I will have them not only speak, but act accordingly. I may never even use the dialogue, but once it gets going, a good portion of it is usually worthwhile and makes the cut.

Tip on building suspense: I zoom in on my POV character—a laser focus to home in on the relevant, visceral details in the scene. I try to engage as many of his/her senses as possible: In moments of intensity, you notice the strangest things—and they're not always the things you can see. I also tend to use shorter paragraphs, shorter sentences. Sometimes even just a single word. Use the enter key. Give your readers some white space. Large, wordy paragraphs can overwhelm their brains, especially in a suspenseful moment. The white space allows them to absorb the few—but critical—words you've given them.

Eden Royce, author of *Root Magic*

Many instructional books on craft tell writers to use their senses to create mood, tone, and atmosphere. Rarely do those books tell you how to do that. Try using a sense you ordinarily wouldn't to describe an occurrence or a locale.

For example, the sense of smell is so powerful; it's one of the strongest triggers of memory for humans. Take one of your favorite scents—dewy flowers, freshly-baked cookies, what have you—and describe it in a horrific way. Twist what's so alluring to you into a smell that clogs, clings, and chokes. Show your character's visceral reaction to that now unbearable fragrance.

Nzondi, Bram Stoker Award-winning author of *Oware Mosaic*

Here is a prompt that I engage in with every novel I write:

Write one or two paragraphs of backstory to why an antagonist/creature is killing by inputting elements that makes the reader sympathetic, giving the creature true purpose other than attributing their actions to random supernatural/evil intent.

CHAPTER FIFTEEN
THE DARK HEART OF HORROR

What makes a story of any genre matter to readers is an emotional core. And since horror *is* an emotion, you could argue that an emotional core is especially vital for stories in our genre. Sometimes the emotional core of a story is easy to determine. At the end of *The Wizard of Oz* (the film), Dorothy chants the emotional core when she's clicking the heels of the ruby slippers together: *There's no place like home, there's no place like home* … Even a giant monster slugfest like *Godzilla vs. Kong* has an emotional core: There can only be one king in one realm, but each king can have their individual realm to rule. Or Enemies can learn to tolerate each other—at a distance. *The Empty Man*'s emotional core is an existential one: Who am I and why am I? The emotional core of *Stars Wars: A New Hope* is individuals can prevail over a monolithic evil if they have faith in themselves, their friendship, and their cause.

You can think of an emotional core as an expression of the main emotional relationship in a story, or you can think of it as the emotional theme, whichever explanation makes the most sense to you. Whether you're attempting to write a great work of literary art or a piece of fun entertainment, a strong emotional core is what makes a story meaningful and memorable to readers—it makes a story *matter*. In this chapter, we're going to work through some exercises designed to help you strengthen the emotional cores that lie at the heart of your stories.

IS TIM TOO LAZY TO COME UP WITH A DIFFERENT LIST?

In the last chapter, I gave you a list of horror movies and asked you to state the Action-Idea for each one. Now I want you to write down the emotional core for them. If you have difficulty coming up with a single sentence to express the emotional core, try listing individual words that relate to it, such as *sorrow, disconnection, self-doubt, hope,* etc. Once you've come up with a list like that, try combining the words into a single statement that expresses the film's emotional core.

The Thing:

_____

_____

_____

Halloween:

_____
_____
_____

The Exorcist:

_____
_____
_____

The Shining:

_____
_____
_____

The Birds:

_____
_____
_____

How did you do? In many ways, I think it's more difficult to determine the emotional core of famous horror movies because their iconic imagery is what immediately leaps to mind when you think of them. Sometimes, you can find the emotional core expressed in characters' dialogue, such as in *The Wizard of Oz*, as I pointed out earlier. At the end of *Halloween*, Laurie asks Dr. Loomis, "Was that the Boogeyman?" and Loomis answers, "As a matter of fact, it was." The emotional core? Our most primal fears may be real and there's no rational explanation for them. But this isn't a test. The specific words you use to express an emotional core don't matter as much as whether you capture the *essence* of the emotional core. For bonus points, show this list to a friend or family member who's also into horror and ask them to identify the emotional core in each film, then compare their version to yours. How similar are they? Are there any major differences? If there are differences, can a case be made for each of your interpretations of a film's emotional core?

TWO CHARACTERS WALK INTO A STORY ...

You can decide on an emotional core when you first plot a story, or you can start writing and allow an emotional core to develop naturally. Since I see so many beginner manuscripts that lack any sort of emotional core whatsoever, I suggest developing at least a rough idea of an emotional core before you write. Plus, knowing the emotional core often means you have a clearer understanding of a story's main conflict, which makes it easier to generate ideas for what happens in your story. Ever get stuck on a story, unsure where to go with it next? Maybe you weren't clear on the story's emotional core. This exercise will give you a simple structure for creating an emotional core in your stories. We'll start with short fiction.

Emotional Cores for Short Stories. Respond to the following prompts:

1. Create two characters (or choose two characters from fiction you've already written). These characters don't have to be massively complex, but they should be developed enough to be at least somewhat distinct.

   _____

   _____

   _____

   _____

2. What is the main emotional connection between these two characters? If they're father and son, what's their relationship like? Be specific. Is the son forever seeking the father's approval—approval the father will never give? Does the father feel like he didn't do a good enough job being a parent to his son and is seeking his son's forgiveness?

   _____

   _____

   _____

   _____

3. Take this emotional core and generate different story ideas that relate to it. For example, the father is a police detective, and the son—in order to impress his father—starts killing people in spectacular ways without leaving any clues whatsoever. The son eventually confesses to his father, but his father refuses to believe him. Or the son is a serial killer, and the father—still a detective in this version—feels his boy became a killer because he spent so many hours on the job and neglected him. He wants to find his son and stop him, but he also wants his son to forgive him for being a bad parent.

   _____

   _____

   _____

   _____

4. Bonus: Generate more than one story idea for the emotional core you came up with.

   _____

   _____

   _____

   _____

How did the exercise turn out for you? Did you come up with something that you might be able to develop into a complete story? Consider writing it, focusing on the emotional core throughout.

Emotional Cores for Novels. Developing emotional cores for novels is different, because you have different emotional connections between different characters, and not all the characters in your novel may be closely connected—or, for that matter, even know—all the others. You'll have groupings of emotional connections. Two characters are married and on the verge of divorce. Three are in a love triangle. Two parents are sick with worry because their young child has been diagnosed with cancer. The mayor is concerned she'll lose reelection, and her husband is urging her to blackmail her opponent into dropping out of the race.

On top of the separate emotional connections between characters, the book itself has a larger emotional core of its own. It's a story about how revenge leads to self-destruction, how loss of a child leads to madness, or how good people can do awful, unimaginable things under the right conditions. An emotional core that shows up in a lot of my work is how we live with the awareness that everything—ourselves, our family and friends, our world, even our universe—is dying, and there's not a damn thing we can do about it. On top of that, I might have a specific emotional core for each story. For example, in my novel *The Forever House*, a group of neighbors must overcome their differences and work together to survive. Or put another way, what connects us is more important than what separates us.

With both short fiction and novels, I sometimes find it easier to start with a primary concept then create characters with emotional connections that relate to that concept. Since I knew in *The Forever House* that I was going to have a group of neighbors be drawn into the house and have to survive its nightmarish inner environments, it was obvious that these people shouldn't all get along in normal circumstances. (Got to have that sweet, sweet conflict going on.) Then I developed the individual characters and their emotional connections to one another in terms of their separate families, as well as emotional connections to their neighbors. It can be a complex process, but here's an exercise that might make it more manageable.

Use a novel you've written, one you're currently writing, or one you've contemplated writing. If you don't have a novel of your own to work with, make up a novel concept for this exercise.

1. What's your novel's concept?

    _____
    _____
    _____
    _____

2. What overall emotional core would work best with this concept?

_____
_____
_____
_____

3. Come up with three different groups of characters (such as a family of three, a newly-married couple, and a widower who lives alone), and create specific emotional connections between them. These connections might relate clearly to the novel's overall emotional core or they might not.

_____
_____
_____
_____

4. Make notes for ways the characters' emotional connections could help create different story events. For example, maybe your character hates her boss, and when she's influenced by the Dark Power that's the main antagonist in your story, she decides to kill him. The character's hatred for the boss results in a scene where, under the influence of the Dark Power, she attempts to murder him.

_____
_____
_____
_____

How did this exercise work out for you? Did you find this process useful in generating emotional relationships and foundations for a novel? Is it a technique you could see yourself using in the future? Why or why not?

AND ... SCENE!

Just as a story has an overall emotional core, so too can individual scenes have them. These scenes can foster character development, move the plot forward, further develop the theme, etc., but underlying each of them is an emotional core of some kind. Even an expository section of a novel, say several paragraphs in an epic fantasy that directly relate the events of an ancient war, can have an emotional core, perhaps possessing a tone that indicts the war was a tragic one that changed the course of the land's history—and not for the better. But usually the emotional core of a scene will arise from character interaction. This core can come from a desire/goal one character has—George desperately wants to ask out Lee but is afraid of rejection. Or it can arise from a conflict between characters—Chloe and Rex think they should take one route to get to their destination, but Arlene is adamant they take another.

For this exercise, you can use three consecutive scenes from a story or novel you've written, or you can make up three new consecutive scenes. Write short descriptions for each of them.

Scene Descriptions

Scene One:

_____

_____

_____

_____

Scene Two:

_____

_____

_____

_____

Scene Three:

_____

_____

_____

_____

Emotional Core for Each Scene

Scene One:

_____

_____

_____

_____

Scene Two:

_____

_____

_____

_____

Scene Three:

_____

_____

_____

_____

How did it go? Was it difficult to come up with an emotional core for each scene, or was it easier than you expected? A short story might be made up of three such scenes, while a novel would be comprised of many more. Do you think this technique would work equally well for both forms? Why or why not?

I COME HERE FOR THE ATMOSPHERE

Emotional cores can also be expressed through setting, creating a specific atmosphere for individual scenes. These emotional settings can be simple—such as a barren wasteland that represents loneliness, desperation, or hopelessness—or a too-tidy house that represents a need for control and order, a sterile anti-home.

Location, Location, Location. List three real-world places that you know well and write down details that communicate their emotional atmosphere. For example, the college where I teach was built in the late 1960's, and outwardly the buildings are blocky gray stone structures reminiscent of a prison. But inside, the hallways are filled with students, some talking with friends as they walk, some walking alone. Overall, the interior tends to have a chill, quiet vibe, which is not at all prison-like.

Make sure to use specific details that clearly communicate the emotional atmospheres of your chosen locations.

Place One:
_____
_____
_____
_____

Place Two:
_____
_____
_____
_____

Place Three:
_____
_____
_____
_____

Did the exercise yield more descriptive details than what you usually put in your fiction? Can you articulate each place's emotional atmosphere in a single sentence? Consider choosing one of the places and using its emotional atmosphere details to write a description of it, one suitable for inclusion in a story.

If, like me, you have trouble inventing real-world settings whole cloth, a technique like this can help make the settings in your fiction much richer.

EMOTIONAL BIOGRAPHY

Writers are used to giving their characters backstories, but often they read more like the dull facts you find on resumes:

> *Albert Inglethorpe grew up in small town just outside Chicago. He studied engineering in college, but he switched his major to sociology halfway through undergrad, and he continued on until he received his doctorate. He met his future wife, Jennifer, in college, and they were married while both were in grad school. Albert found a teaching position at a college in Tallahassee, Florida, and they moved there just before the birth of their first child, Alexa. Steven came along a couple years later. Jennifer was an English major and she writes freelance nonfiction articles on a variety of subjects. The kids are both in high school now, and the family is, on the whole, happy.*

What's missing from this character bio is any emotional detail. Yeah, Albert got married and has kids, and I told you the family is generally happy. But it gives me almost nothing to work with when writing about the Inglethorpes. Writers will provide emotional backstories for characters, but often it's only when those backstories connect implicitly to the plot. A vampire hunter who, when she was a teenager, was forced to kill her own mother after she fell under the curse of the undead. A character who survived a plane crash years ago has finally gotten over their fear enough to take a trip on a plane, and some kind of monstrous birdlike creature attacks the craft in the air. These parallels are both too neat, too convenient—and they're clichés. The "character experienced something awful in the past and is now experiencing the same thing again (or something very close to it)" is a common trope in horror, suspense, and thriller fiction.

In real life, we experience many different emotional events during the course of our lives, events which shape us and, in some cases, come to define us. These events are not connected to some larger story we're going to live sometime in the future, but they can influence us going forward, making some things easier and some things harder. So instead of giving your characters no emotional background or shopworn tropey ones, consider giving them a varied, more realistic emotional biography.

Take a character from one of your stories, one you created for a previous exercise, or make up a new one now. Write responses to the following questions. (It's up to you how detailed you want your responses to be.)

1. What was the worst day of your character's life?

    _____

    _____

    _____

    _____

2. What was the best day?

    _____

    _____

    _____

3. When did your character first truly understand that the world isn't a fair place?

    _____

    _____

    _____

    _____

4. When did your character first truly understand what death was and what it means?

    _____

    _____

    _____

    _____

5. Who did your character love most as a child?

    _____

    _____

    _____

    _____

6. What's your character's biggest regret in life (so far)?

    _____

    _____

    _____

    _____

7. When did you character feel deeply betrayed?

    _____

    _____

    _____

    _____

8. When did you character feel most loved/affirmed?

    _____

    _____

    _____

    _____

9. When did your character fall in the love for the first time?

    _____

    _____

    _____

    _____

10. When did your character first have their heart broken?

    _____

    _____

    _____

    _____

11. When did your character first feel like an adult? (Assuming the character is an adult.)

    _____

    _____

    _____

    _____

12. When did the character experience a major loss that *wasn't* the death of someone they cared for?

    _____

    _____

    _____

    _____

13. What did the character do that they are most ashamed of?

    _____

    _____

    _____

    _____

14. When was the character the most terrified they've ever been?

    _____

    _____

    _____

    _____

15. When was the character the most overjoyed they've ever been?

_____
_____
_____
_____

16. When did you character feel the most contented?

_____
_____
_____
_____

17. If your character could go back in time and relive an experience, what would it be?

_____
_____
_____
_____

18. If your character could have a memory surgically removed from their brain so they would never have to recall it again, what would it be?

_____
_____
_____
_____

19. What's the greatest challenge your character has ever faced?

_____
_____
_____
_____

20. What's their greatest achievement?

_____
_____
_____
_____

21. What's their greatest loss (in terms of something they tried to do but failed)?

_____
_____
_____

22. What's the one secret your character will never tell anyone?

    _____

    _____

    _____

    _____

23. Add any other questions you can think of to this list and answer them.

    _____

    _____

    _____

    _____

As with any kind of character bio, you don't have to use all the details you come up with, and you can change any of them when you use a character in a story. But an emotional background like this can be useful in myriad ways. It can give you some sense how a character will react in a specific situation. If the character is betrayed in the current narrative, that may trigger their feelings about how they were betrayed in the past. Items in their emotional background may influence their choices. For example, someone who fell off a roof as a child is now afraid of heights, so they refuse to climb to a high place to escape a threat. (Or it makes it a much greater challenge for them to try.) The items can also give you ideas for whole stories or scenes in novels as well. You can also fill out a generic one, meaning a list that isn't focused on a single character and in which the items don't have to be consistent. You can use this as an emotional background generator sheet, and take items from it to apply to characters you work on in future stories.

VOICES FROM THE SHADOWS

Ramsey Campbell, award-winning author of _The Wise Friend_, _Somebody's Voice_, and the Brichester Mythos trilogy

One exercise I've found useful at intervals throughout my career is identifying some element I depend on as a writer and discovering what happens if I do without it for the duration of a tale. As early as 1962 I tried telling a Lovecraftian tale ("The Will of Stanley Brooke") in unadorned prose, mostly through dialogue. It wasn't very good—at sixteen years old I was unequipped to depict the characters, who come across as sketchy imitations of the kind of cast you'd find in a standard country house crime story—but it taught me to try out different narrative voices. My most extreme experiment was "A Street Was Chosen," a tale told wholly in the passive voice as the report of an experiment on people identified only by letters and numbers. It proved—even when read aloud—how much you can pare away from horror fiction without robbing it of power, perhaps even adding some by distillation. More recently, the venturesome Adam Nevill's "Hippocampus" is a horror story wholly without characters, for which it demonstrates it has no need. So I recommend the general principle as an exercise to all our writerly readers: Find something you routinely use in your fiction—perhaps an element of the prose, or reliance on dialogue as a way of conveying narrative, or presenting the characters from within (or entirely from outside)—and test how your writing works if you deny yourself one of them. And may I suggest a related creative approach, if indeed you haven't already employed it? Try telling a story in a voice unlike your own—a character's inner voice, the further from your usual vocabulary the better—and from their viewpoint, unfiltered by the author. May all this engage your imagination, and I know you'll do that to ours. And one trick that works for me is always to compose at least the first sentence before sitting down to write, which avoids having to stare at the blank page and having it stare back at me.

Kealan Patrick Burke, Bram Stoker Award-winning author of *Kin* and *Currency of Souls*

There have been days where my mind has been flooded with so many ideas, they begin to cancel each other out, like a crowd of people impatient for their turn at the microphone, each one insisting their voice is the one that should be heard above all others. Days like this can be as frustrating as those in which inspiration is low because an abundance of good ideas does not always translate to words on the page, especially if you're finding it difficult to focus on a single one. Your brain becomes a chokepoint. Sometimes, to counter the chaos, I'll ignore every one of those voices and write an opening paragraph to something completely different, something that has no accompanying idea, a stranger, if you will, lurking quietly behind that jostling crowd. An engaging opening paragraph will intrigue the reader. It should also intrigue you too. The best ones serve as roadmaps to a story even you didn't know, but now cannot possibly ignore. Here's an example you're free to use:

"Everyone remembers the day they stopped believing in magic. For me, it was that sunny summer afternoon back in 1989 when The Sheriff of Aisle Nine shot Danny Burrows with a bullet from an imaginary gun."

I have no idea where this paragraph leads, but the need to answer those questions means you've looked beyond the crowd, and that's always where the best stories are found. So, who is The Sheriff of Aisle Nine, and what did he do to cause the death of magic for our narrator? And should the story lead to a different kind of magic, you can always come back and alter that opener now that you've made it your own. Perhaps there was no Sheriff of Aisle Nine. Perhaps it was the narrator's father, who shot Danny Burrows with a rifle the boy gave him as a gift. Perhaps it's a metaphor? Perhaps it's a dramatic turn in a series of novels the narrator worshipped as a child? Who knows?

But there's only one way to find out …

RC Matheson, bestselling, Emmy Award-winning author, screenwriter, and producer

When plotting, I try to do the next most interesting thing. This presupposes one knows what's interesting; a necessary gamble.

For pace, I prefer to start conversations mid-way. Bail before they end; dodge the expository voids of intros and outros. I prefer evasive dialogue; disguising intent and plot. Stories can be told in various ways, but all roads must lead to Oz: The inevitable truth or lie. In writing anything dark, I seek understatement; not describing but eliciting. I leave much out and believe in a strong piece of writing, the reader does half the work. My goal is to provide dots, not connection. For me, less is still too much.

John Claude Smith, author of the Bram Stoker Award-nominated novel *Riding the Centipede*

I've made the addition of reading a tale out loud when I think it is completed an essential part of the final revision process. Why? Hearing the words is different than simply reading them. Especially for dialogue, but it's great for the all-around feel, latching onto the rhythms within the paragraphs and individual sentences. Fascinating discoveries abound. I realized this when I was set to do a reading for a podcast—the reading was lost as the recording process ran into a glitch—and in the process of practicing beforehand, reading the already completed and published tale, I found a few spots within the text that required fine-tuning. Nothing major, but enough to let me realize I needed to do this all the time. It reveals things one might not see while simply reading the manuscript. Recently, I was revising a novel and spotted an interesting rhythm in a chapter that, upon hearing it, I was able to accentuate for the unique flow the chapter required. So, yes, speak up and listen to the words.

Yvette Tan, award-winning author of *Waking the Dead*

Find a strange-sounding word or phrase that catches your attention and write a story around that. The challenge is that you have to include that word or phrase in your story in such a way that it doesn't stand out, or if it becomes central to the story, that it doesn't read like a writing exercise. "Seek Ye Whore," one of my stories that people like the most, was written using this exercise.

CHAPTER SIXTEEN
A MATTER OF STYLE

Style, in terms of fiction writing, is the way a story is told. It's separate from content (the events that occur in a story), and two authors, given the exact same story outline to follow, will produce two different—maybe very different—stories because of their individual writing styles. But although writing teachers talk about story and style as if they're two separate things, ultimately a story is the sum of all the elements that comprise it, from concept to punctuation. Readers may say they read only for story, but usually what they mean is that they like fiction with a fast-paced, easy-to-read style. (And readers who claim they read primarily for language mean they enjoy stories with well-written, elevated prose. Otherwise, they'd read the goddamn dictionary.) Bottom line: Story and style are one.

Some writers believe that style is a natural outgrowth of writing. Write long enough and your individual style will emerge. Others believe that style is the result of conscious choices writers make as they compose their stories. (Spoiler alert: Both of these views are true.) The human body develops naturally, but the choices we make in terms of health and nutrition throughout our lives affect the way it develops. It's the same with writing. So if you want to become a better writer, one of the ways to do that is to improve your writing style—which is what this chapter is all about.

Many years ago, I posted a comment on a message board about how horror was the most poetic of genres. People were quick to respond that *all* genres could be poetic, depending on a writer's style. I'd been struggling to express an insight I'd had about horror writing, and I'd done so poorly, but since I didn't understand this insight well enough to explain it clearly, I dropped the subject. Years later, I realized that what I was trying to express was that in horror, we use language in heightened ways to evoke an emotional response, which is what poetry often does. We work hard to create an atmosphere of unease or dread, to describe things in ways that get under readers' skins, to use immersive points of view to show what it's like to be *truly* afraid. All of these effects are created by style. Stephen King could make a children's playground on a sunny summer day seem terrifying by the *way* he writes about it. I'm sure he could do the same for something as simple as a glass of water.

Horror *is* style. So if you want to write better horror, you need to improve your writing style, and that's what this chapter is designed to help you do.

FICTION WRITING ASSESSMENT FORM

Everything in a piece of writing works together to create style, so the first step in improving your style is to take stock of where you're at currently.

Choose one of your stories that you think is among the best you've ever written, then use this form to analyze it, rating each element on a scale of 1 to 5, with 5 being the best. Look for strengths in your writing as well as areas where you feel you could improve. You can also use this form to analyze work from writers you admire to get a better sense of how they do what they do, and you can also use it to give feedback to critique partners.

Characters

Engaging, interesting characters:
Well-developed characters:
Clear, believable motivations:
Clear character goals:

_____
_____
_____
_____
_____
_____
_____

Point of View

Point of view is effective for story:
Clear, consistent:
Avoids point-of-view shifts:

_____
_____
_____
_____
_____
_____
_____

Description

Varied types of description used:
Types of description well-blended:

_____
_____
_____
_____
_____
_____
_____

Dialogue

Natural–seeming:
Reveals character:
Advances story:

_____
_____
_____
_____
_____
_____
_____

Plot

Interesting:
Logical:
Innovative:
Surprising:

_____
_____
_____
_____
_____
_____

Conflict

Sharply defined:
Drives the story:
Reveals character:

_____
_____
_____
_____
_____
_____

Exposition

Kept to a minimum:
Well-blended:
Used only when needed:

_____
_____
_____
_____
_____
_____

Scenes

Focused:
Vivid:
Effective transitions between:

_____
_____
_____
_____
_____
_____

Pace

Well-controlled:
Forward-moving:
Varied:

_____
_____
_____
_____
_____
_____
_____

Language

Word choice:
Precision:
Effective imagery:
Effective rhythm:

_____
_____
_____
_____
_____
_____
_____

Grammar

Rules adhered to:
Rules "bended" where needed:

_____
_____
_____
_____
_____
_____
_____

Insights and Action Plan

_____

_____

_____

_____

_____

_____

_____

What insights did you gain from your self-assessment? What next steps will you take to improve your writing?

HEIGHTENED SENSES

Several years ago, I was one of the presenters at my college's annual writers' workshop. One of my colleagues, a romance writer, presented a session focused on a technique she called *heightened senses*. In romance fiction, she explained, whenever the two lead characters are together, they experience each other's presence with heightened senses. This strengthens their attraction to each other and makes it hard for them to resist. These characters don't literally have enhanced senses; that's just the way the author writes them. (You could say that the characters are paying more attention to their senses *because* of their attraction, if you like.)

Horror writers use the same technique, except we employ it to depict our characters' experience of fear. For example:

Non-Heightened Description

Emily entered the dark room and heard the sound of something sharp scrape the hardwood floor.

Heightened Description

Emily opened the door to darkness. She stood at the threshold for a moment to give her eyes time to adjust, but the darkness only seemed to become thicker and more impenetrable the longer she waited. Her imagination, surely, but she shivered as she stepped into the room. She felt the firmness of the hardwood floor beneath her feet, strong and solid, even if she couldn't see it. She found its support reassuring, an anchor in a sea of shadow. The air in the room felt cold and damp, like the atmosphere in a forest after a late Autumn rain, and she thought she could detect the faint hint of loam in the air. If it wasn't for the floor, she might've thought she was standing on wet soil beneath a starless night sky, large trees looming over her like silent sentries, watching, waiting to see what she'd do next.

A sound then, coming from off to her right, metallic and grinding, sharp steel drawn over rough stone. She tried to draw in a breath, couldn't, then the sound came again, louder this time, closer ...

Using heightened sensory detail like this is what helps create an immersive point of view. In the non-heightened example, I simply narrated what Emily saw and heard. In the heightened example, I tried to make you feel the sensory impressions just as Emily did. For those moments, I wanted you to *be* her. And while my second example won't garner me any accolades, it's far more successful than the first.

To practice the heightened senses technique, I want you to take the following non-heightened descriptions and turn all five into sinister heightened ones suitable for a horror story.

1. Waiting nervously in a doctor's office.

   _____
   _____
   _____
   _____

2. Standing at a bus stop close to midnight.

   _____
   _____
   _____
   _____

3. Driving down a country road in the late afternoon.

   _____
   _____
   _____
   _____

4. Watching birds eat seed from a bird feeder.

   _____
   _____
   _____

5. Walking down the sidewalk and hearing a barking dog coming toward you.

   _____
   _____
   _____
   _____

How did it go? Was it difficult for you to write with heightened language? Did you like the effects it created? Do you feel your descriptions were not detailed enough? Were they too detailed? Which of the ones you wrote do you think was most successful? Least? Why?

MULTILEVEL FICTION

We experience the world as a deluge of sensory data through which we're constantly sifting in order to make some sense of it all. We don't pay equal attention to all the details simultaneously, though. If we did, we'd go mad. Instead, we identify which bits of information are most important to pay attention to at any given time, and which ones we can safely ignore (at least for now). In short, we experience reality on multiple levels, so when we write fiction, we want to simulate this experience on the page as much as possible. It helps create verisimilitude and the suspension of disbelief, which is what helps readers imagine that what they're reading is real.

In order to recreate this multilevel experience, we layer different types of details in our scenes and alternate between these layers as a scene progresses. Maybe we use a sensory description like sight first, followed by describing a character's movement, then we add a couple lines of dialogue, then we describe what the character hears, then we detail the character's reaction to this sound as a thought, and so on. There's no magic formula for writing multilevel fiction, other than the basics: Alternate between levels in whatever way a scene calls for, and try to vary the types of details so that your scenes don't all read alike.

Following is an exercise designed to help you write multilevel fiction. It may be more time-consuming than many of the exercises in the book, but I think it's time well spent, and I urge you take your time with this one so you can get the most out of it you can.

1. Outline a short scene, then write several versions of the scene, focusing on one story element at a time.

    _____
    _____
    _____
    _____

2. Write the scene as all-action (movement).

    _____
    _____
    _____
    _____

3. Write the scene as all-dialogue.

_____
_____
_____
_____

4. Write the scene with only the viewpoint character's thoughts and reactions.

_____
_____
_____
_____

5. Write the scene with only description.

_____
_____
_____
_____

6. Write the scene with only exposition (background information about people, places, and things).

_____
_____
_____
_____

7. When finished, combine all five versions into one, alternating between them as the scene progresses.

_____
_____
_____
_____

How did your combined scene turn out? Is there anything you could do to make it better?

If you want bonus points, you can do this exercise again, only this time pick one of the elements—such as dialogue or description—to be the dominant level in the scene. The others will be there still, but they'll recede into the background somewhat. When you're finished, compare your new multilevel fiction exercise to your first one. Which is superior? Why?

_____
_____
_____
_____
_____

MONSTER ATTACK!

We spoke about creating monsters in Chapter Seven, and now it's time to put your monster to the test. This exercise isn't about monsters, though. It's about point of view—or maybe I should say *perspective*. You're familiar with the basic voices in English: First Person (I, we, us), Second Person (you), and Third Person (he, she, it, they). But for this exercise, I want you to think in terms of which specific character's point of view is effective at any given moment in your story, or rather, from which vantage point you wish to write a scene from.

Imagine your monster is attacking a character and that a second character is watching from a (relatively) safe distance. You have a choice of four perspectives to write the scene from: The character being attacked, the character observing, the monster, and an omniscient godlike perspective. Which you ultimately use in a scene depends on the effect you want to create for your readers.

Here we go. Write a short monster-attack scene from each of the following perspectives:

1. The victim:

    _____

    _____

    _____

    _____

2. An onlooker:

    _____

    _____

    _____

    _____

3. The monster:

    _____

    _____

    _____

    _____

4. An omniscient perspective (you can use a distant omniscient, meaning you don't show us any of the characters' thoughts or feelings, or you can use a close omniscient, meaning you can head-hop at will—although be careful not to overdo it):

    _____

    _____

    _____

    _____

Start writing!

When you're finished, read over your scenes. What different effects were created by using these different perspectives? Which do you think is stronger and more interesting? Which do you think readers will respond to more strongly? Why?

_____
_____
_____
_____
_____
_____
_____

FILTER WORDS

Writers love words, and we use a lot of them—sometimes too many. Unnecessary words like *just* or *that* clog our sentences, and we may have an excessive number of adverbs that, instead of strengthening our descriptions, only weaken them. When we edit our work, we cut these excess words, but some words are not only unneeded, they interfere with depicting a strong point of view. These are filter words.

Compare these two examples:

Janet saw the swamp monster rise from the muck. She screamed.

The swamp monster rose from the muck. Janet screamed.

In the first example, readers are kept at a distance from the image of the swamp monster because of the words *Janet saw*. The swamp monster is filtered through these words. But if we were Janet, we wouldn't see ourselves seeing the monster. We'd just *see* it. The monster would appear and we would scream. The second example conveys this reality. The readers see the monster, then they see Janet scream. They experience the event the same way she does, without a filter. Going through your stories and eliminating as many filter words as possible can sharpen your prose significantly. Following is a list of filter words, and I keep a print-out of this list on my writing desk so I can refer to it whenever I'm editing. I urge you to do the same.

(Note: Sometimes I keep filter words because I want a slight distancing effect in a sentence, but generally I try to eliminate them.)

Filter Words List

See / saw
Hear / heard

Think / thought
Touch / touched
Wonder / wondered
Seem / seemed
Decide / decided
Know / knew
Feel / felt
Look / looked
Notice / noticed
Realize / realized
Watch / watched
Sound
Can / could
To be able to
Note / noted
experience / experienced
remember / remembered

Now for an exercise.

Rewrite the following sentences to eliminate filter words and make them stronger.

1. Bob thought about the time that a cobra bit him on the thigh.

   _____
   _____
   _____
   _____

2. Barbara heard a wolf howl from somewhere off in the distance, and the sound made her shiver.

   _____
   _____
   _____
   _____

3. Natalie watched with horror as the Chainsaw Maniac cut her friend Robert in half.

   _____
   _____
   _____
   _____

4. Steve wondered if the hazy figure he saw up ahead was an actual ghost or just a trick of the light.

   _____

   _____

   _____

   _____

5. Ned seemed to be acting strange, his movements jerky and uncoordinated, and Leroy didn't know what to think about that.

   _____

   _____

   _____

   _____

How did your non-filtered versions turn out? Do you think they're stronger? Did they feel awkward to write? We're so used to using filter words that it sometimes feels like something's wrong when we try to write without them. Like anything else, it gets easier with practice.

CHECK YOUR ISMS

Sexism, racism, homophobia, transphobia, ageism, ableism, sizeism, classism, anti-intellectualism … Today, people are much more aware of the negative attitudes we may harbor—consciously or not—toward others who are different from us (or who we at least perceive to be different). Hopefully, we do our best to identify these attitudes and then eliminate them from ourselves. But the roots of these attitudes can run deep, and getting rid of them is easier said than done.

Horror has a history of using these -isms in its fiction, so much so that many of them have become tropes in the genre. Horror is about fear of the unknown, our attitudes toward death, our struggles with the violence and darkness inherent in our human nature. And *difference* often equals *monstrous* for humans. Given all that, it's no wonder that tropes like the primitive tribespeople who possess secret occult knowledge, the grotesquely overweight villain, the cross-dressing serial killer, backwoods cannibals, and sinister old people have become genre staples. How can we do better?

1. First, become aware of any prejudices or stereotypical views of people you might harbor, whether consciously or subconsciously. This might require some uncomfortable self-examination on your part, as well as some difficult conversations with friends, relatives, and significant others.
2. Learn to listen when people in marginalized groups talk about experiencing prejudice or being viewed as a stereotype. Learn what depictions and attitudes people find ignorant, insulting, and harmful.
3. When you write, make sure your characters are well-developed individuals, not just types.

4. Use sensitivity readers who are members of groups your characters belong to.
5. Avoid using these offensive horror clichés in your work:

- Women characters who exist only to be victims.
- Rape as an "edgy" extreme horror trope.
- Evil/monstrousness signified by a character's appearance or disability (I'm looking at you, Disney!).
- People of different races and cultures depicted as either evil/monstrous or possessing special magical abilities and who exist in the story only to help the protagonist.
- Intelligence levels (high or low) portrayed as evil/monstrous.
- Old age as a sign of evil/monstrousness.
- Mental illness as evil/monstrous.
- Cishet sexuality depicted as the norm with all other sexual identities depicted as evil/monstrous.

6. Don't use other groups' legends, folklore, history, and cultural beliefs as fodder for your horror.
7. Don't attempt to tell THE story of a culture or group you don't belong to. I'm male, and I often write female characters, but I'd never attempt to tell some kind of definitive story about what it means to be a woman in twenty-first century America. Same if I write a character of a different race or sexuality from my own. I focus on them as individual humans facing problems (weird, scary ones).
8. Don't give a character a prejudice of some sort as a shorthand indicator that they are a bad person. It's lazy writing. Characters can have negative attitudes toward marginalized groups without being completely evil. (That doesn't mean they'll be sympathetic characters, though.)

Here are some exercises that might help you identify and deal with -isms in your writing.

1. Make a list of stereotypical views of people that you've held in the past and may still hold today. Be honest. You don't have to share this list with anyone. It's simply to help increase your self-awareness in this area. Use this list to help you check your writing for any unconscious -isms during revision, and if you find any, eliminate them.

_____

_____

_____

_____

2. Write about times when you've been stereotyped. What happened? How did it make you feel? Did it give you more empathy for other people who experience stereotyping?

_____
_____
_____
_____

3.   Make a list of all the various groups that you belong to. These groups will include gender, race, and sexuality, but they should also include other aspects of your life, such as whether you're a parent or childless, if you're a college graduate or not, grew up in one state or another, have this hobby or that one. Make this list as long as you can. When you're finished, read it over. The complexity you see is the same kind of complexity anyone might have. Remember this when you create characters for your stories. Consider making a "group list" like this for your characters.

_____
_____
_____
_____

VOICES FROM THE SHADOWS

Catherine Cavendish, author of *In Darkness, Shadows Breathe*

When writing any form of horror, we are told of the importance of engaging the senses, but how often does that actually result in "seeing" and "hearing" alone? We are there, in our character's POV. We're writing about the birdsong, or the sound of a howling wind, and we are talking about the rain lashing on the window. Good start, but, hang on a minute …

Many worthy academics (and others) have expended considerable time and energy on determining precisely which senses stimulate humans most and it comes down to this—all of them. Of course, some of us are more stimulated by what we see (Visual), others by sound (Aural), but many of us respond strongest to those of smell (Olfactory) and taste (Gustatory), and don't forget touch (Kinaesthetic). There's a whole science about this—known as Neuro-Linguistic Programming (NLP), and it has taught me a lot.

I remember visiting a friend in hospital some time ago. My walk to her ward took me past the kitchens. It was around two p.m., the doors were open and the familiar smell of boiled cauliflower wafted its way toward me. Instantly, I was transported back to my school days and the awful school dinners, compete with boiled-to-death cauli which landed on your plate like a mushy, indistinct, gray mush. I even caught the tasteless sensation of it in my mouth. Sound familiar?

The same applies whenever I smell Dettol disinfectant. That takes me back to even earlier schooldays.

Your reader could respond best to any of the five senses (or Representational Systems as our NLP friends call them). Blend them all together and you will capture your readers and transport them fully into your story. It is a natural and enjoyable way of creating great atmosphere, as well as ratcheting up the tension right when you need it. (What does fear taste like? Or smell like?)

Here's a great exercise you can try, which has certainly helped me:

Pick a season. Go to a forest or wood—maybe even a local park—at a time when there are few, if any people about. (It makes it easier to concentrate on the nature around you.)

Close your eyes and let your other four senses take over, one at a time.

Concentrate on what you can smell. How would you describe the scent of (e.g.) the pine trees? The wildflowers? The leaves? The air itself? Go into as fine detail as you can, and either record it, or write it down while you're still there. I usually sit on a fallen tree to perform this exercise.

Repeat—each time concentrating on one particular sense. When not analyzing the visual sense, keep your eyes closed. What do the dead leaves feel like? What is the texture of that tree bark?

Make sure you revisit that same spot in each of the four seasons. Note the differences. The scent of the air after a summer rainfall. The true sound of the winter wind lashing against the branches, the sound their creaking makes. The smell of new leaves in spring, or fallen ones in autumn.

Let your imagination take over and give each of your senses full rein.

Easy? Yes.

Now all you have to do is apply it to your writing.

Have fun with your senses and let your readers experience them.

Elizabeth Engstrom, author of *When Darkness Loves Us* and other tales of dark suspense

While my novels are all lightly outlined right from the beginning, I leave plenty of room for the magic of creativity. I generally start my writing day with this question: What's the worst thing I can do to my characters today?

Kathryn Ptacek, the one-and-only Gila Queen and author of *Ghost Dance* and *In Silence Sealed*

Years ago, I came up with an exercise for February (short month). I would write a story beginning—a sentence, a paragraph, a page or two or three—every day for a week. In following years, I wrote a story start every day in February. Last year, I went beyond that and wrote starts for 100 days. This exercise gets me to sit and focus and actually write something. I have finished some of the stories and sold them to various markets. I really have fun with these brief beginnings, and I encourage every writer to try the exercise for at least a week.

Eve Harms, author of *Kendra Temples: The Demonic Diaries*

I have a dirty little trick I sometimes use when figuring out how to further a story's plot. I ask myself: How would the protagonist hurt someone they care about, or themselves, to get what they want? What character flaw does their harmful action come from, and what's the fallout?

J. A. Sullivan, horror writer and contributor to *Kendall Reviews*

Whenever I'm in a writing slump or fighting the dreaded writer's block, I get things flowing again with a "Found Objects" exercise. I'll glance through the classified ads, pick a couple of items at random, and spend 10 minutes writing a story around why someone would want to buy or sell those items together. Don't think about it too hard, just let your dark imagination go wild and see where the story takes you. For example, I saw a kitchen knife set and a compost bin for sale. What pops into mind? Grab a pen, set a timer, and go!

CHAPTER SEVENTEEN
THE ART OF SUSPENSE

Suspense is a heightened version of that basic question at the heart of all storytelling: What's going to happen next? It's an excellent technique for getting readers to race through your novels—hands trembling, hearts pounding, sweat beading on their brows—so they can find out what happens to your characters in the end. It's one of the most important tools horror writers have to help us write kick-ass stories, so it's worth practicing to get right.

Which is why we're here, isn't it?

Some important elements for creating suspense:

- **The anticipation of something bad happening.** Let your readers know something awful is going to happen to a character.
- **Give the audience a superior viewpoint.** Make readers aware of something the characters aren't—especially something unpleasant and most likely life-threatening.
- **Use time constraints.** Give your characters a deadline of some sort. It puts more pressure on them and ramps up the tension the longer the story goes on.
- **Isolate your protagonist.** Make it difficult—if not impossible—for your main character to get help from anyone else. If they're on their own, they're in danger and have to work all the harder to solve the story problem.
- **Apply pressure.** Is anyone chasing your character? Police? Mobsters? A pack of werewolves? A coven of witches? Has one of your character's friends or family been taken hostage? Create more pressure on your character as the story progresses.
- **Create dilemmas.** Give your character impossible choices. They can only save one of two friends. The other will die. Your character can't go to the police because the bad guys will kill their family if they do. (This also puts more pressure on them.) Etcetera.
- **Complicate matters.** Add other problems that don't necessarily relate to the main plot but which make your character's job harder. Bad weather. A road shut down for repair. A burning oil lamp accidentally knocked over during a fight which starts a fire. Make your character suffer some really bad luck during their story.

- **Be unpredictable.** Try to avoid clichés in suspense scenes, and try to avoid having your scene flow in an obvious direction. Your character manages to wrestle a gun away from the antagonist, but the character has a violent dislike of guns (maybe one of their siblings died in a mass shooting). Readers will expect the character to be unable to use the gun. What they won't expect is the character tossing the gun away, grabbing a baseball bat, and beating the antagonist unconscious. Readers thought your character was completely nonviolent, when really your character only has negative feelings toward guns.

Enough background. Turn the page and let's get started!

THE SUSPENSE IS KILLING ME

What do *you* find suspenseful? Make a list of the most suspenseful moments you can remember from books, movies, TV shows, comics, etc.—moments that have stayed with you over years. I'm 57 as I type this, and I first read Stephen King's *Salem's Lot* when it came out in 1975. The most suspenseful scene for me had nothing to do with the vampires, but rather when Ben Mears talks about when, as a child, he saw an image of the hanged body of Hubie Marsten. The way King built up to that … It gives me a cold queasy feeling whenever I think about it.

This is *your* list. If you watched a segment on *Sesame Street* when you were a kid and found it to be unbearably suspenseful, put it down. Your items only have to have been suspenseful to *you*. And they don't all have to be scary moments. Suspense can be exciting and fun, too.

When you finish your list, go over it and see if you detect any themes or commonalities in the things you found suspenseful. Any insights you can gain on what makes something suspenseful for you will help you create suspense for others.

For extra credit, make a list of the most failed suspenseful scenes you've read or watched, scenes that tried to create suspense but—as far as you're concerned—absolutely blew it. (For me, that's the entirety of *Paranormal Activity*, which I think of as *Very-Normal Activity*. That film held no suspense for me at all, although the audience I saw it with in the theater was on the edge of their seats the entire time.) Once you finish this list, try to determine what the creators of those scenes could've done to make them suspenseful for you.

_____

_____

_____

_____

_____

_____

_____

ANTICI ...... PATION!

As I said earlier, suspense is created by the anticipation that something bad is going to happen. (Remember when we talked about Anticipation as part of Anticipation-Confrontation Point-Aftermath in Chapter Fourteen? A lot of the same stuff applies here.) The characters in a story might experience this anticipation, but they might not be aware that something bad is coming—at least, they're not aware at first. But the audience knows right from the beginning, and knowing that something bad is getting closer … closer … *closerrrrr* … drives us crazy. This is why in a movie theater, someone who can't stand the suspense any longer will shout, "Get out of there, dumbasses! That house is haunted!"

The way to create this anticipation is to—wait for it—have nothing happen. This doesn't mean your characters aren't doing something. It means that the bad thing, whatever it is, doesn't appear right away. In other words, the thing your audience most wants to have happen, doesn't. Not for a while, anyway. As writers, we use details to create an atmosphere of suspense and we increase it step-by-step, moment-by-moment, until … *bam!* Hello, Bad Thing! (Or if it's a lame-ass horror movie, a character yanks open a closet door expecting to be confronted by a monster, and a yowling cat runs out. Fake scares are the worst.) Here's an example of anticipation in action:

Laura stood at the door, right hand trembling as it rested lightly on the knob, the metal making soft rattling sounds beneath her cold flesh. It was *in there. The Mirror. She always thought of it like that, Mirror with a capital M. She hadn't seen it since she was a child, but she knew it was still in the room—she could* feel *it. She imagined she could hear it calling to her, whispering her name over and over, speaking so fast the words ran together to form a murmured chant.*

Lauralauralauralauralauralauralauralauralauralaura …

"No," she said and gave her head a quick shake of denial. Neither the word nor the gesture had much force behind it, though. The voice—whether anyone else could've heard it or it was only in her mind—was real, and she knew it.

A flash of memory then, so strong she gasped as if hit with physical force. She was nine, looking up at the mirror on the wall—gleaming glass enclosed within a frame fashioned from actual gold—watching as the first trickle of blood, its crimson a startling violation on the wall's white paint, emerged from behind the mirror. The line of blood began to slowly descend, and her eyes followed its progress, as if mesmerized.

Drink, *the mirror said.* Drink of my essence, and we shall be one.

Laura waited until the line of blood stretched almost all the way to the floor. Then moving with dull, mechanical motions, she got down on her knees, scooted close to the wall, leaned forward, opened her mouth, extended her tongue …

A hand touched her shoulder and she screamed. She spun around to see her husband looking at her, expression a blend of bemusement and concern.

"Damn it, Martin! You know *how much I hate fake scares!"*

In one sense, nothing happens in this scene. Laura stands at the door then Martin spooks her. But a hell of a lot is happening in Laura's interior world, all of it designed to make readers dread Laura seeing the Mirror again, but also make them *want* Laura to step into the room so they can see something awful happen.

Now you write a scene of Anticipation where "nothing" happens, but the step-by-step details create an atmosphere of increasing suspense. When you're finished, find someone to read it and give you feedback. Was it suspenseful for them? Ask them if there's anything you could do differently to make it even more suspenseful for them.

_____

_____

_____

_____

_____

_____

_____

GET TO HIGHER GROUND

A great way to build suspense is to give your audience a viewpoint superior to your characters. It's as if your audience are gods gazing down from on high, aware of so much more than limited mortals could ever be. One of the examples I used in *Writing in the Dark* was similar to this scenario. Imagine you're standing at a hotel window, high above the street below. From your vantage point, you can see two streets that meet in an intersection, but the building next door blocks the drivers' view of the opposite street. You see a delivery truck hurtling toward the intersection coming from one direction, and a bicyclist coming from the other. They can't see each other, and so have no idea they will collide in mere seconds. But you do, and despite your godly vantage point, there's nothing you can do to prevent the terrible tragedy that's about to occur.

A scene like this can be written from an observer's point of view, but it's difficult to put a character in the exact right place at the exact right time to witness something—and without anyone else knowing that character is present. And if you do manage to figure out a way to get a concealed witness at the scene, you can only use the trick once in a piece of writing; otherwise, the readers won't believe it. The best way to write scenes like this are from an omniscient—sometimes called authorial—point of view. Regardless of what voice the rest of the story is in, first, second, or third, superior view scenes tend to be written in third-person omniscient. You, the author, write as if you're a god watching and narrating the action for your audience. They also tend to be relatively short and you only have one in a short story or a handful in a novel.

They go something like this:

Larry, seated in his rowboat, cast his line with a practiced flick of his wrist. He watched the silver lure arc through the air, plummet toward the water, and then hit with a plunk. As it sank, the bobber, a red-and-white plastic ball, touched the surface and wobbled a few times before finally matching the gentle rhythm of the waves. What Larry didn't see—because he was facing the other way—was the dark shape that emerged less than six yards from the port side of his boat, a slick black form with two dark green eyes that peered at him with unblinking, inhuman interest.

Larry loved being out on the lake by himself. No wife, no kids, just him, his fishing pole, a warm breeze, and the water. He loved his wife and kids, no question, but sometimes a man needed some alone time, you know? What Larry didn't know was that Joyce and the kids were just as relieved to be away from him. They loved him, sure, but he had a big personality, was the kind of guy who took up a lot of space in the world. Talked too much, too loud, gestured too big, and had a temper that, while he controlled it most of the time, still leaked out now and then, usually with him snapping at one of the kids and making them cry. It was good that Larry went off by himself now and again, Joyce thought. Otherwise, he'd never relax, and he'd end up being harder to live with than he normally was.

Larry watched his bobber float in the water roughly five yards from the starboard side of his rowboat. Shore was half a mile away, home seven miles farther. The late afternoon sun was still warm, but he could feel a hint of chill in the air. Gonna get cold tonight, *he thought.* Might be a good night to put a few logs in the fireplace.

Maybe he should say to hell with it and pack it in for the day. He'd been here for almost two hours, and he hadn't had so much as a nibble. Sure, it was relaxing to be out on the water whether he caught anything or not, but given a choice, he'd much prefer to catch something, maybe a nice-sized bass that he could bring home for tonight's supper. But it looked like that wasn't going to happen today, so …

His boat rocked then, and he saw waves roll past, large ones, as if a motorboat had sped close by. But he hadn't heard an engine. The wind had *picked up over the last few minutes. Maybe that had caused the waves. Hopefully, they'd settle down soon. He returned his attention to his bobber.* Thirty more minutes, *he told himself.* No more.

The thing in the water, which was far larger than the small portion of its head that was visible, was trying to decide if Larry would be good to eat. It had awakened from its long slumber several days ago, and it had been swimming slowly around the lake, staying underwater, building its strength. It had never seen a human before, let alone the strange hollowed-out log it floated on. The human smelled *like it might taste good, but the creature hadn't survived for several million years by taking chances. But it* was *hungry, and while it didn't possess the cognitive ability to think in ways humans would understand, it made a decision which, loosely translated, was* Nothing ventured, nothing gained.

It glided forward.

If you're writing a first-person narrative, you can probably get away with your main character saying something like, *I didn't know it then, but at the same time as I walked into the bank, Martha Stephenson was fighting for her life in her living room only a quarter of a mile away.* The implication is that the narrator eventually learned of these events and thus can talk about them during their telling of the story.

I tend not to use first person when I write fiction, so for superior view scenes, I use omniscient third, like with poor Larry and the lake monster. I write in second person sometimes, but since with second person, the author is the narrator telling "you" what "you're" doing, it's easy to write superior view scenes. Second person is always from an omniscient point of view. Here's an example using the scenario I mentioned earlier—the bike and the truck.

> *You're riding your bike down the street, and you're feeling good. Patty said yes when you asked her out at lunch, and the Denslow account looks like a lock. Now you're heading home to take a shower and put on some decent-looking clothes before you meet Patty for dinner at this new Italian place on 45th Street. What you don't know is that there's a Samson's Furniture delivery truck barreling towards the intersection. The driver, Bruce McAllister, is pissed at Manny, his supervisor. Bruce has a habit of taking his sweet time with deliveries—the slower he goes, the less work he has to do in a day, right?—but customers keep complaining, and Manny's had enough of it. He told Bruce that if he didn't straighten the fuck up and fly right, he'd be out on his ass looking for a new job before he knew what happened. Bruce knows Manny means it this time, so he's been driving fast all day, cursing Manny's name the whole time.*
>
> *You're going to meet Bruce in just a few seconds—quite forcibly, in fact—but you won't know it. In fact, you won't know anything ever again.*

All right, enough of my words. It's time for you to make some of your own.

Write a superior-view scene in either first person, second person, or third-person omniscient. If you want, try all three and see which way you like best. When you're finished, reflect on what it felt like to write a superior-view scene. Was it easier than you thought? Harder? Can you see yourself using this technique in a short story or a novel? Which length do you think the technique is better suited for? Only one? Both? Why?

_____

_____

_____

_____

_____

_____

_____

PUTTING ALL THE ELEMENTS TO WORK

For this exercise, I'm going to give you a scenario, and you're going to turn it into a good suspense story.

Scenario: Jackie wants to kill her girlfriend, Sylvia. Jackie belongs to a cult—which Sylvia is unaware of—and Jackie intends to provide her as a sacrifice during one of the cult's mystic rituals. Each cult member is responsible for bringing a loved one to be killed during the ritual. The fact they love them is what makes their deaths a true sacrifice. Sylvia knows Jackie is into some weird stuff, but she has no idea just *how* weird. It's their six-month anniversary, and Jackie suggests they go camping. Sylvia isn't big on the outdoors, but she agrees. What Sylvia doesn't know is that Jackie plans to pitch their tent near where the cult is going to conduct their ritual. Sylvia intends to bring Jackie to the cult the first night they're there.

Since the scenario already provides for **anticipation** and a **superior view**, we'll move on to the remaining elements of suspense.

Time Constraints. Make a list of time constraints that you could add to this scenario. These constraints can affect any aspect of the story, the characters, the cult, the kind of ritual it is, etc.

_____
_____
_____
_____

Apply Pressure. Make a list of ways you could put pressure on any of the characters—Jackie, Sylvia, the cultists …

_____
_____
_____
_____

Create Dilemmas. Jackie already has one built-in dilemma, assuming she truly loves Sylvia *and* she's a true believer in the cult's goals. What other dilemmas can you come up with for any of the characters?

_____
_____
_____
_____

Be Unpredictable. The scenario I gave you has several predictable possibilities. Jackie will have a change of heart and save Sylvia. Jackie will allow Sylvia to be sacrificed. Jackie tries to save Sylvia but the cult catches them and sacrifices them both. Try to come up with some unpredictable developments, ones which may or may not be specifically related to the plot. Make a list.

_____

_____

_____

_____

Put It All Together. Go over your lists, pick your favorites from the ideas you came up with, and put them together to make a story that you think would be effectively suspenseful. You don't have to write the entire story. Just make notes.

_____

_____

_____

_____

VOICES FROM THE SHADOWS

Tim Lebbon, award-winning author of *Eden*

One tip for getting to know your characters before you even start writing is to interview them. I do this a lot—write twenty questions (place of birth, favorite band, first childhood pet … that sort of thing), and even though a lot of your character's answers won't even find their way into your book/story, it'll still give that character a real rounded feel for you. Just like … a real person! Which is what you aim your characters to be. The questions can be as straight or outlandish as you like, and sometimes this exercise can throw up some quirks or habits that can really form a large part of the story you immerse them in. It's almost like getting to know your characters before you consciously know anything about them.

David Wellington, author of *The Last Astronaut*

As horror writers we seek to evoke both dread—the creeping realization that something horrible is about to happen—and terror, the visceral, right-now reaction to Bad Things. You most likely have the dread down pat. Dread is the idea behind your story, the premise. Today, work on terror. As an exercise: Write a scene where you're running away from a monster. Here's the catch: Your scene should contain zero exposition. No description of the monster, no reasons why you're running. Instead, focus on the sensations, the experience of being chased. Think of the physiological effects of fear: The heart racing, the cold sweat, the prickle on the back of your neck. Think of what fear can make you do. Does it paralyze you, like a rabbit unable to escape the wolf? Do you break for wide open spaces, or try to hide somewhere small and cramped? There's no time to think! Start writing now, and don't stop until you get away … or get caught.

Stephanie M. Wytovich, Bram Stoker Award-winning author of *Brothel*

Sometimes when I'm sitting down to write, I'll use my tarot deck as a companion. I'll shuffle it, cut the deck, and pick three cards off the top. If I'm looking to brainstorm and just freewrite, I'll write about the images, the numbers, and the suite of the cards I pulled to see if it prompts anything. Other times, I'll do the same but use the cards as an invitation to the beginning, middle, and end of a story. It's a fun and intuitive way to write, get to know your characters, or just experiment with the writing process and invite a little magic into your craft.

Red Lagoe, author of *Dismal Dreams*

Almost anyone can write a spooky scene that takes place in a crumbling cemetery on a foggy night. But what if the setting is a dog park on a sunny day? This is where creative use of language helps to set a creepy mood. I like to start by looking at verbs in the scene.

The sun, instead of shining, can burn, blind, or assault. On a moonlit night, bare branches might not reach for the moon, but rather claw at the moon. Instead of blanketing a landscape, snow could suffocate it. Using stronger, evocative language can drastically shift the mood. Inject sinister-sounding verbs (bleed, strangle, gouge, sever, blister, scar) into scenes to make them darker and more menacing.

Mark Morris, author of the *Obsidian Heart* trilogy and editor of *New Fears*

This may not work for everybody, but I've found that when I'm putting ideas together for a story or a novel, one of the elements that brings it to life is to get the location right. For me, locations are incredibly evocative. They're like characters in their own right, and invariably spark off ideas, moods, entire scenes in my head. My first novel *Toady* was set in a traditional British seaside town in the winter, and thinking about incongruous things like snow on a beach and the incoming tide eating it away sent my imagination into overdrive. My latest novel is set on a small Nordic island, and simply researching the flora and fauna, the landscape and the climate has enriched and enlivened the story to no end, adding layers of atmosphere and texture that may not otherwise have been there.

CHAPTER EIGHTEEN
LET THEM FIGHT!

The characters in horror stories tend to be ordinary people without superpowers or special combat training. Put into threatening situations, they're no more or less capable of defending themselves than the rest of us. Reading about a bad-ass monster slayer cutting a bloody swath through a horde of supernatural baddies may be fun, but there's no real tension to it. The hero is too powerful for us to believe she's in any real danger, and she's too strong to experience the same kind of fear that we would if we had to fight monsters. Horror works best when characters feel threatened, in over their heads, and helpless. Because of this, fight scenes in horror are different than they are in adventure-type fiction. They tend to be more grounded in reality—at least in terms of *how* characters fight if not *what* they fight. The exercises in this chapter are designed to help you write more effective and convincing action scenes in your horror fiction.

Ready to get started?

Lights … camera …

Action!

ARE YOU READY TO RUMBLE?

How battle-ready is your protagonist? Not just physically but psychologically? Here's a questionnaire you can fill out to help you determine just how prepared your characters are to throw hands.

1. PHYSICAL CONDITION: How physically fit is your character?

   _____
   _____
   _____
   _____

2. PSYCHOLOGICAL CONDITION: How mentally prepared is your character to fight?

   _____
   _____
   _____
   _____

3. FIGHT TRAINING AND/OR EXPERIENCE: What experience or training, whether official (such as a stint in the military) or unofficial (such as getting into fights a lot as a kid) does your character have, if any?

    _____
    _____
    _____
    _____

4. ATTITUDE TOWARD VIOLENCE IN GENERAL: How does your character normally feel about violence, especially about the thought of committing it themselves?

    _____
    _____
    _____
    _____

5. ATTITUDE TOWARD VIOLENCE AS IT'S HAPPENING: How will they respond psychologically in the midst of a fight? Will they put their emotions aside and do what has to be done? Are they terrified but still able to fight? Are they hesitant to commit fully to the fight? Do they start out fine but become more upset as the violence worsens? How do they feel about inflicting pain on someone else? Does it sicken them? Satisfy them? Do they hate it but do it anyway because they have to? Do they seek to cause minimal damage? Do they seek to take out their antagonist as quickly as possible to end the violence?

    _____
    _____
    _____
    _____

6. RESPONSE TO EXPERIENCING PAIN DURING A FIGHT: How does your character react to experiencing pain during a fight? Some people have never been in a fight before, let alone been hurt during one, and they may find pain terrifying, so much so that they hesitate to continue fighting or even try to break off the fight. Some people ignore the pain until the fight is over. Some people are further motivated by pain.

    _____
    _____
    _____
    _____

7. REACTION TO THE AFTERMATH OF VIOLENCE: How does your character respond once violence is over? Do they feel sick and shaky? Do they throw up? Do they feel exhilarated? Are they tired? Are they emotionally numb? Are they horrified by what they've done? Are they disturbed that they possessed a capacity for violence that they weren't aware of? How do they deal

with any injuries they've sustained? How do they function with these injuries moving forward?

_____
_____
_____
_____

The answers to these questions will help you write better fight scenes because you'll have a clearer idea of what your character will and won't do in a fight, and how they'll react during and after a battle.

TELL ME WHAT YOU WANT, WHAT YOU REALLY-REALLY WANT

One of the most important things about writing a fight scene is to make sure your protagonist (or, for that matter, your antagonist) has clear goals. Let's say your character is hiking in the woods one day, and they're attacked by a vicious Lizard Man. Your character's **immediate goal** would most likely be to get away from the Lizard Man. (Remember when we talked about fight vs. flight in Chapter Thirteen?) But Lizard Man's too strong and fast for your character to escape, so their goal changes. Now they have no choice but to stand and fight if they wish to live. But they know there's no damn way they're going to hurt Lizard Man, let alone actually kill him, so their **underlying goal** remains the same as their initial one: To escape. Everything they do in the fight is to help them achieve that goal. They'll have reactions to the moves Lizard Man makes, of course, which amount to **short-term goals**. *Lizard Man is reaching for my throat! I'd better dodge to the side if I don't want my neck snapped like a fucking twig!* But they never lose sight of their underlying goal—unless, of course, the circumstances change drastically during the course of the fight. Let's say that during the fight with Lizard Man, the character's young child wanders into the scene. (Don't ask me why, just go with it.) The character's goal would shift from escape to protecting their child. They now have a **new or altered goal**.

Create a character or use one of your existing ones. Ask yourself what would they do in the following scenario: They're exploring the basement of an old house when a living corpse bursts through the floor, jumps to its feet, and attacks. The corpse's movements are fast, although it's not very coordinated, and it's stronger than an ordinary human.

Your antagonist in a fight scene has goals too. In this scenario, the corpse wants to feed on your character's soul, but to do that, it needs to press its open mouth to your character's and literally inhale the soul.

Now that we've established a scenario, fill in details for the following items:

Antagonist's Immediate Goal: We'll start with this because the antagonist is the aggressor.

_____
_____
_____
_____

Protagonist's Immediate Goal: The character's first response to being attacked.

_____
_____
_____
_____
_____

Protagonist's Underlying Goal: The character's ultimate goal in this scene. It might be the same as the Immediate Goal, but it might not be.

_____
_____
_____
_____
_____

Antagonist's Underlying Goal: The corpse's ultimate goal in this scene. As with the protagonist, this might or might not be the same as its immediate goal.

_____
_____
_____
_____
_____

Antagonist's Short-Term Goals: Actions the corpse takes to help it achieve its goal of draining the protagonist's soul.

_____
_____
_____
_____
_____

Protagonist's Short-Term Goals: What are some of the character's responses to moves the undead creature makes during the fight? You can create a brief outline of the fight here if you like.

_____
_____
_____
_____
_____

Antagonist's Altered Goal: Does anything happen that changes the corpse's underlying goal or does the corpse's underlying goal remain the same throughout the scene?

_____
_____
_____
_____
_____

Protagonist's Altered Goal: Come up with something that happens during the fight which changes the character's underlying goal.

_____
_____
_____
_____
_____

How did this exercise turn out for you? Did having clear motivations throughout the fight—even if they shifted along the way—for both the protagonist and antagonist help you plot an effective scene? Did they help you picture the events more clearly? Do you feel confident you could write the scene based on what you've come up with here?

_____
_____
_____
_____
_____

HOW FAR IS TOO FAR?

A character who has never been in a fight before has no idea how they'll react or what they'll do until the time comes. This is one of the things I like most about *Sean of the Dead*. Sean isn't a person anyone would normally peg as a leader and warrior, but once the zombie outbreak hits, that's exactly what he becomes. You need to know your character's **perceived limits** when it comes to violence as well as they're **functional limits** when violence occurs. You also need to know their **breaking point**, the thing that will push them beyond their functional limits to commit an act of violence they never could've imagined doing. This is their **absolute limit**.

Once again, it's questionnaire time!

1. PERCEIVED LIMITS: What does your character imagine their limits will be in a fight? Are they willing to punch someone but not stab them? Will they hit someone on the head with a blunt object? How hard? What do other characters perceive are the limits for this character when it comes to committing violent acts?

_____
_____
_____
_____

2. FUNCTIONAL LIMITS: Once a fight begins, what are the actual limits that your character has—actions they take that might surprise them, that they did not think themselves capable of, and actions they may start to perform but find themselves unable to follow through on?

_____
_____
_____
_____

3. BREAKING POINT: What would happen during a fight that would cause your character to perform an act of violence that would normally be shocking or abhorrent to them? Seeing a friend killed? Hearing the antagonist threaten their children? Becoming so terrified that they snap and become temporarily insane? When they reach this point, do they commit a single act of violence or do they go into berserker mode and attack?

_____
_____
_____
_____

4. ABSOLUTE LIMIT: Once your character has reached their breaking point, how far is too far for them to go when it comes to committing violence? Will they stop short of killing someone? Will they stop once an opponent is neutralized or will they continue causing them pain? Will they stop when they first spill their opponent's blood? Or do they have no limit and they'll continue beating their opponent until they're nothing but a mess of broken bones, crushed organs, and bloody goo?

_____
_____
_____
_____

The answers to this questionnaire will give you an even clearer idea of what your character will or won't do in a fight. And while it would be ridiculous to push your characters past their breaking point in every fight they find themselves in, consider pushing them to that point at least once in your story. This _is_ horror we're talking about, after all.

PLOTTING FIGHT SCENES USING SCENE AND SEQUEL

We discussed using the technique of Scene and Sequel as a plotting tool in Chapter Fourteen. Now we're going to talk about it as a way of structuring fight scenes.

To quickly recap:

- A character has an **Overall Story Goal**.
- The character takes steps to achieve that goal. These are called **Subgoals**.
- A **Scene** is a story unit in which the character takes action in order to achieve a Subgoal.
- Scenes end in **Disasters**. Maybe setbacks would be a better term. Either the character doesn't achieve their subgoal, or they do, but achieving it brings about unintended consequences that make things worse for them.
- A **Sequel** is a story unit in which the character processes the outcome of a Scene and decides on their next subgoal. This leads directly into the next Scene.
- If necessary, sequels can be **Deferred** until later, but the rule is that every Scene must have a Sequel.

A fight scene can be viewed as a fast-moving series of Scenes and Sequels. None of the Scenes and Sequels last very long—perhaps only a split second in some instances—and characters don't have time to think during a Sequel. They have to act fast because their antagonist isn't going to stand around and wait for them to figure out what to do. They either have to think quickly or act instinctively. Here's an example of a fight broken down into Scenes and Sequels:

Daniel, the senior counselor at Camp Hackemup, hears a noise outside his cabin. He goes outside to check it out, figuring that it's probably some of the campers playing a prank on him, only to discover the legendary masked killer Jason Myerson standing there gripping a very large blood-stained machete.

Daniel's Overall Goal: Not to get killed.

First Subgoal: To get the hell away from Myerson.

Scene: Daniel turns and runs. Unfortunately, he's not thinking straight (most characters don't think clearly during a fight unless they have a lot of battle experience), and he runs back into his cabin. He locks the door behind him. (Returning to his cabin is a **Disaster**. He'd have been much better off running away from the cabin, where he had room to maneuver and might've found help.)

Sequel: Daniel realizes that he's made a mistake. He knows Myerson will break into the cabin and come after him, so he needs to find a weapon. (This is the next Subgoal.)

Scene: Daniel begins frantically searching his cabin for a weapon. A few seconds later, Myerson breaks down the door and enters. (Myerson entering is the Disaster.)

Sequel: Daniel says "Fuck!" and searches even more frantically. (This is the next Subgoal).

Scene: Daniel's search is successful. He finds a hunting knife and grabs it. Myerson continued moving after breaking in and he now grabs Daniel's knife hand by the wrist and squeezes it hard. (This is the Disaster.)

Sequel: Daniel knows that Myerson will break his wrist any moment, so he decides to headbutt him. (This is the new Subgoal.)

Scene: Daniel headbutts Myerson. He strikes the killer hard enough to make him release his grip and stagger backward, but the impact causes Daniel's head to explode with pain and his vision blurs. (This is the Disaster.)

Sequel: Daniel considers trying to run past Myerson to reach the doorway, but he's dizzy and his vision is too wonky to trust. Myerson recovers quickly and starts toward Daniel. Daniel decides to stab Myerson. (This is the new Subgoal.)

Scene: Instead of backing away from Myerson, Daniel steps forward to meet his attack. He rams the hunting knife into the killer's abdomen. Myerson lets out a grunt of pain, then he hits Daniel with a backhanded blow, and Daniel flies through the air, crashes into the wall, bounces off, and hits the floor. (This is the Disaster.)

I could go on, but you get the idea. (Besides, you know that Daniel is dead meat. Only a Final Girl can defeat a masked slasher.)

Another great thing about using Scene and Sequel to write fight scenes is that the technique helps you stay in the moment as your write. It's less likely that you'll gloss over—or completely omit—an important step in the battle.

Your turn. If you like, you can pick up the fight where I left off and continue to plan out Daniel's battle with Myerson using Scene and Sequel. Or if you'd rather, you can come up with your own fight scenario and develop it using Scene and Sequel. Either way, start writing.

_____

_____

_____

_____

_____

_____

_____

What was using Scene and Sequel like for you? Did it help you structure the fight sequence more effectively? Did it also help you think of more actions to include in the fight? Did you find it constraining and awkward? If so, using Scene and Sequel tends to get easier for people the more they practice it.

Bonus Exercise

If you have a fight scene in a story, reread it, viewing it through the lens of Scene and Sequel. Rewrite it using Scene and Sequel and see if that section of your story improves.

_____

_____

_____

_____

_____

_____

VOICES FROM THE SHADOWS

Angela Slatter, award-winning author of *All the Murmuring Bones*

This tip is very small and it can basically be summed up as "withholding." If I were editing the below paragraph, the word I would remove to create a sense of suspense and tension is "him"—it's the second last word in the piece.

> *She caught Adeline staring at her as Charlie wandered off towards to the house. As if Wendy was lying or something. She'd seldom seen her sister so serious, so determined. Adeline had been joking around when they first arrived, when she'd given the invitation, too. But now she was straight-faced, maybe sullen; Wendy was about to ask why when they heard him screaming.*

The reason I'd delete that is because you're going to tell the reader soon enough who is screaming, but if you remove "him" from here, then there's an ever-so-small chance for the reader to believe the screaming isn't coming from the character of Charlie. It leaves the potential for it to be someone else, which means you've given the reader a moment of suspense and unknowing—who else might be there? It's a moment of tension—so you're changing and controlling the pace by the simple removal of one tiny word. Suspense is about dropping a trail of breadcrumbs for the reader—and sometimes it's also about picking up some of those breadcrumbs so it's not too easy for them to see what's coming. Therefore you'd have:

> *She caught Adeline staring at her as Charlie wandered off towards to the house. As if Wendy was lying or something. She'd seldom seen her sister so serious, so determined. Adeline had been joking around when they first arrived, when she'd given the invitation, too. But now she was straight-faced, maybe sullen; Wendy was about to ask why when they heard screaming.*

Grady Hendrix, bestselling author of *The Final Girl Support Group*

Count your words. I keep a schedule book on my desk and at the end of every day I log my word count. It's evolved a little and is more of a work diary these days (so if I spent three hours answering emails I write that in) but the most essential thing is my word count. I started counting about seven years ago when I was writing *Horrorstör* and I thought I was being productive. I wasn't. Having my daily word count staring me in the eye, in black and white, was a huge wake-up call. It showed me how productive I was, or wasn't, being and just seeing the number made me determined to do better. Pro Tip: I kept my word count on my calendar app for 5 years until a digital hiccup outside my control (Apple stopped updating the app) wiped it clean. I do it in pen and ink now because that belongs to me and nothing except fire can erase it.

Villimey Mist, author of the *Nocturnal* series

I watched a lot of horror movies and TV shows before I embarked on the whole writing journey, but I've noticed that they've helped me a lot when it comes to writing horror stories. I usually center around the scenes of the characters and their motives whenever I watch movies as well as whenever I write. For me, if I can imagine just one scene with the main character along with one emotion perfectly, be it either the beginning, the middle or the end, then usually the rest of the story comes rushing forward as well. If you can connect the emotion to the character, it will definitely help forming the layout of the story. That's what I did with one story of mine, "Kokkuri-san." A girl wanting revenge popped into my head. Her anger was so vivid that I immediately explored the reasons why and added a Japanese supernatural element to it and the result became entwined to Japanese bully culture.

Mort Castle, Bram Stoker Award-winning author of *The Strangers*

I've heard writers state that the hardest part of writing a story is getting started: writing that first line. Problem solved: Steal it.

- Get an anthology (preferably with many contributors whose work you are not familiar with) or a short story collection (by an author whose work you do not know).
- Do not read the book.
- Copy the first sentence of every story.
- Choose one for your first sentence. You know it's good because, hey! It was published, right? This might be a sentence that really gives you a yank for a spiritual, psychic, creative, or cursed reason. Or you can choose one at random.
- There's the first line of your story.
- Write the rest.
- Of course, when the story is in its final draft, change that first line so greatly that even its original author or his lawyer will not recognize it.
- Or, more often than not, you can just throw it away.

Chuck Wendig, *New York Times* **bestselling author of** *Wanderers* **and** *The Book of Accidents*

If you can surprise yourself—or better yet, scare yourself—then you're going to do the same to your readers. And doing it to them is doing it for them. Think of it like a public service.

CHAPTER NINETEEN
THERE ARE NO LIMITS, BUT ...

One of the things horror creators have to consider is the issue of extreme and violent content. Some decide whether to include such material in their fiction on a case-by-case basis. Does the story need extreme content? Then they include it. If not, they leave it out. Others decide based purely on artistic preference. If they think horror fiction is better with extreme content in general, they use it. If they think it's more effective without, they don't. Still others decide based solely on marketing concerns. Extreme horror has a smaller audience than, for lack of a better term, not-so-extreme horror, so if writers want to reach the widest possible audience with their work, they limit the amount of violence, gore, and sex in their fiction.

I'm in the use-whatever-I-need-to-at-this-particular-moment-in-the-story camp, so while I'm comfortable writing extreme horror, I don't classify my work that way. A lot of reviewers said that my novel *Your Turn to Suffer* was dark, brutal, and extreme. I didn't think it was any more or less those things than most of my other horror novels, but hey, I'm just the writer. What do I know? Besides, what's extreme content to one person is mild to another.

I do believe that extreme elements, like any other content, should be used in service of the story rather than an end in and of themselves. A "story" that's nothing but a series of torture scenes that has no point other than to titillate readers with how awful it can be—as if it's some sort of literary endurance test—isn't much different from a child pulling a booger from their nose and holding it up to gross out their friends. But horror fiction that uses extreme elements to hold a mirror up to the darker parts of society, as nightmarish fuel for a tale that still possesses all the elements of effective fiction, or as meta-commentary on the genre of extreme horror fiction itself ... that, as they say, is an entirely different story.

Remember the -isms exercise in Chapter Sixteen? We talked about how in horror fiction women often serve only as objects to be used for violence, sexual assault, and overall degradation. Nowhere is that more common than in extreme horror. Maybe those creators who treat women this way in their fiction (which is by no means all authors of extreme horror) are reflecting negative societal attitudes toward women without realizing it. Maybe they've absorbed the tropes of violating women from extreme horror content they've read and viewed. Or maybe they're just misogynistic assholes. Whenever I write extreme horror, I do my best to dole out the punishment equally to everyone, and always in service to the story. And no matter how minor a role a character may play in one of my stories, I do my best to portray them as a human being, not just a piece of sacrificial meat, and I give them as much dignity as I can during whatever time they have on stage. I suggest you do the same.

Moving on.

In this chapter, we're going to work through exercises that will help you identify where you're at on the Extreme-o-Meter (pat pending) as well as the best ways to present extreme content to readers. If extreme horror isn't your thing, you can always skip this chapter, but I'd suggest reading it anyway. Violence, death, s-e-x, and all the spurting fluids that come with them can appear in otherwise sedate horror, so if you're going to sever a character's carotid artery in the middle of your homage to Victorian ghost stories, you might as well be good at writing about the red stuff.

THE EXTREME-O-METER

First off, what does *extreme horror* mean to you? One of my friends was afraid of *The Munsters* when he was a child. That show was extreme for him back then. I have other friends who have to stifle yawns while watching *A Serbian Film*. I'm not sure they consider any content truly extreme. Let's find out what's extreme to you.

1. How do you define "extreme horror"?
    _____
    _____
    _____
    _____

2. Are there any works of extreme horror—written or cinematic—that you've enjoyed? If so, list some of your favorites.
    _____
    _____
    _____

3. Conversely, are there any works of extreme horror you didn't enjoy? If so, list them.
    _____
    _____
    _____

4. Are there any scenes you've read/watched in a work of extreme horror that were too much for you? What were they? Why were they too much for you? (For example, my wife has no problem watching monsters chomp on people in a movie, but she can't stand seeing humans hurt other humans. Monsters are imaginary, but people actually do hurt other

people in the real world, so scenes of extreme human-on-human violence are too much for her.)

_____

_____

_____

_____

5. Are there any elements of extreme horror that you refuse to read/watch? Concepts or images that would make you slam a book, turn off the television, or close your browser? If so, what are they?

_____

_____

_____

_____

Remember when I mentioned Jack Ketchum's advice to write from the wound in an earlier chapter? Consider exploring the types of extreme content that you've had an adverse reaction to. It's my most fervent wish that you *can't* write about horrific violence from personal experience, but as an artist, if there are ideas that you have a strong reaction to, no matter what kind of reaction it is, they can be worth exploring. There's something powerful there, and investigating it could result in some amazing fiction. But as I also said in an earlier chapter, you don't have to traumatize yourself to write stories. In the end, do whatever's best for you.

RESTRAINT? WE DON'T NEED NO STINKIN' RESTRAINT! (OR DO WE?)

When people think about writing extreme horror, they think about going balls-to-the-wall, take-no-prisoners, heavy-metal-rock-and-roll-hail-Satan-fuck-the-world *crazy*. And you can do that. There's a lot of energy in that approach, and if you can transfer that energy to the page, readers will respond to it, just like an audience at a rock concert will cheer for a kick-ass guitar solo. But that's not the only way to write about extreme content, and it's not always the best way.

In the 1943 movie *The Leopard Man*, a black leopard is on the loose in a small New Mexico town. A series of murders occur for which the leopard is blamed, but one of the characters begins to suspect the leopard may have only committed the first murder, and the rest were committed by—pardon the pun—a copycat. A *human* one. (Skip the rest of the paragraph if you want to avoid spoilers.) A young girl is the first to be killed. Because the leopard was loose, she was too afraid to go out at night and buy some cornmeal from the grocer as her mother wanted. Her mother forces her outside, locks the door, and tells her not to come back without that cornmeal. She needs it to make tortillas for Father's dinner. Frightened, the girl hurries to the grocer's, gets the cornmeal, and rushes home. Along the way, something begins to pursue her. (We aren't shown what.) In her panic, she drops the cornmeal and starts running. The whatever-it-is chases her. She reaches her home and pounds on the door, but her mother asks if she's brought the cornmeal. She says she dropped it and begs to be let in. Her mother refuses to unlock the door, believing her child is being overly dramatic, and tells her to go back and get some more. The girl turns toward the street and watches, paralyzed with terror, as something approaches her. (We still don't see what it is.) The next shot is the mother inside, hearing her girl scream, followed by a pool of blood flowing beneath the door. We learn in the next scene that the girl was horribly mutilated and died. We never see her body.

An extreme act of violence occurred, but it was depicted in a restrained way. Did that make it more successful than if we'd gotten to see the leopard attack the girl? The *concept* is better. Not showing the leopard means we don't know who or what the killer really is, setting up the story's prime mystery. And in general, people's imaginations can usually conjure up something worse than anything writers and filmmakers can show them. But the scene fails somewhat in its execution. We hear the girl scream, but that's all. We don't hear the leopard make any sounds, and there's no impact on the door when the cat presumably leaps upon the girl. The girl screams only once, not for very long, and the scream isn't the scream of someone being torn apart by a wild animal. It's the scream of an actor being told by a direction to scream, but not to make it *too* screamy. "*After all, this is 1943, darling.*"

One of the reasons the original Splatterpunks back in the 80's—Skipp & Spector, David J. Schow, Richard Christian Matheson, and others—decided to write extreme horror is that it's more honest in its depiction of violence. Violence isn't neat, tidy, and sterile. It's vicious, brutal, bloody, and it hurts like a motherfucker. If a monster rips someone's throat out, they're going to bleed—a *lot*. If a serial killer eviscerates someone, their guts will spill onto the ground in a glistening wet mess.

That's what's missing from the scene of the girl's death in *The Leopard Man*. Honesty, or to put it another way, realism. We should hear the noises the leopard makes as it kills the girl. We should hear her scream repeatedly, each scream successively more agonizing until she can scream no longer. Maybe we'll hear blood gurgling in her throat, hear her thick wheezing as she struggles to breathe. Each time the leopard lunges at her or bats her body around, there should be a *thud* at the door as the girl collides with it. And as a bit of artistic license, I'd have each thud get louder, and the last one would threaten to rip the door off its hinges. Then silence would fall, and the girl's blood would flow beneath the door. I'd extend the scene a few moments longer. I'd have the mother look at the blood in shock, then unlock and throw open the door. Maybe I'd have the girl sitting with her back to the door, and the top half of her mutilated body falls backward across the threshold and onto the floor of the home. Or maybe I'd just have one of her injured arms flop onto the floor and leave the rest of her body unseen. I'd add claw marks on the front surface of the wooden door, along with splattered blood.

All of those details are realistic (more or less). They're *honest*. And they'd be terrifying if the scene was filmed correctly. This revised scene has some extreme details added, but there's also restraint applied in order to make the scene more frightening and disturbing. Restraint can be one of the extreme horror writer's best friends. And when it's applied early, you can ease up on the reins the further you go into a story, allowing you to "turn up the sound" as you go until by the end you're blasting away at full volume.

All right. Time to get extreme! If you don't normally use extreme elements in your horror fiction—actually, *especially* if you don't—consider doing the following exercise anyway. If nothing else, you might add a few new tools to your horror writer's toolkit, and you may find a whole new area of the genre opening up for you.

Here's a scenario. You can use it for this exercise or make up a scenario of your own.

A supernatural creature called a Hider disguises itself as human in order to camouflage itself and walk among its prey unnoticed. (I just made this creature up, so if you want to use it in a story, feel free.) When it attacks a victim, it cuts them open with its long claws, devours their organs (it liquefies them and slurps them up), then climbs inside the hollowed-out body. Since the Hider is supernatural, it morphs to fit the contours of the body, and the wound seals up (although it leaves a visible, seam-like scar). The host's brain is still there for the Hider to access, so it can speak in the host's voice and knows basic information about their life. The camouflage starts to decay almost as soon as the Hider dons it, and within a few days its rotted to the point where the Hider needs to discard it and find a new victim.

The scene I want you to write is the Hider attacking a victim, killing them, cutting them open, eating their insides, donning their body like a new suit of clothes, then walking off. I want you to write three versions of this scene. (I listed them from least extreme to most, but you can write them in any order you prefer.)

1. Write a quiet horror version of the scene, where no violence or blood is shown, only implied.

_____

_____

_____

_____

_____

_____

_____

2. Write a medium extreme version (like the revisions I made to the scene from *The Leopard Man*, half quiet, half extreme). Some violence and blood will be shown. How much is up to you.

_____

_____

_____

_____

_____

_____

_____

3.   Write a full-tilt extreme version with blood and guts flying everywhere. (Extreme horror often skirts the edge of absurdism—which is why some people find it funny. Try not to cross that line with your extreme scene. Try to take it seriously.)

_____

_____

_____

_____

_____

_____

_____

Compare the three versions you wrote. Which one was easiest to write? Which one was the hardest? (Implying is harder than showing, so I wouldn't be surprised if you found the quiet version harder to write.) Which one was the most fun to write? Which was the least fun? Which of the three scenes do you think was most successful? If you don't normally write extreme horror, what was it like for you to try your hand at it? Can you see yourself writing extreme horror—or at least adding some extreme elements from to time—in the future?

LET'S TALK ABOUT SEX

When my earliest horror novels first came out, I was surprised that some readers—who didn't bat an eye at my depictions of violence and death—were uncomfortable with the sexual elements in the stories. Even if the sex was bizarre and twisted (and it often was), sex itself is a normal part of human life. Why would some readers be weirded out by it? But over the years, I've come to believe that people are often uncomfortable with sexual content in stories because humans are uncomfortable with sex in general, regardless of whether it's a normal part of life or not. There's such intimacy, such trust, such *risk*—physical and emotional—when it comes to sex that it's no wonder our attitudes toward it are complicated. I don't consider sex part of extreme horror, unless it's melded with violence, injury, and death somehow. Otherwise, I classify sexual elements in horror as erotic horror, and I think most horror folk do too. But that doesn't mean extreme horror can't contain elements of erotic horror, or vice versa. But because some people have strong reactions to sex in horror stories—because it's beyond some readers' *limits*—I thought we'd discuss it in this chapter.

So keep going, you naughty-naughty readers, if you dare …

SEXUAL CONTENT QUESTIONNAIRE

Answer the following questions. You don't have to show your responses to anyone, so I hope you'll feel free to be honest.

1. How do you feel about sexual content in fiction/film?

    _____
    _____
    _____
    _____

2. How do you feel about sexual content in _horror_ fiction/film?

    _____
    _____
    _____
    _____

3. What, if any, types of sexual content in horror fiction/film make you uncomfortable?

    _____
    _____
    _____
    _____

4. What are some of the most memorable scenes involving sex that you've experienced in horror fiction/film? (You can define _memorable_ however you wish.)

    _____
    _____
    _____
    _____

5. Are there any sexual scenes/content in horror fiction/film that you had a negative—perhaps extremely negative—reaction to? If so, what were they and why did you have such a strong reaction to them?

    _____
    _____
    _____
    _____

6. What sort of sexual content do you _never_ want to read/see in horror fiction/film? Why?

    _____
    _____
    _____
    _____

7. Have you written scenes with sexual elements in them? How did you feel while writing them? Comfortable? Uncomfortable? How successful were those scenes in your opinion?

_____
_____
_____
_____

8.   Read over your answers. Do you see any commonalities or patterns in them? Is there anything about your answers that surprised you? Do you see anything that indicates how you might feel about using sexual content in your writing? If so, what conclusions can you draw?

_____
_____
_____
_____

SEXY TIMES IN HORROR TOWN

For this exercise, we're going to do something similar to the extreme horror exercise. I'm going to give you a scenario, and you'll write three scenes with sexual content, each more intense than the last.

Scenario: A succubus or incubus (take your pick) has lured a human into bed. The demon intends to feed on the sexual energy generated by their lovemaking. The more intense the sex, the more the demon will feed, and the greater the risk of the human dying. Unknown to the demon, the human they've chosen as prey is a psychic vampire. He or she thinks the demon is a human, and they intend to feed on him/her by draining all their life energy while they have sex. (The psychic vampire needs sexual contact to make a strong connection to its prey. It also needs its prey to lower their mental defenses, which happens during intense sex.) As they make love, they wage a battle—one they're not aware of at first—to see who will get to feed on who. Eventually, they both realize what's happening, and the sex becomes rougher and more intense as one tries to defeat the other.

(Hmmm … This sounds like a situation that could work in a sexy paranormal romance novel. Too bad I don't write that stuff.)

If you're embarrassed to write sex scenes, remember that you never have to show the results of these exercises to anyone.

1.   Write a restrained PG-13 or mild R version of the scene.

_____
_____
_____
_____
_____
_____

2. Write a somewhat-but-not-too restrained version of the scene, something that would get a solid to hard R or NC-17 rating. Perhaps even a mild X.

    _____
    _____
    _____
    _____
    _____
    _____
    _____
    _____
    _____

3. Write a solid X to XXX version of the scene, something so hot that your computer begins to smoke before you're halfway finished.

    _____
    _____
    _____
    _____
    _____
    _____
    _____
    _____
    _____

Once you finish, go take a cold shower if you need to. When you come back, read your scenes and ask yourself similar questions to those you answered after doing the extreme horror exercise. Which one was easiest to write? Which one was the most difficult? Which was the most fun? Which was the least? Which do you think was most successful? Did you have any problems writing the scenes, especially the XXX one? If so, what made you uncomfortable? If you don't already include sexual content in your fiction, do you think you're more likely to in the future, even if only periodically and in a limited fashion? Are you ready to chuck the whole horror thing and set off on a new career as an author of super-steamy dark erotica? (If so, you'll probably make more money.)

VOICES FROM THE SHADOWS

John Everson, Bram Stoker Award-winning author of _Covenant_ and _Voodoo Heart_

When you think your story is done—edited, polished and ready for prime time—read your work aloud. I bet you will find a pothole or three still! You don't need an audience for this (although if you have any kind of open mic night for writers in your area, that's always the best way. There's nothing like the live feedback loop of a real audience.) But you can do this at home. Read it to yourself in front of a mirror.

But read it all the way through, in full voice (no quickly mumbling your way through it—that defeats the purpose.) When you edit on a page, your inner ear doesn't pick up the same things that your outer ear will. When you speak prose out loud, you will hear dialogue that sounded genius in your head suddenly revealed as unnatural, awkward and stilted. You will hear words that you have repeated too many times on the same page. You will hear when it takes wayyy too long to get to the point because you realize as you're reading that your mouth has to go on and on to get to where you're trying to take the reader.

I've always really enjoyed doing live readings, and a long time ago I used to go to a writers' group every month or two that met in a bar in Chicago to read my latest short story. It's a great way to see if the crowd cringes as you hope when you think you've delivered a gruesome twist or laughs where you think you've framed a perfect joke. But it also helps you hear the places where your prose is simply flat or fat. I don't think I've ever done a live reading where I haven't realized—in both published and unpublished work—that I could have trimmed words or phrases to make the prose tighter and more effective. Sometimes I have edited as I was reading and dropped words on the spot that I realized were extraneous before I spoke them. It's a great tool. It won't fix a flawed plot, but it will help you polish your prose.

Philip Fracassi, author of *Boys in the Valley* and *Beneath a Pale Sky*

If I had two bits of writing advice to offer a new writer it would be these:

First, be yourself. Your unique voice and perspective are what will make you stand out against the crowded market. Don't imitate what you've read, or worry about your plot being too similar to another story. It's your vision that will make your work something fresh, and something readers respond to.

And second, don't let yourself get bogged down during a draft. I used to keep the insert from a Fortune Cookie taped to my laptop that said, "When skating on thin ice, your safety is in your speed." I apply that to my work constantly. Sometimes writers spend more time thinking about writing than actual writing. Don't be afraid to cut loose on an idea and just write. Sometimes, if you stop to think about it for too long, you'll fall through that ice. Don't be afraid to just start skating! And when you do, don't stop until you get to the end. Revisions will always be waiting across the pond.

Damien Angelica Walters, author of *The Dead Girls Club*

One of the most helpful writing tips I have is to stop the day's writing in the middle of a scene. The blank page can often feel larger than it is, those initial words holding an enormous amount of import. Beginning in the middle of a half-finished scene allows you to dive back in without having to determine where to start and how to draw a reader in. If it feels too disjointed to leave a scene in the middle, try leaving it with only a paragraph or two to finish and see what happens.

Lucy Taylor, author of Bram Stoker Award finalist novelette "Sweetlings"

Dialogue can make or break a scene. I try to write it in a way that highlights each character's speaking style and emotional state. Regional idioms can tell the reader a lot about the character speaking. For example, I love the way my neighbors from Maine say, "this wicked good/fast/sharp such and such" or a Wyoming friend's use of the word "hoosegow" to mean jail (as in "throw him in the hoosegow"). An unusual or infrequently used word can also add color, as well as giving an idea of the speaker's age, education, or origin. For example: "Why confront the ruffian? He'll just prevaricate."

I also find it helpful to read dialogue aloud. Do I have the right cadence and flow? Have I maintained a distinctive voice for each speaker? Above all, I don't want my characters to start sounding alike.

Angela Yuriko Smith, author of *Suite and Sour* and editor-in-chief of *Space and Time Magazine*

It's easy to get stuck in the same old tropes when writing in the speculative genre. I find science news is an easy way to find fresh ways to see an old story. There is always some horrific and wonderful mystery happening in the real world. Just today I read about crested rats that eat poisonous bark to style their hair with the toxic saliva and golden poison frogs. If I wanted to dress up something boring I might mix this real science in. What about a vampire (I know, yawn) who sucks on golden poison frogs (*phyllobates terribilis*) before kissing his victims? He'd be immune to the poison effects, as an undead, but his victims may become paralyzed and appear to faint. How easy would it be to escort a new friend from a nightclub like this? Perhaps he discards the frogs in the mouth of the corpse, leading to a detective hunt for a serial killer who leaves corpses drained of blood. What if the story took place in cyberpunk Brazil, post deforestation? How does a thinner ozone layer affect the hyper sun-sensitive undead? This is a silly example, but you get the idea. Truth is stranger than fiction, and strange truth is as close as the nearest clickbait science news search. Just don't go so far down the rabbit hole you forget to come back and write about it.

CHAPTER TWENTY
THE EVIL SPREADS

Congratulations! You've made it to the final chapter. Reward yourself with a cookie or something. In this one, we're going to focus on exercises that will help you market and sell your fiction. Don't get the wrong idea—you're still going to have to write. I'm not going to let you get off that easy.

When it came to deciding what areas to cover in this chapter, I chose topics that I get the most questions about as a writing teacher. I'm not going to pretend that these exercises will help you with everything you'll ever need to know about the business of writing. That sort of education never stops. But hopefully, you'll still get something of value from this chapter that will help you market yourself better. Here are the topics we'll be covering:

- Determine Your Publishing Goals
- Improving by Examining Both Rejected and Accepted Stories
- Market Ranking
- Persistence when Submitting
- Branding
- Coming up with Ideas for Theme Anthologies
- Pitches (and Synopses)

Let's get to it!

PUBLISHING GOALS

If someone asked you what your publishing goals are, could you tell them? Do you even have specific goals?

I'm not sure I did when I was starting out almost forty years ago. I wanted to be a writer, I wanted to write cool weird stuff—horror, fantasy, science fiction—I wanted to write and publish novels and short stories, and that's about it. Following are some questions that might help solidify your publishing goals. After all, if you want to hit a target, it helps to know what you're aiming for.

1. What do you want to publish?

   _____
   _____
   _____
   _____

2. How do you want to be involved in publishing? (Do you want to do more than just publish your writing? Many writers do other publishing-related work, such as freelance editing or designing books covers, as additional income streams.)

   _____
   _____
   _____
   _____

3. How do you feel about traditional publishing?

   _____
   _____
   _____
   _____

4. How do you feel about indie publishing?

   _____
   _____
   _____
   _____

5. Do you have any concerns or fears about publishing?

   _____
   _____
   _____
   _____

6. What would publishing success mean to you?

   _____
   _____
   _____
   _____

I'VE NEVER READ A STORY SO ... (SELECT ONE)

☐ **FANTASTIC**
☐ **MEDIOCRE**
☐ **AWFUL**

Want to improve your odds of getting published? (And if you answered NO, why the hell are you reading this book?) A good way to do this is to go over fiction—short stories, novellas, novels—that you've written, submitted to an editor or agent, and got a response from, whether yea or nay. If you're an indie writer, you can do the same thing by examining reviews of your work. In this case, you'd be looking for positive and negative feedback. (Traditionally published writers can also examine their reviews, but I suggest looking at editor and agent feedback first.) If you haven't started sending any work out yet, maybe you can ask beta readers, friends, or family for some feedback. (You'd need to find people who'll be brutally honest with you, though.)

Whatever feedback you choose to work with, you want to look at both praise and criticism, and you want to chart the responses. Your chart doesn't have to be anything fancy (unless you're into making fancy charts). Write STRENGTHS and OPPORTUNITIES FOR IMPROVEMENT at the top, draw a line down the middle, and viola! Insta-chart! As you go through your feedback, make notes in the appropriate columns. I did this when I was in my early twenties, after I'd been submitting stories and gathering rejections for a couple years. I don't remember where I got the idea, whether I came up with it myself or I read about it someplace like *Writers' Digest*. (Tell you what—let's pretend I invented it. It makes me look smarter.) It was a revelatory exercise. By picking out patterns in the feedback, I was able to identify stuff I did well and stuff I *didn't* do so well. If I was lucky, sometimes editors would give me suggestions on how I could improve. (I'm talking about rejections with comments. I ignored form rejections for this exercise.)

What did I do once I'd finished? I started working on my Opportunities for Improvement, naturally. This exercise was a huge learning step for me early in my career, and maybe it'll work for you too. Give it a shot and see. And if you do try it, do these things afterward:

Look for patterns. If three or more people made the same comment on your stories, such as "Too much exposition," then it's a good bet you need to work on that. If three or more people praise an aspect of your writing, such as characterization or description, then you'll want to keep getting better at those. None of us can be great at everything we do, but we can maximize our strengths and work on our weaknesses until we at least get competent in those areas. Your strengths are what will help you get published and read. And if your weaknesses are no longer *too* weak, they likely won't matter in the long run.

See if you can get a sense which comments are more important than others. If editors tell you that you need to proofread your text more thoroughly, that's an extremely important comment. If your manuscript has issues with grammar and spelling, editors won't finish reading it, let alone offer to publish it. If someone said something piddly-ass like, "I rejected this story because it used the word *admonish* in two separate places. I loathe that word!" then you know you it's a comment that's *way* down on the importance scale.

Work on improving the easiest things first. It's what I generally do whenever editors ask me to make revisions. It builds confidence and makes the revision process seem not so daunting.

Make peace with the fact that improving in the larger areas—like plotting, dialogue, etc.—will take some time. Get started, work steadily, a journey of a thousand miles begins with a single step, etc., etc.

Make two lists: 1) I AM AWESOME and 2) STUFF TO WORK ON. Keep them somewhere you can see them as you write. I have sticky notes affixed to my writing … I'm not sure what to call it. Hutch? There's a cabinet as well as open storage areas above the flat working surface. At any rate, I write things on the notes I want to see whenever I sit down to work. If you see the I AM AWESOME list (which is where you write your strengths) seeing the STUFF TO WORK ON list won't be so bad.

Unlike the other exercises in the book, this one takes some time to do, maybe a year or two if you're just starting out, but I highly recommend you try it. It worked wonders for me.

RANK YOUR MARKETS

Unlike the last exercise, this one's fairly simple. Make a list of markets you want to sell your fiction to. You can have one list for short fiction and one list for novels. You can also have a list ranking agents if you're getting ready to look for one. Organize your lists from best to … well, not *worst*. Not as best? After all, I wouldn't list a market you think is crap and would never submit to in a million years. How about "Put your dream market on top and rank them in descending order."

How you define *best* is up to you, and your definition—and your list—can change over time. Best can mean any of the following:

- The market that's the most prestigious in the field (or just to you)
- The market that pays the most
- The market that has the largest circulation (so more readers see your fiction)
- The market you love to read yourself and would be thrilled to sell a story to
- The market which has an editor you'd like to work with

Don't let anyone else tell you how you should rank your markets. It's your choice, and any way you order them is fine. Hell, you can rank them by which has the prettiest covers if you want. It's your career, no one else's.

_____

_____

_____

_____

_____

_____

_____

THE RULE OF TWELVE

I am about to commit an act of … not exactly plagiarism, but I didn't invent the Rule of Twelve. I read an article about it in a volume of *Writer's Market* many years ago, but I forget the author's name. I no longer have that volume, and while I've done multiple Internet searches trying to find her, I haven't been successful. This hasn't stopped me from sharing the Rule of Twelve with my creative writing students, but that's in a classroom situation. But I'm about to share the author's technique with you, and I'm unable to give credit. I'm still going to do it, since it's one of the most valuable writing and publishing techniques I've ever come across, and I want you to be aware of it. But if any of you reading this has any idea who the author of "The Rule of Twelve" is, I'd appreciate you sending me an email to let me know her name.

So, at risk of having the Citation Police breaking down my door in the middle of the night, here is the Rule of Twelve.

As I said, I was reading *Writer's Market* many years ago when I came across "The Rule of Twelve." The title intrigued me, so I started reading. The author said that she would write a story, send it out to be published, and after two rejections, she figured it wasn't any good, put it away, and concentrated on writing a new story. I thought, *Hey, I do that!* I read on, even more interested now. The author decided she was giving up on her stories too easily. She decided that when she sent them out, she would keep sending them out until they sold. No matter how many times it took. She made a submission chart and started submitting her stories. And what she discovered was that her stories sold on average the twelfth time out. By using the Rule of Twelve, she started selling her fiction regularly, and she urged her readers to do the same.

When I finished the article, I decided I'd give the technique a try. I did so, even making and using a chart just like the article's author, and you know what? My stories sold on average the *ninth* time out. I continued following this method, and my success rate continued improving. Soon I was selling stories the sixth time. Then the fourth. Third. Second. Then first. After this, they continued selling the first time out—not only because I'd improved as a writer but because I was doing a better job of targeting receptive markets—and I stopped recording the number of submissions.

What's magnificent about this technique is that it's a way to give structure to persistence—a way that doesn't depend on the writer's emotions. It doesn't matter if you're bummed out by the latest rejection.

You know you have to keep sending your stories out until they're sold, no matter how long it takes, so you send the damn thing back out.

If you find it hard to continue submitting your work for publication time after time, and if—like me—you gave up on your stories after only a couple rejections, I urge you to give the Rule of Twelve a try. Who knows? Maybe you'll beat my initial average of nine times, then you can message me on social media and taunt me about it.

ALWAYS BE BRANDING

Branding, branding, branding. Some days, it seems like that's all writers talk about on social media. One reason, I think, is that it's something writers can do that makes them feel like they're taking steps to advance their careers that doesn't actually have anything to do with writing. *Why no, I haven't written anything yet. But I have figured out my brand.* Writing and submitting (or self-publishing) risks rejection or bad reviews. Working on branding is far safer. I also suspect the emphasis on branding was driven by indie authors who, without a publisher to do marketing for them, were trying to find the best ways to market themselves and their work on social media—advertising venues that are free and open to all. I think traditionally published authors eventually started adopting indie marketing strategies because, hey, most trade publishers don't have massive advertising budgets (or if they do, they only spend money on sure bets, like authors who are already bestsellers), so they needed to get word about their stuff out there too.

I say all this to tell you that if you don't want anything to do with branding, that's cool. I sometimes see writers, usually newer ones, say things about marketing like *You gotta do this, and you gotta do that!* My friend, in the writing world, you don't gotta do a damn thing you don't want to. (Unless, of course, you signed a contract.) Brand, don't brand, whatever. But here are some exercises to help you brand better, if you'd like to give them a try. Some of these exercises also appear in *Writing in the Dark*, but I think they're important enough to repeat here, especially for those of you who read this book first. If you've read *Writing in the Dark* and didn't try the branding techniques I discussed there, now's your chance.

Branding Basics. Write down the following:

1. The genre(s) you write in:

    _____
    _____
    _____

2. The subgenre(s) you write in:

    _____
    _____
    _____

3. Specific qualities your writing has: Fast-paced, strong characters, action-packed, creeping menace, intricately-plotted, etc.:

   _____

   _____

   _____

4. Credentials: Well-published, veteran, award-winner, skilled craftsperson, high-quality writing, etc.:

   _____

   _____

   _____

If you have trouble coming up with anything to write for the above items, ask a writer friend who's familiar with your work to help. Many times, others see us more clearly than we see ourselves.

Three Words. List three words that you associate with your writing style. This list will help you to hone in on your brand. Again, if you have trouble thinking of any, ask a friend or perhaps look to any reviews your work has gotten. For instance, many of the reviews for my novel *Your Turn to Suffer* mention the words *weird*, *brutal*, and *dark*.

_____

_____

_____

One Sentence. Create a one-sentence tagline that describes your brand. For example: Sally Monroe writes YA stories with elements of snark and vulnerability. You can also write a slightly shorter tagline. Here are three examples from horror writers:

1. Ronald Kelly—Southern Fried Horror
2. John F. D. Taff—King of Pain
3. Gaby Triana—Gothic Horror with a Twist of Lime

The great thing about these shorter phrases is that they can fit on websites more easily, as automatic email signatures, on business cards, on merch, etc.

Now try to try to create short, medium, and long(ish) branding statements using the information you've generated. Longer branding statements can work well in author bios and—if they're not too braggy in tone—in query letters to editors or agents. Share your branding statements with writer friends to get their feedback. Post them on social media and ask your followers for feedback if you're comfortable doing so. And remember you're not stuck with your brand forever. You can change it whenever you want (although I wouldn't change it every couple of weeks), and it may also change naturally with time as your writing changes.

_____

_____

_____

VARIATIONS ON A THEME

One great thing about the horror field: A lot of theme anthologies are published, especially in the small press, and they can be a way to break into print and start building your bibliography as well as your reputation as a writer. I haven't done an official count, but I wouldn't be surprised if at least half of the almost two hundred stories I've published appeared in theme anthologies. The problem with theme anthologies—especially when they're open submission—is that editors get a ton of stories, so it can be very competitive. And a lot of the stories editors see don't do anything original or interesting with the theme. The following exercise will help you develop original ideas for theme anthologies that will stand out from the crowd and (hopefully) make it onto the final table of contents.

- **Hone in on the theme.** If the anthology's theme is rabid weasels, then not only does your story have to contain at least one rabid weasel, it needs to address the _theme_ of rabid weasels. It's not enough to stick a rabid weasel into a story you've already written and call it a day.
- **Think of the most obvious story ideas. Everyone else will write these. Come up with something better.** For the rabid weasels anthology, you know people are going to write stories about a pet weasel turning evil, a wild weasel attacking someone, a weasel apocalypse, a were-weasel, an evil person who commands weasels, etc. Other writers will immediately fall back on standard horror tropes. Be more original than that.
- **Don't go with your first, second, or even third idea.** You're probably still thinking about using the same tropes everyone else is. Don't. Do try to think of ways to put fresh, interesting spins on tropes.
- **Follow the editorial guidelines.** If the anthology's guidelines say that there should be 3.5 weasels in each submission, and all the weasels should have orange fur, then that's what you put in your story. Don't send a story that you think is "close enough" to what the editor wants. Give them _exactly_ what they want.
- **My formula: A twist on a theme + something weird I observed + a personal connection to the theme.** This works for me. You might give it a try. For the weasels anthology, I might go with a character who's plagued by weasels in his mind. Who else is going to think of mind weasels? It's spring as I write this, so I'm seeing lots of animals in my suburban neighborhood. They're not particularly weird, but instead of squirrels in trees and birds at bird feeders, I'll make my character start seeing weasels in their place. As for a personal connection, I've never seen a weasel in the wild, but I saw weasels in Loony Tunes cartoons as a kid, and there are

230 WRITING IN THE DARK: THE WORKBOOK

the weasels in *Who Framed Roger Rabbit?* I'll give that detail to my character, although I'll make up my own cartoon. Maybe I'll have the character be fascinated and disturbed in equal measure by the weasel cartoons. Maybe I'll make it so that the character was able to escape a difficult home life by watching the weasel cartoons. I'd still have a lot of work to do to come up with a finished story, but this formula will give me enough so that I should be able to come up with a decent submission.

Your turn. I'm going to give you a list of anthology themes, and I want you to come up with story ideas for them using my formula: A twist on a theme + something weird you observed + a personal connection to the theme.

- Space vampires
- An Earth ruled by kaiju
- First dates from Hell
- Ghosts and sorrow
- Small-town cults

_____
_____
_____
_____
_____
_____
_____

How did your ideas turn out? If you had to pick the best one—the idea which would make the most successful story—which would it be? Did you have difficulty coming up with ideas for any of the themes? If so, why? Were any themes easy for you? If so, why? What was it like using my formula? Did it work for you? Why or why not?

Bonus Exercise: Tinker with my formula, subtracting some elements, adding some of your own. See if you can come up with a formula that not only works better for you, but that reflects your individual writing process and style.

_____
_____
_____
_____
_____
_____
_____

PITCH PERFECT (OR CLOSE ENOUGH) AND GOOD FOR SYNOPSES TOO!

I don't know about you, but I hate pitching to editors and agents (at least ones I don't already know). Trying to encapsulate a novel into what's essentially a short sales message always feels awkward, and when I read over it—or listen to myself speak it if it's an in-person pitch—it seems clunky and forced. Still, I have a decent success rate pitching, so I must not suck too badly at it. But if you're as uncomfortable pitching as I am, this exercise will hopefully help you feel more relaxed (maybe just a little?) about the process.

And if you hate writing synopses, this technique is good for that as well, just like the title says.

There are written pitches, in-person pitches, and remote pitches (phone, Skype, Zoom, etc.). The following technique is good for all three types. You can use one of your own novels for this exercise, or you can use a novel written by someone else or a movie that you're familiar with for practice.

1. First create a one-sentence tag (This is a horror thriller that is very much Freddy Krueger meets Rambo).

    _____
    _____
    _____

2. Then add a slightly longer explanation (This is a story about an ex-military black ops captain who stumbles into a nightmare world where dreams can kill you, and it's presided over a devil-like creature who feeds on peoples' fears.)

    _____
    _____
    _____
    _____
    _____
    _____

3. Then write a short summary of the plot (one you could read aloud in just a couple minutes). Detail the main character's goal and challenges in the story, any major subplots, how your main character finally wins/loses/dies/is damned to Hell for all eternity (hey, we're talking horror here), why this story will interest readers, and what makes it different from other novels in the genre.

    _____
    _____
    _____
    _____
    _____
    _____

Now that you're done, you should have a kick-ass pitch to deliver to an agent or editor! Try your pitch out on some friends and see what they think. Ask them to offer suggestions for revision. A good pitch can always be made better.

VOICES FROM THE SHADOWS

Kathe Koja, award-winning author of *The Cipher* and *Velocities: Stories*

The best and most durable writing advice I know is this: Write what you love. Every day, every time. If you don't love it, stop.

Gwendolyn Kiste, Bram Stoker Award-winning author of *The Rust Maidens* and *The Invention of Ghosts*

Here's one question I always ask myself as a horror writer: What scares me? Of course, there's not a static answer to this. Growing up, I was afraid of sleep; it utterly terrified me. To be honest, I'm still not fond of it, and that unnerving relationship with sleep has definitely worked its way into my fiction. However, as I've gotten older, my fears have changed, and now include losing those close to me or even losing myself and who I am.

As an author, it can be easy to fall into the trap of believing there are certain things you should be writing about. But when you're crafting a horror story, don't be worried about what things you think others will find scary. Always ask yourself: What am I afraid of? You'll end up with stories that resonate far more with readers because those stories even scared the author who wrote them.

Horror craft tip I use:

My work tends to be character driven—particularly when I started out, the characters came first. In order to make their reactions to the story's horror elements authentic, I practice what I call character immersion. I carry around a notebook and spend time, sometimes weeks or months depending, getting into their heads. I experience a situation and ask myself how my character would handle it, what feelings it would bring for them, based on their personality and back story. No characters should be two dimensional—I want my supporting cast to be as real as the main character. That way we're all experiencing the fear together. If I know them, then I can be more effective in determining what scares them.

Laurel Hightower, author of *Crossroads* and *Whispers in the Dark*

If I'm brainstorming for new projects, I free associate about what sensory experiences in particular scare me. What movies have I watched that produced the most effective fear reactions, and how did they accomplish that? For example, in *Ghosts of War*, the soldiers are following a particularly disturbing noise that's echoing throughout the mansion where they're stationed. It's loud, permeates the entire house, and can't be associated with a common cause. The longer it goes on, the more ominous it gets. In that sequence, what was effective for me was the alien nature of the sound, and that it filled the soldiers' temporary home. There's no respite, only fear. Then I look at ways to utilize that concept in my own work, to produce a similar sense of unease for my characters. When I'm hammering all this out in my brainstorming document, something always comes to the surface—I've plumbed my own subconscious to identify what scares me, so now I can go about tinkering with how to use it to scare my readers.

Cynthia Pelayo, author of *Into the Forest and All the Way Through*

Two writing tips that have helped me substantially are character interviews and using a timer.

A character interview is exactly what it sounds like, you sit down with your journal and you interview your character. I do this for all of the characters that appear in my works. It does not need to be shown to anyone, and all of this information will not necessarily make it into your manuscript. It shouldn't. What this detail does is start to fully bring to life the character in your head.

For the timer, there are a few apps you can download for free, or you can just use your watch or your phone. I write in devoted blocks of time. For example, I'll set my timer app on my computer to 25 minutes. I will then write for those 25 minutes straight, not editing, not going back, just writing straight through. I will take a five-minute break and then repeat. I do this for a few rounds a day, maybe not all at once. Maybe once in the morning, once in the afternoon and twice in the evening, whatever my writing goal is for that project. This specifically helps me get what I call my "zero" draft down, the draft no one will see, but still the draft where I tell myself the story. Everything after is really cleaning, revising, shaping and improving.

Kristine Ong Muslim, British Fantasy Award-winning co-editor of *People of Colo(u)r Destroy Science Fiction!*

I get story ideas from Reddit and Creepypasta. Those stories of mine in LitHub, in *World Literature Today*, in other fancy places—they contain improvised, expanded, sometimes adulterated bits and pieces of subreddits and creepypastas. Along the ragged margins of the world's dark lore and endlessly captivating urban legends are the lies that people tell each other to affect normalcy. Try combing the labyrinthine horror-related subreddits. It really worked for me.

END OF THE LINE

I hope the exercises in this book helped you better hone your writing skills, and maybe even gave you a few ideas for stories you'll eventually write and share with the rest of us. I also hope that, like after a really good writing conference, you come away feeling inspired, recharged, and ready to work. Reading articles and books on how to write not only helped my development as a writer, they were models for my own essays on the writing craft. I hope that this book, as well as *Writing in the Dark*, might inspire some of you to share your experience and insights about writing, especially horror writing, with others. As I said in my introduction, we need everyone we can to help spread the dark gospel of Horror. Write articles, blog posts, social media posts, books … Make videos, do AMA's, present workshops, serve on conference panels, teach classes … Not because these are all good ways to promote yourself and your work (not that there's anything wrong with that), but because it's in the spirit of paying it forward. In one sense, writing is a solitary pursuit, but in another it's a group effort. We learn from each other all the time, whether from reading others' fiction and articles or taking their workshops and classes. We're lifelong learners, but we're also lifelong teachers … or, if you prefer, lifelong *sharers*. Share what you know, what you can do, and what you've experienced about the craft, business, and life of writing in the dark.

We can't wait to learn from you.

APPENDIX A
VOICES LIKE BARBED WIRE
BY TIM WAGGONER

I've lived in Ash Creek most of my adult life, so when I pull into the parking lot of a fast-food restaurant that doesn't exist, I am—as you might imagine—more than a little surprised. I'm scared, too, but at the same time hopeful. Maybe I'll finally find what I've been searching for here—some small measure of peace.

I park my Prius between two vehicles that I can't identify. One is a monstrously large sedan that looks like it belongs in the 1950's, its body shimmering in the sunlight as if it's made from mother of pearl. The other vehicle has seven wheels and looks like it's been constructed from odds and ends of silvery wire soldered together. The other cars in the lot are equally strange, but I find them comforting rather than upsetting. They're an indication that I've come to the right place.

When I get out of my car and take a breath, I find the air has a chemical tang to it, as if an industrial factory is close by. There isn't one to my knowledge, but up until a few moments ago, I didn't believe there was a restaurant here, so what do I know? The asphalt of the parking lot is dry and cracked, and there are no lines painted on it to indicate parking spaces. Vegetation grows upward from the cracks, some of it ordinary grass, but there are also weeds of a kind I can't identify. Sickly yellow-green things that are covered with thistles and which terminate in round crimson bulbs that glisten wetly. These bulbs sway slowly back and forth despite the absence of a breeze. I ran over several of these plants while driving into the lot, and I flattened them, the bulbs bursting open like tumors, squirting reddish-brown goo. The substance reminds me of how my daughters used to mix paints when they were little, adding more and more colors until they created a muddy brown soup.

It hits me then as it often does, so strong and unexpected that I'm unable to prepare myself.

An image of two girls sitting on a couch, one twelve, one seven. My daughters, Nancy and Lauren. Nancy's eyes are wet, but she's smiling, desperately trying to hold back her tears. Lauren is crying openly, tears streaming down her cheeks like tiny waterfalls. The girls are holding hands, fingers interlaced, gripping tightly. It's this detail that hurts my heart the most, I think.

I wish this wasn't happening! Lauren wails. *I wish this was a dream!*

Nancy's response to what her father and I have just told them is more restrained, and all the more awful for it.

That's okay, she says, lips trembling with the effort of maintaining her smile. *It's okay.*

The memory of their voices—of their shock and pain—nearly drives me to my knees. I can't breathe, and I wonder if the grief and guilt will finally kill me, and I'll fall dead in the parking lot of a place that shouldn't be real. But the memory retreats and I begin breathing once more. My heart is racing, but I don't think it's going to give out on me this time. I feel as much disappointment as relief from this knowledge.

Pandora's is the name of the restaurant, and it's spelled out in large red plastic letters on the front of the building, which—despite the oddities of the parking lot and the vehicles within it—looks pretty much like any fast-food joint. Beneath the name is a cartoonish depiction of a wooden box, the lid partway open, inside black shadows which almost seem to be swirling, like eddies of dark water.

How appetizing, I think, and although I'm still unsteady on my feet, I feel a little better. False bravado is better than none, right?

I go inside.

The weird chemical tang is stronger in here, as if the restaurant itself is producing it. My throat starts to hurt immediately and my eyes sting. I try not to think about what that odor is or what it might be doing to my body. At first glance, the interior looks the same as any other fast-food place: Tiled floor, counter staffed by dull-eyed uniformed workers, menu above them displaying options and prices, along with photos of what's meant to be tempting food selections. Sandwiches, fries, and shakes, but not the normal offerings. The sandwich meat is greenish and covered with what looks like scales, and the seeds on the bun aren't seeds at all, but rather tiny eyes. The fries look more like small sections of bone sprinkled with salt, and the shake cups are filled with a purple-gray substance that looks like something that's been squeezed out of an infected wound. My stomach lurches, and I almost turn around and get the hell out of there, but the girls' voices come to me again.

I wish this wasn't happening! I wish this was a dream!

That's okay. It's okay.

I take a deep breath through my mouth so I don't have to smell the chemical stink, and then I approach the counter. The woman at the register is in her twenties, bald with a tattoo of a large purple eye on her forehead. Her left eye remains closed while her right blinks rapidly and continuously. Her short-sleeved uniform is blue, and she wears a square brown hat shaped like a wooden box. Her nametag reads OND. When she speaks, her voice is bright and chipper, but she doesn't smile.

"Welcome to Pandora's, where you won't believe what's in the box. Will this be cash, credit, or etheric transfer?"

I try to speak, but my throat's so raw—thanks to the chemicals in the air—that it takes me a couple tries to produce sound.

"I'm, uh, actually here to meet someone. Mr. Lim?"

Ond's right eye stops fluttering, just for a couple seconds, before starting back up again. She doesn't answer with words but instead raises her arm and point toward the dining area. Her hands are twisted and lumpy, as if she suffers from severe arthritis, but her face doesn't change expression as she points.

I turn my head to look where she's pointing, and I see a dozen people scattered around the dining area, some sitting alone, some with companions. They all look like the sort of people that would drive the strange vehicles outside, but only one captures my full attention. An older man sitting alone and eating a sandwich, a pile of fast-food sandwich wrappers on the table before him.

Mr. Lim, I presume.

I thank Ond, who gives no indication that she hears me—or maybe she simply doesn't care—and I walk over to Mr. Lim's table. The man's body odor hits me when I'm within five feet of him, a feral smell, like the scent of big cats in a zoo enclosure. His stink leavens the chemical odor and actually comes as something of a relief. He's a thin man in his fifties—about a decade older than me—and he's wearing an army jacket, jeans, and sneakers. His clothes are worn, colors faded, but overall clean enough. He's several days overdue for a shave, and his bristles are as white as the tangled thatch of hair on his head. There's a TV screen hanging from a ceiling mount. The sound is muted, but instead of news, it's playing a series of black-and-white images that look like clips from snuff films. Mr. Lim keeps his gaze focused on the screen as he eats. Although *eating* is too nice a word for what he's doing. He's *devouring* his sandwiches, tearing into them with the speed and ferocity of a starving dog. He has three other sandwiches waiting for him on the table, all wrapped in yellow paper. I do a quick count of the crumpled wrappers piled in front of him, and I get ten. Assuming he hasn't been sitting here all day and pacing himself, he's evidently ordered fourteen of Pandora's sandwiches for his meal, and while he's eaten the majority of them, it appears his appetite is nowhere near satisfied. I wonder if he's eating the sandwiches with the green-scaled patties, but I decide I don't want to know.

He doesn't look away from the TV to acknowledge my presence, so I stand there, unsure what to do. On the screen, a naked middle-aged man holding an electric drill approaches an equally naked teenage girl duct-taped to a wooden chair. The terror in her eyes is so strong it's almost a living thing in and of itself, and I cast my gaze downward, unable to bear witness to what happens next. I try to tell myself that it's not real, just some slasher flick, but I know better.

I almost leave then, but I hear my daughters' voices once more—maybe because the woman in the video is so young—and my gut cramps with pain. As bizarre and frightening as this place is, it's nothing compared to what that memory does to me and I stay right where I am.

"Sit down," Mr. Lim says through a mouthful of food. He still doesn't look at me.

I hesitate for a moment, then I sit down opposite him, my back to the TV. He continues eating, one sandwich after the other, until he's finished. It doesn't take long. When he's done, he wipes a bit of ketchup from the corner of his mouth and licks it off his fingers. At least, I hope it's ketchup. He lowers his gaze to mine then, and I see he has the most beautiful pair of sky-blue eyes that I've ever seen. The eyes of an angel.

I'm about to introduce myself when he asks, "Who referred you?"

His voice sounds normal, but my ears hurt when he speaks, as if his vocal cords transmit an ultrasonic signal that I can't consciously detect. I find my voice faster than I did with Ond.

"Marsha McLean. A friend from high school. She said you helped her and could help me."

"Said?"

"Uh, yeah. I posted about my problem on social media—just venting, you know?—and she sent me a private message about what you did for her and how I could find you."

Marsha gave me Pandora's address, but no result came up when I entered it into my GPS app on my phone. I figured it was just a glitch of some kind, and I set out searching for the restaurant. I drove up and down the street five times before I finally found it. A gas station was on this corner the first four times I drove by, but on the fifth, Pandora's sat where the station had been.

Mr. Lim raises and lowers his chin, as if to indicate my answer is satisfactory.

"I remember her."

He turns halfway in his chair and waves to get Ond's attention. She looks at him blankly, then she nods and shuffles toward the kitchen. He then turns back to me.

"What's your problem?"

I tell him about the memory that plagues me, the night Jacob and I told our girls that we were divorcing.

"I'm their mother. I'm supposed to protect them from hurt, not be the cause of it."

When I finish, I feel exposed, as if I've revealed too much. But I have to tell him my story, don't I? How can he help me otherwise?

Marsha's problem was similar to mine. She lost her husband to cancer, and she was holding his hand in the hospital room when he died. She didn't regret being there for him, but every night she dreamed of that last moment with him. When it became too much for her to bear any longer, she told a friend, and this friend told her about a man she'd heard of who could solve any problem. A man named Mr. Lim. It took Marsha some time to track him down, but she did, and when she finally met him in person, he was indeed able to help her. Somehow, he removed the memory of her husband's death from her mind, and she's slept fine ever since. I pray he can do the same for me.

"What do you want me to do?" Mr. Lim asks.

"You took away a painful memory from my friend. I'd like you to do the same for me."

He looks at me for a moment with those unearthly blue eyes, and then says, "I can do that."

The relief that fills me is so overwhelming that it's all I can do not to burst into tears.

"But I'll need you to get something for me first."

Before I can ask what it is, Ond approaches the table carrying a tray of fresh sandwiches wrapped in yellow paper. Fourteen of them. Despite her arthritic-looking hands, she carries the tray without difficulty and sets it in front of Mr. Lim. Without looking at either of us or speaking a word, before she turns and shuffles back toward the counter. Given the way he was eating before, I expect Mr. Lim to tear the paper off one of the sandwiches and cram it into his mouth. But instead he calmly tells me what he wants me to do.

When he's finished, he asks if I understand. I don't really, but I'll do whatever it takes to be free of the voices.

Satisfied, he picks up one of the sandwiches, unwraps it slowly, almost lovingly, and then falls upon it with an animalistic snarl.

As I wrote earlier, I've lived in Ash Creek for a long time, but I grew up on a farm outside a small town called Waldron. It wasn't a very successful farm. My dad inherited it from his father, but his heart wasn't in it. He didn't like the work and had no head for business. He grew soybeans mostly, and he didn't do a good job of it. By the time I was married and Nancy was born, he'd sold the farm, moved with my mother to a smaller house in town, and started doing odd jobs as a handyman.

One summer when I was six, I was playing in a field that Dad never planted nor maintained. I was running through the field, laughing as I chased butterflies, when my foot snagged on something. Fiery pain shot through my ankle, and I cried out as whatever had hold of me drew taught, sending me falling to the ground face first. I put out my hands to break my fall, and the impact hurt my wrists, but that pain was nothing compared to the agony in my ankle. Crying, teeth, gritted, I rolled onto my back and sat up. I bent over to examine my foot and saw my sock and shoe were both covered in blood. There was so much of it, and it was so *red*, that the sight of it almost made me pass out. I sat there whimpering for several moments until I worked up enough courage to examine my wound more closely.

Rusty barbed wire was wrapped tight around my ankle, the points caught so deep in my flesh that I imagine they touched the bone. I had no idea where the wire had come from, but later Dad told me there used to be a fence around that field when he was a kid, and the length of wire that caught me must've been left over from that time, lying in the field all those years like the world's most patient serpent, waiting for someone to come along so it could strike.

I needed stitches and a tetanus shot, of course, and I walked with a crutch for a couple weeks while the wound healed. Luckily, no tendons were damaged, at least not badly, and I was back to running again before summer's end. But not in that field. Never again.

The pain of that rusty wire biting through my skin and muscle down to the bone was the worst I'd ever experienced in my life—including labor with both of my girls. Until the night Jacob and I gave them the news we'd both hoped never to have to tell them. Until I saw their faces. Until I heard their voices.

It's worse in my dreams. There the memory plays and replays with vivid colors and crisp sound, like an expensive Hollywood production. I don't sleep much. Hell, who am I trying to fool? I hardly sleep at all. You'd think that the memory, painful as it is, would've faded over the years, especially since the girls are grown and in college, Lauren at Northern Kentucky University for her undergrad, Nancy at Wichita State for her graduate degree. But the memory has only become sharper with the passage of time. My brother once told me that's because I have a sick need to punish myself. Maybe so, but knowing that doesn't make the memory go away.

I'm careful about what I watch on TV. Commercials are the worst. You never know when kids will be in one. And I'm cautious about the movies I see in theaters. I only go to shows that start after 9 pm in the hope I won't run into any parents taking their little ones to see the latest animated extravaganza. But for all my precautions, I still hear my girls' voices throughout the day, so many times that I no longer bother counting.

I'm back at Pandora's less than an hour later. I'm carrying a white cardboard box with the logo for Pets and More printed on the side. Mr. Lim is finishing the last of what I assume to be another set of fourteen sandwiches. The mound of crumpled wrappers on the table is so large now that there isn't room for them all, and several have fallen to the floor. I wait for him to finish his sandwich—I know it won't take long—but I don't look up at the TV. I don't what to see what it's showing. As before, Mr. Lim pays no attention to me until he's finished. He then glances over at me, then his gaze flicks to the box and he grins. His teeth are overlarge and so white they gleam. He sweeps the wrappers off the table to make room, and I gently set the box down before him. My heart pounds, and my stomach roils with nausea.

Mr. Lim leans over the box, closes his eyes, and inhales deeply, as if he's drawing in the scent of a fine wine. He reaches out with trembling hands and opens the box. His lips are moist and I realize he's drooling. He peers inside, then he turns and give me an angry glare.

"I don't eat anything that's still alive," he says, voice dripping with disgust. "I'm not a *savage*." He picks up the box and shoves it toward me. I don't want to take it, but Mr. Lim releases the box, and if I don't grab hold of it, the box and its contents will fall to the floor. So I catch it, and there's a panicked scuttling from inside.

I look down at the rabbit, a black-and-white fluffball that looks back up at me with frightened eyes.

"I … You can't …"

"What I *can* do is give you the relief you desire," he says. "But I don't work for free."

I don't look at Mr. Lim. Instead, I continue looking at the bunny. After the divorce, Nancy and Lauren begged me to get them a pet, but back then I lived in a small two-bedroom apartment, and I didn't want to deal with looking after an animal on the days the girls were with their father. And by the time I found myself a new house, the girls were older and had stopped talking about pets. So they never had any growing up. One more regret to add to my list.

I wish this wasn't happening! I wish this was a dream!

That's okay. It's okay.

I take hold of the rabbit by the scruff of its neck and pull it out of the box. I let the box fall to the floor, put one hand around the rabbit's neck, the other hand on its head, and I quickly turn them in opposite directions. There's a snapping sound, and the rabbit spasms once and then falls still. I toss the dead creature onto the table, and Mr. Lim gazes at it for a moment, gorgeous blue eyes shining. Then he snatches it up and brings it to his mouth. It takes him longer to finish it off than it does a Pandora's sandwich, but that's because he has the fur, bones, and internal organs to deal with, too—all of which he eats. When he's done, his army jacket is splattered with crimson, and the lower half of his face is a red smear. As he starts to lick blood from his fingers, I say, "Now will you do it?"

Between finger-licks, he glances at me and says, "It's already done."

I don't feel any different, and doubt must show on my face, for Mr. Lim sighs and says, "Why did you come to me?"

"So you could remove one of my bad memories. The worst one."

"And which one is that?"

I open my mouth to reply, but then I realize I have no idea. I remember everything about my interactions with Mr. Lim from the moment I first stepped into Pandora's, but I can't recall which memory I wanted him to take from me.

I smile in wonderment.

"I can't believe it! It's *gone!* Thank you, thank you *so—*"

He waves away my thanks. Ond approaches with a tray of fresh sandwiches, and Mr. Lim turns his attention to whatever new atrocities are playing out on the TV screen. I take this as my cue to go, only too happy to take my leave of Mr. Lim and this strange place.

As I push open the entrance door, a mother and her two young daughters enter. The faces of all three are mottled, the flesh swollen and gently pulsating. I try not to stare as they pass me, then I continue outside and walk toward my Prius. I don't hear any voices in my head, and I don't know if I should be relieved by that.

I'm a phlebotomist, and I took the day off work so I could meet with Mr. Lim. It's still early enough that I could go to the hospital and put in a few hours, but I feel so good, so much *lighter*, that I decide to take the rest of the day to celebrate. I don't know exactly what burden Mr. Lim relieved me of, but given that I'm so happy I'm almost giddy, I know it has to be a huge one, and no longer being tormented by memory like that is definitely worth celebrating. I feel so great that I don't question how Mr. Lim performed this miracle or even what he is precisely, or where exactly Pandora's is in relation to what I've always thought of as the real world. In truth, I don't really care about those details, and I suspect that if I had answers to my questions, I wouldn't like them.

I'm debating whether to get a relaxing massage at my gym or a strong margarita at my favorite Mexican restaurant when my phone starts buzzing. I left my purse on the floor of my passenger seat both times I went into Pandora's, but I moved it back onto the passenger seat before I left the parking lot. I reach inside, remove the phone and accept the call without looking to see who it is. Like most people, I usually screen my calls to avoid salespeople or political polltakers, but right now I'm too happy to care who it is.

"Hello?"

"Hi, Mom!"

I frown. "Who is this?"

Silence on the other end for several seconds.

"Mom, it's *me. Nancy.*"

I'm not sure why this woman is calling me *Mom*, but I search my memory, trying to recall if I know a Nancy. There's a nurse named Nancy that I've worked with a few times when I've been on nights, but this isn't her. She's in her late sixties, and this woman is young, in her twenties, maybe. Besides, why would that Nancy call me *Mom*?"

"Sorry, you must have the wrong number." I pull the phone away from my ear, intending to disconnect, but before I can the woman—Nancy—speaks hurriedly.

"Is this some kind of joke, Mom? Please tell me it is, because if it's not, you're scaring me."

I should disconnect anyway. If there's anyone joking here, it's her. But I don't. Instead I put the phone back to my ear.

"I'm sorry but not only don't I know a Nancy, I don't recognize your voice."

The pause is longer this time, and I think *she's* ended the call, but then she says, "Do you remember the hospital where you work?"

"I'm not sure what disturbs me more: That she knows where I work or the forced calm in her voice, which does a poor job of masking the fear underneath.

"Yes."

"Go there. Right now. Tell them you're having trouble remembering things. I'll book a flight and be in Ohio as soon as I can. I'll call Lauren and—" She breaks off. "Do you remember Lauren?"

My silence is answer enough.

"I'll call her, and I'm sure she'll come, too. She's close enough to drive, and she'll get there first. Don't worry, Mom. You're going to be okay. Everything's going to be okay. I love you."

She sounds on the verge of tears as she disconnects. I hold the phone to my ear a moment longer before returning it to my purse. This incident is as strange as anything I experienced in Pandora's, and while I have no idea who Nancy or Lauren are, there was something about Nancy's parting words, something about the way she repeated *okay* that chilled me. Whoever these girls are, they must be part of the memory Mr. Lim removed from my mind. I wanted that memory gone, *needed* it desperately. My continuing sanity depended on it. So maybe I shouldn't think about this too closely, shouldn't try to recover that which I worked so hard to be free of.

To hell with the massage and the margarita, and to hell with the hospital. I needed to go home. *Now.*

I pressed down on the gas and prayed I wouldn't catch the attention of any cops on the way.

A couple hours later, I'm sitting in Pandora's parking lot again. It isn't as full as it was earlier, but the vehicles here now are just as weird as the ones before. I was afraid that I wouldn't be able to find the restaurant again, that once my wish was granted, the place would go back to wherever it came from, never to return. But I found it again, and on the first try. I've been sitting here for five minutes, gripping the steering wheel and looking straight ahead. Once I got home, I checked my phone and found contacts for both a Nancy and a Lauren. No last names, though. I checked my text messages and found conversations with both women. The latest exchanges were about their upcoming Spring Breaks. Their schools didn't do their Spring Breaks during the same week. Lauren's was first, and Nancy's was the week after. The three of us wanted to take a cruise, but we were having trouble figuring out the logistics of the trip.

I have no memory of these texts.

There are saved voicemails from both girls, too. I didn't recognize either of their voices. There are pictures on my phone, most of which are of one or two young women who I assume are Nancy and Lauren. I'm in some of those pictures, but I have no memory of them being taken. I checked my social media accounts and found more pictures of them, along with their comments on my posts. I checked out their profiles, went through their pictures, saw bits and pieces of two lives I know nothing about. I saw both girls are connected to Jacob on social media, and they share his last name—Haynes. That was my last name, too. I didn't change it after the divorce. It seemed like too much of a hassle, and Jacob and I don't have hard feelings toward each other, Well, not *too* many. I haven't spoken with him in years, not since he remarried, but I'm tempted to call him now and ask him about Nancy and Lauren, if they really are who I fear they are. I have others I could call, too. My own mother. My brother. But there's no point. I understand what happened—if not exactly why—and I know what I need to do.

I get out of my car and head into the restaurant once more.

Ond is still standing behind the counter, and the place still smells like a chemical factory. The dining area isn't as full as it was earlier, but the people that are here are strange, just like—Mr. Lim is sitting at the same table, a new mound of crumpled wrappers in front of him and scattered piles of them on the floor around his feet. He has only one sandwich left, but he seems to be in no hurry to eat it. Maybe he's finally full? He holds onto the sandwich with both hands, almost as if cradling it. His jacket is still stained with rabbit blood, thick and wet. He's watching a woman use a butcher knife cut off a man's balls on the TV. I'm so relieved he's here. I was afraid he might have left while I was gone. I then wonder if he ever leaves, or if he's always sitting here, devouring one sandwich after another, watching an endless parade of televised murder and mutilation, doing favors for people willing to pay his price.

I head over to the table on the edge of panic. I don't have any memories of Nancy and Lauren, but now I believe I *should* have, and I'm horrified at what I must have lost, what I must have willingly given up. I don't know what I was thinking, and I don't care. I just want my memories back. But before I can speak, Mr. Lim turns to me with a smile that's almost, but not quite, mocking.

"No one realizes that when you remove *one* memory, all the others associated with it have to go, too. It's like a house of cards. Take one from the bottom and the entire structure collapses. You'd be surprised how many of my clients come back after they understand this, but I must say, you may have set the record for the fastest return visit."

"So you can give them back—the memories?"

"Of course, I can!" He sounds offended at first, but then he smiles again, slowly this time. Slyly. "But like I told you earlier, I don't work for free."

He unwraps the sandwich, crumples the paper, and tosses it to the floor. He lifts the sandwich up for my inspection and removes the top bun to reveal a bloody hunk of raw meat sitting there. A very particular cut of meat.

"It's hard to find a steady supply," he says. "Especially when you have an appetite like mine."

I remember how during my first visit, when I told him Marsha had *said* something to me about him, he questioned my use of the word. Now I know why. Marsha can type just fine, but she can't *say* anything. She went through this same ritual, as I imagine most of Mr. Lim's customers do—if they want back what they so foolishly gave away.

He replaces the top bun and gobbles the sandwich down. Afterward, he wipes away a splotch of crimson from his lips which I now know for certain isn't ketchup, and then points to the counter. Ond holds a butcher knife that looks very much like the one wielded by the ball-cutter on the TV. I think of how scared Nancy sounded on the phone even though she fought so hard to sound calm. I think of Lauren, who even now is driving back to Ohio from Kentucky, worried sick that her mother had a stroke or is suffering from early-onset dementia. I'll see her soon, Nancy too, and when I do, I may not be able to say I love you, but I will hug them, hug them *hard*. I think they'll get the message. Most importantly, I'll remember them. Remember everything, good times and bad.

I walk to the counter and stick out my tongue. Ond takes hold of the tip between a thumb and forefinger and pulls it taut. Then, without any change in her expression, she raises the knife and cuts. It hurts worse than the barbed wire around my ankle, but still not as bad as—I hear my girls' voices again, and as Ond heads back to the kitchen with her grisly prize, I smile with my empty mouth, blood pouring over my chin and splattering onto the counter with a sound sweet as music.

APPENDIX B
ANALYSIS OF "VOICES LIKE BARBED WIRE"

I'm assuming you've read the preceding story. If not, you might want to do so before continuing.

When I decided to do a DTHSD (Dread, Terror, Horror, Shock, Disgust) analysis of one of my stories as an example in Chapter Eight, I picked "Voices Like Barbed Wire" because it has a mix of all five elements. I didn't intend to use it for anything more. In fact, I wasn't even going to include it in the book. Instead, I thought I'd put it on my website and provide a link for anyone who might be interested in reading it. Then, as I was proofreading the complete first draft, I realized that for the example to be worthwhile, it had to be easily available for people as they read the book. So I stuck it the back. I figured that was good enough and continued proofreading. As I did so, I remembered that in *Writing in the Dark*, I included one of my earliest stories, "Scary Christmas," and critiqued it from my current point of view as a writer forty years older than the kid who wrote it. I began to think, *What if I analyzed "Voices Like Barbed Wire," too?* But I didn't want to do a generic analysis of it. Then it occurred to me. I originally included it as an example for one of the exercises. What if I talked about all the other ways the story connects to the different principles I put forward in this book (and in *Writing in the Dark*)?

And then I told myself, *If you do that, you're going to have to tell everyone where you got the idea for the story. Are you sure you want to share that?*

No, I am not. But I'm going to do it anyway.

I'll link my analysis to corresponding chapters in the book, so you can more clearly connect it with the writing advice and exercises I've presented. Oh, and if you have *Writing in the Dark*, it might be interesting for you to read "Scary Christmas" and then re-read "Voices Like Barbed Wire" to see how my writing has evolved over the last four decades.

CHAPTER 1: WHY HORROR MATTERS

This story deals with the theme that memories, even bad ones—hell, even the *worst* ones—make us who we are, and while they're hard to bear, we may be better off with them than without them. So the story deals with a theme that most readers can relate to. They can also ponder the choices the narrator makes in the story and think about what choices they might make in the same circumstances. The story might make them think about one of their worst memories, and its place in their life and the makeup of their identity.

CHAPTER 2: THINGS UNKNOWN

Everything about Pandora's restaurant, Ond, and Mr. Lim are unknown. Mr. Lim's power to remove memories is defined as an ability he has, but *how* he does it isn't defined.

CHAPTER 3: EVERYTHING YOU KNOW IS WRONG

Reality is violated only inside Pandora's (and in its parking lot). I decided to keep the weirdness contained in this story so I could focus on the narrator and her character arc.

CHAPTER 4: HELLO DARKNESS, MY OLD FRIEND

I love to mix subgenres of horror in my fiction. This is a blend of character-based, surreal, weird, and extreme horror, with some dark fantasy thrown in for good measure. I don't consciously decide what proportion of these elements will go into a story. Once I have a basic concept, I start writing and see where the story goes.

CHAPTER 5: STRANGE NOTIONS

Once in a McDonald's, I saw a thin man in an army jacket sitting at a table eating a cheeseburger, with a large pile of crumpled cheeseburger wrappers sitting in front of him. (Maybe he'd been eating with some buddies, and they'd already departed? I couldn't see how anyone could eat that many burgers in one sitting.) I whipped out my phone, wrote a short description of the man on my notepad app, and later, when I was looking for a story idea, I decided to use him.

Sometime earlier I'd written the phrase "voices like barbed wire" in my notepad, but I can't remember where I got it from. When I decided to use it as the title for this story, I created the flashback of the narrator getting injured by barbed wire when she was a kid so that the title would better fit the story. The *voices* part of the title was easy. I chose that title because the girls' voices were prominent in the story.

I've used the idea of memory removal in other stories, most notably in my first *Nekropolis* novel. My hero needs information, so he goes to a vampire librarian who feeds on memories instead of blood. The price for information—one random memory given by the asker. I'm not sure why the concept appeals to me so. Probably because it speaks to the value of memory and its role in forming our identities.

I can't recall were I got Mr. Lim and Ond's names. I have a vague memory of seeing those words somewhere—maybe they were typos I made when writing something else? At any rate, I wanted odd names for these odd characters.

The reason why I chose this particular memory as the narrator's worst is because it's *my* memory. That was how my two daughters reacted when they were twelve and seven and my ex-wife and I told them we were getting divorced. The words the daughters in the story use are the exact ones my girls spoke. This is one of my absolute worst memories. By that point, I knew my marriage couldn't be saved, no matter how hard I'd tried, and overall it was best for the entire family, the girls included, if my ex and I divorced. But I was the girl's father. I was supposed to protect them, not hurt them so deeply. I do my best to keep this memory walled off and I try not to touch it. My idea of Hell is being forced to relive that moment over and over for eternity.

Why did I choose to use such a personal memory in this story? Because it would provide a strong emotional core. It would help characterize the narrator, make her seem more real, and—hopefully—sympathetic to readers. My real emotions would fuel her fictional emotions. Plus, no one ever had to know I used one of my own worst memories in the story. That's what's great about fiction, right? We can reveal *and* hide in plain sight at the same time.

I definitely went with Jack Ketchum's "Write from the wound" advice with this story. Using this memory was cathartic for me, because now I have additional, more positive experiences associated with it. The experience and personal catharsis of writing the story, the satisfaction of seeing readers react positively to the story when it was first published, along with the satisfaction of having it chosen for a best-of anthology—and, of course, now having used it in this book as well. I still try to avoid thinking about this memory, but when I do recall it these days, it's still bad, but not as bad as it was. That's another reason why horror matters. Sometimes it can help save us as readers *and* as writers.

In terms of my formula Weird Idea + Personal Observation + Emotional Core, this story follows it. Weird Idea: A deal with a bizarre supernatural entity for removal of a painful memory. Personal Observation: The guy I saw in McDonald's. Emotional Core: My memory.

CHAPTER 6: DONE TO DEATH

As I said in Chapter Eight, this is a revamped Deal with the Devil story, filtered through my imagination. Hopefully, readers will feel the power of the Devil trope through Mr. Lim without any of the trope's attendant baggage. Instead of a character asking to be given something, as so often happens in Deal with the Devil stories, I had my character ask for something to be removed.

CHAPTER 7: WHERE NO MONSTER HAS GONE BEFORE

As I said, Lim is a reworked devil, and Ond is a reworked devil's servant. I gave Lim an unending appetite for a very grotesque type of sandwich, and I made Pandora's a weird lair for him. I didn't have Lim talk much so I could maintain a sense of the unknown about him. I wanted him to seem unearthly and inhuman. Chatting with the narrator would've humanized him too much.

CHAPTER 8: THE HORROR WRITER'S PALETTE

I already analyzed how I used Dread, Terror, Horror, Shock and Disgust in this story in Chapter Eight.

CHAPTER 9: THE HORROR HERO'S JOURNEY

I hadn't thought about it until now, but I suppose my narrator's journey in this story is The Poor Bastard Escapes with Severe Wounds and Scars. Although she does manage to get her memory back, so she trades one scar for (at least to her mind) a lesser one (the loss of her tongue).

CHAPTER 10: DOWN TO THE BONE

I used an immersive point of view in this story. As I've said elsewhere, I think it's the most effective way to write fiction in general and horror in particular. How well I succeeded with this point of view is up to you to decide.

CHAPTER 11: MORE THAN MEAT

Hopefully, I portrayed the narrator as a fully realized person (as much as is possible in a short story) and treated her with dignity.

CHAPTER 12: HURTS SO GOOD

There's a mix of pain types in this story: Mental, emotional, physical, and—if you consider the theme of identity—spiritual too. I'd say emotional pain predominates, which makes sense given that a painful memory lies at the center of the story.

CHAPTER 13: THE PHYSIOLOGY OF FEAR

This isn't a story where the main character is put into a situation where she feels intense fear. No one attempts to hurt her (not in any way she doesn't choose), and Pandora's, Ond, and Mr. Lim are weird and disturbing, but they don't inspire intense fear. If they did, who would stick around to make a deal with Mr. Lim? So not a lot of fear details in this one.

CHAPTER 14: TELL ME A SCARY STORY

You can go through and see how I used Scene and Sequel in this story. As I said in Chapter Fourteen, I don't consciously plan out my fiction using this technique, but I use it instinctively. As I reread the story, it seemed to me to work on a Scene and Sequel level.

CHAPTER 15: THE DARK HEART OF HORROR

I've already established that the story centers on an emotional core. Hopefully it's a strong and effective one for readers.

CHAPTER 16: A MATTER OF STYLE

I said elsewhere in the book that I tend not to use first person much, but in this case it seemed the best choice because of how deeply personal the memory was, and how deep the loss of it hit the narrator. I used present tense so that readers could imagine the story was being told as it happened, as if we're riding along in the narrator's mind as events progress. I thought this might make it a little more believable when the narrator loses her memory. Sure, she's telling the story after she gets her memory back, but I wanted the section of the story when she'd lost the memory to feel more immediate, more *now*. I didn't want readers to be 100 percent certain she'd get her memory back. If the story had been told in past tense, you would've been sure her memory was returned. In present tense? Not so much.

I also discussed -isms in Chapter Sixteen. When I was proofing the book and reread "Voices Like Barbed Wire" again, I noticed several -isms that I hadn't been aware of before. In the original version, I described the naked man on the TV as fat. Why? Because I wanted the image on the screen to be as unsettling as possible (but leaving the actual violence as implied). Hardcore porn plays with different combinations of body types and sexual practices that are viewed as, if not taboo, then at least uncommon by society at large. (How common they actually are is another matter.) I also wanted a contrast between someone small and someone big to add to the implication of violence. (I didn't spend a ton of time thinking this through when I wrote the scene. It was more of an instinctive decision based on the general feel I wanted Pandora's to have.)

But when proofing the story again, I wondered if my use of *fat* constituted sizeism. After all, there was no reason the man had to be fat. So I changed the description, making him middle-aged to make him seem more predatory since the girl is described as young. Does that constitute ageism? I'm sixteen years older than my wife, and the looks we sometimes get in public make it clear that a lot of people aren't comfortable with our age difference, and some obviously disapprove of it. I decided that since I could base the choice of *middle-aged* on my own experience, I could leave it.

The second -ism I discovered was that I'd originally described the mother and kids who enter the restaurant of having discolorations like port-wine stains on their faces. They didn't actually have them. Whatever they had only *resembled* port-wine stains. But I decided the description could be views as ableist, so I changed it.

A third -ism—one I didn't change—is that in the snuff film playing on TV a woman is portrayed as a victim (or rather soon-to-be victim) of violence, with a decided sexual edge to the scene. As I mentioned elsewhere in the book, women who exist solely to be victims of sexual violence is a misogynistic cliché in extreme horror. I left this one in because I thought Mr. Lim watching this kind of scene would further make him seem more sinister, more devil-like.

Was it the right choice to leave this image in? I honestly don't know. One of the things about horror fiction is that it deals with dark material, and authors have to constantly negotiate with ourselves what we put in our stories, how we present it, and try to determine what effect it will have on readers and whether that effect is the one we want. And we need to check to make sure we aren't perpetuating harmful stereotypes in our work. With the fat man, I was perpetuating the stereotype of a fat body being viewed as grotesque, especially when sex is involved, as well as someone with a fat body been viewed as monstrous (since he's about to kill his victim). With the family with port-wine-like patches of skin on their faces, I was perpetuating the stereotype that people who have skin conditions are monstrous. I decided that the stereotype of the young, helpless female victim who exists only to be tortured and killed was something that might appear on a snuff film—especially one a being like Lim would watch—so I left that element as it was.

I have no idea if these choices were right ones. I do my best to write effective horror fiction without perpetuating harmful stereotypes, and I know there are times I'm going to fail. I just need to keep educating myself on -isms and try to do better keeping them out of my fiction.

CHAPTER 17: THE ART OF SUSPENSE

I tried to build suspense through the description of Pandora's parking lot, then its interior, then the narrator's meeting with Ond, then Mr. Lim. I did it by not immediately revealing what Lim's price is for removing the narrator's memory (or what's in the sandwiches he eats), and by slowly revealing what memory the narrator lost. I tried to build a bit of suspense at the end before the narrator learns the price of regaining her memory.

CHAPTER 18: LET THEM FIGHT!

I tend to focus on the characters and the emotional core in short stories, so I usually don't have fight scenes in them. I do have them in my novels. There's more room in books, and you've got to fill them up with something, right? I've never really thought about why I don't have fight scenes in short stories as a rule. Maybe fight scenes work best when there are other types of scenes surrounding them, and there just isn't enough room in short stories to do that? Or maybe short fiction is more rewarding for readers when it focuses on character rather than action? Short stories back in the days of the Pulps would be all action, but only comics seem to continue the tradition of short-form action in literature these days. I don't have any real insights to offer here, just some thoughts.

CHAPTER 19: THERE ARE NO LIMITS, BUT ...

There are touches of extreme horror here, along with some body horror. I attempted to keep the extreme elements fairly restrained. I wanted them to add to the overall feeling of weirdness and uncertainty in this story, so readers wouldn't know for certain what might happen in Pandora's. I also needed to include these elements to foreshadow the ending—not specifically what occurs, but that this is a story in which that *type* of thing could occur.

CHAPTER 20: THE EVIL SPREADS

There's not much I can say about the story in terms of how it was published. I'm privileged at this point in my career to have editors ask me to submit stories, and that's what happened in this case. Later, I decided to send it for consideration to *Year's Best Hardcore Horror*. I wasn't sure if it was hardcore enough, but the editors thought so and accepted it. And now I've used the story in this book as well. I suppose I can say that this is an example of getting a single story in front of as many eyes as possible, finding ways to re-market your work and finding different uses for it.

That's it for my analysis. During the process of writing it, I took a break, and my wife Christine and I took our two dachshunds Lucy and Bentley for a walk in the park. During the walk, I told Christine that I was writing this analysis. I said that it seemed more than a little self-indulgent to be writing so much about one of my own stories in this way. Yeah, it seemed like it might be a good idea, educationally speaking, to show how all the different principles I discussed in the book worked in a piece of my own fiction. Christine told me that she thought readers would find the analysis valuable. I don't know how valuable it was, but I hope at least you found it useful.

And now, since this is a book of exercises, why don't you take one of your stories and analyze it using the principles from all the chapters in the book to see what insights you gain? After all, this book may be over, but the learning never ends.

FORBIDDEN KNOWLEDGE
RESOURCES FOR FURTHER LEARNING

Websites

Diversity in Horror: **diversityhorror.blogspot.com**

Horror Writers Association: **www.horror.org**

International Thriller Writers Association: **www.thrillerwriters.org**

Jane Friedman: **www.janefriedman.com**

Ladies of Horror Fiction: **www.ladiesofhorrorfiction.com**

The Science Fiction and Fantasy Writers of America: **www.sfwa.org**

The Seers' Table: **horror.org/category/the-seers-table**

Tim's Blog: **writinginthedarktw.blogspot.com**

Tim's YouTube Channel: **www.youtube.com/c/timwaggonerswritinginthedark**

Women in Horror Month: **www.womeninhorrormonth.com**

Books on Writing and Writers

Aristotle's Poetics for Screenwriters, Michael Tierno

Body Trauma: A Writer's Guide to Wounds and Injuries, David W. Page

Capturing Ghosts on the Page: Writing Horror & Dark Fiction, Kaaron Warren

The Complete Idiot's Guide to Writing a Novel, Tom Monteleone

Creativity for Life: Practical Advice on the Artist's Personality, and Career from America's Foremost Creativity Coach, Eric Maisel

Danse Macabre, Stephen King

Dark Dreamers: Conversations with the Masters of Horror, Stanley Wiater

Dark Thoughts on Writing, Stanley Wiater

Dark Visions: Conversations with the Masters of Horror Film, Stanley Wiater and Tanya Wiater

The Dead Stage: The Journey from Page to Stage, Dan Weatherer

End of the Road, Brian Keene

For Exposure: The Life and Times of a Small-Press Publisher, Jason Sizemore

Forensics and Fiction: Clever, Intriguing, and Downright Odd Questions from Crime Writers, D.P. Lyle

Horror 101: The Way Forward, Joe Mynhardt (ed.)

Horror 201: The Silver Scream, Joe Mynhardt and Emma Audsley (eds.)

The Horror ... The Horror: An Autobiography, Rick Hautala

The Horror Writer: A Study of Craft and Identity in the Horror Genre. Joe Mynhardt (ed.)

How to Write Horror Fiction, William F. Nolan

How to Write Tales of Horror, Fantasy, and Science Fiction, J.N. Williamson

Instigation: Creative Prompts on the Dark Side, Michael A. Arnzen

It's Alive: Bringing Your Nightmares to Life. Joe Mynhardt and Eugene Johnson (eds.)

The Kick-Ass Writer, Chuck Wendig

Many Genres, One Craft: Lessons in Writing Popular Fiction, Michael A. Arnzen and Heidi Ruby Miller (eds.)

Mark My Words: Read the Submission Guidelines and other Self-editing Tips, Lee Murray and Angelia Yuriko Smith

Murder and Mayhem: A Doctor Answers Medical and Forensic Questions for Mystery Writers, D.P. Lyle

Now Write! Science Fiction, Fantasy, and Horror: Speculative Genre Exercises from Today's Best Teachers, Laurie Lamsen (ed.)

On Writing: A Memoir of the Craft, Stephen King

On Writing Horror: A Handbook by the Horror Writers Association, Mort Castle (ed.)

Out in the Dark: Interviews with Gay Horror Filmmakers, Actors, and Authors, Sean Abley

Plotting and Writing Suspense Fiction. Patricia Highsmith.

The Readers' Advisory Guide to Horror, Third Edition, Becky Siegel Spratford

The Scream Writers Handbook: How to Write a Terrifying Screenplay in 10 Bloody Steps, Thomas Fenton.

Shooting Yourself in the Head for Fun and Profit: A Writer's Survival Guide, Lucy A. Snyder

Southern Fried and Horrified, Ron Kelly

Starve Better: Surviving the Endless Horror of the Writing Life, Nick Mamatas

Supernatural Horror in Literature, H.P. Lovecraft

Techniques of the Selling Writer, Dwight V. Swain

Thrill Me: Essays on Fiction, Benjamin Percy

To Each Their Darkness, Gary A. Braunbeck

Where Nightmares Come From: The Art of Storytelling in the Horror Genre. Joe Mynhardt and Eugene Johnson (eds.)

Wonderbook, Jeff Vandermeer

Write the Fight Right, Alan Baxter

A Writer's Tale, Richard Laymon

Writers Workshop of Horror, Michael Knost (ed.)

Writers Workshop of Horror 2, Michael Knost (ed.)

Writing for Emotional Impact, Karl Iglesias

The Writing Life, Jeff Strand.
Writing Monsters, Philip Athans
Writing the Paranormal Novel, Steven Harper
Writing Horror Fiction, Guy N. Smith
Writing the Uncanny: Essays on Crafting Strange Fiction. Dan Coxon and Richard V. Hirst (eds.)
Yours to Tell: Dialogues on the Art & Practice of Writing, Steve Rasnic Tem and Melanie Tem

ABOUT THE AUTHOR

Tim Waggoner has published over fifty novels and seven collections of short stories. He writes original dark fantasy and horror, as well as media tie-ins, and his articles on writing have appeared in numerous publications. He's won the Bram Stoker Award, the Horror Writers Association's Mentor of the Year Award, and he's been a finalist for the Shirley Jackson Award, the Scribe Award, and the Splatterpunk Award. He's also a full-time tenured professor who teaches creative writing and composition at Sinclair College in Dayton, Ohio.

BIBLIOGRAPHY

Novels

Lord of the Feast. Flame Tree Press, 2023.

A Hunter Called Night. Flame Tree Press, 2022.

Zombicide Invader: Planet Havoc. Aconyte Books, 2022.

We Rise Again. Flame Tree Press, 2022.

Halloween Kills: The Official Movie Novelization. Titan Books, 2021.

Your Turn to Suffer. Flame Tree Press, 2021.

The Forever House. Flame Tree Press, 2020.

Alien: Prototype. Titan Books, 2019.

They Kill. Flame Tree Press, 2019.

Blood Island. Severed Press, 2019.

Supernatural: Children of Anubis. Titan Books, 2019.

The Mouth of the Dark. Flame Tree Press, 2018.

The Teeth of the Sea. Severed Press, 2017.

Kingsman: The Golden Circle: The Official Movie Novelization. Titan Books, 2017.

xXx: The Return of Xander Cage: The Official Movie Novelization. Titan Books, 2017.

Resident Evil: The Final Chapter: The Official Movie Novelization. Titan Books, 2017.

Supernatural: Mythmaker. Titan Books, 2016.

Eat the Night. DarkFuse, 2016.

Dream Stalkers. Angry Robot, 2016.

Dark Art. Past Curfew Press, 2014.

Grimm: The Killing Time. Titan Books, 2014.

Night Terrors. Angry Robot, 2014.

The Way of All Flesh. Samhain Books, 2014.

Supernatural: The Roads Not Taken. Insight Editions, 2013.

Supernatural: Carved in Flesh. Titan Books, 2013.

Ghost Town. Pocket Books, 2012.

The Nekropolis Archives. Omnibus. Angry Robot, 2012.

Ghost Trackers. Pocket Books, 2011.

Nekropolis: Dark War. Angry Robot, 2011.

Nekropolis: Dead Streets. Angry Robot, 2010.

Nekropolis. Angry Robot, 2010.

Lady Ruin. Wizards of the Coast, 2010.

Last of the Lycans: Monarch of the Moon. Actionopolis, 2010.

Stargate SG-1: Valhalla. Fandemonium Books, 2009.

Cross County. Wizards of the Coast, Aug. 2008. Reprinted by Prologue as *Beneath the Bones,* F&W
    Publications, 2012.

Blade of the Flame 3: Sea of Death. Wizards of the Coast, February 2008.

Blade of the Flame 2: Forge of the Mindslayers. Wizards of the Coast, March 2007.

Ripped from a Dream. Black Flame, October 2006. Omnibus reprinting *A Nightmare on Elm Street:
    Protégé.*

Darkness Wakes. Leisure Books, December 2006.

Godfire 2: Heart's Wound. Five Star/Thorndike Books, Oct. 2006.

Godfire 1: The Orchard of Dreams. Five Star/Thorndike Books, July 2006.

Blade of the Flame 1: Thieves of Blood. Wizards of the Coast, May 2006.

Pandora Drive. Leisure Books, April 2006.

A Nightmare on Elm Street: Protégé. Black Flame, October 2005.

A Shadow Over Heaven's Eye. White Wolf Publishing, July 2005.

Like Death. Leisure Books, January 2005. Reprinted by Apex Publications, 2011.

Dragonlance, the New Adventures: Return of the Sorceress. Wizards of the Coast, Inc., 2004.

Defender: Hyperswarm. I-Books, 2004.

Dragonlance, the New Adventures: Temple of the Dragonslayer. Wizards of the Coast, Inc., July 2004.

Necropolis. Five Star/Thorndike Books, 2004.

Dark Ages: Gangrel. White Wolf Publishing, 2004.

The Harmony Society. Prime Books, 2003. Reprinted by Dark Regions Press, 2012.

Dying for It. Foggy Windows Books, 2001.

Nonfiction

Writing in the Dark. Guide Dog Books, 2020.
The Art of Writing Genre Fiction. With Michael Knost. MyBookPress, 2018.
The Men of Letters Bestiary: Winchester Family Edition. Insight Editions, 2017.

Collections

A Little Aqua Book of Marine Stories. Borderlands Press, 2018.
Love, Death, and Madness. Crossroad Press, 2018.
Dark and Distant Voices. Nightshade Press, 2018.
CD Selects: Tim Waggoner. Cemetery Dance, 2017.
Bone Whispers. Post Mortem Press, 2013.
Broken Shadows. Delirium Books, 2009.
All Too Surreal. Prime Books, 2002.

Chapbooks

"Skull Cathedral." Squid Salad Press, 2008.

Novellas and Novelettes

"Some Kind of Monster." Apex Books, 2020.
"Raiders of the Poisoned Plains." Deadlands anthology. Pinnacle, 2019.
"A Kiss of Thorns." DarkFuse, 2017.
"The Winter Box." DarkFuse, 2016.
"The Last Mile." DarkFuse, 2014.
"Deep Like the River." Dark Regions, 2014.
"The Men Upstairs." DarkFuse, 2012.
"A Strange and Savage Garden." Brimstone Turnpike. CD Publications, 2008.
Republished by Samhain Books, 2014.
"Long Way Home." Thrillers II, CD Publications, 2007.
"The Blade of the Flame." *Tales of the Last War*, Wizards of the Coast, 2006.

CPSIA information can be obtained
at www.ICGtesting.com
Printed in the USA
LVHW011211161122
733176LV00005B/32

9 781947 879461